Meeting the
Medicine Men

Meeting the Medicine Men

*An Englishman's Travels
among the Navajo*

Charles Langley

NICHOLAS BREALEY
PUBLISHING

BOSTON • LONDON

First published by Nicholas Brealey Publishing in 2008.

Nicholas Brealey Publishing
20 Park Plaza, Suite 1115A
Boston, MA 02116, USA
Tel: + 617-523-3801
Fax: + 617-523-3708

Nicholas Brealey Publishing
3-5 Spafield Street, Clerkenwell
London, EC1R 4QB, UK
Tel: +44-(0)-207-239-0360
Fax: +44-(0)-207-239-0370

www.nicholasbrealey.com

© 2008 by Charles Langley

12 11 10 09 08   1 2 3 4 5

ISBN: 978-1-85788-507-1

Library of Congress Cataloging-in-Publication Data

Langley, Charles, 1950–
  Meeting the medicine men: an Englishman's travels among the Navajo /
Charles Langley.
    p.   cm.
  1. Navajo Indians—Religion. 2.Navajo Indians—Medicine.
3. Shamans—New Mexico. 4. Traditional medicine—New Mexico.
5. New Mexico—Social life and customs. 6. Langley, Charles. I. Title.

  E99.N3L365 2008
  978.9004'9726–dc22

2008002900

SOME READERS MAY FIND the events recorded within these pages hard to believe and I certainly would not blame them for that. Nevertheless, these things did happen and for the most part they happened pretty well as I describe. The places I name also exist and so do the people. However, those who allowed me into their homes also trusted me to keep their secrets. With this in mind I have deliberately jumbled people, places, and events so that, while those who were present may occasionally recognise themselves, no one else will. That aside, I believe I have made a true record of at least one small part of the remarkable spiritual life of the Navajo people. In these uncertain times many of us from other nations might also wish we had the wisdom and strength of our Paleolithic ancestors to gird around us.

—*Charles Langley*

To all my relations

Contents

CHAPTER ONE

Lucky Day   1

*"By the time I washed up in the United States,
I had reached that stage in life where a man less
lucky than me might have found himself slipping
towards a graceless old age."*

CHAPTER TWO

The Skin-Walker   29

*"For the next two weeks Reuben escorted me to the
remoter parts of Navajo territory and displayed me
to various Medicine Men."*

CHAPTER THREE

Blue Horse   53

*"Whatever it was did not return the next night, nor
the night after, and even if it had, in deference to
my hosts' wishes I would have taken no action."*

Contents

Foreword

MY NAME IS EMERSON JACKSON, SR. I am a Navajo full blood, born and raised on the Navajo Indian Reservation in the Four Corners area of the United States. My first language is Navajo, my first name of Nóódaʼ yéę Binálí is Navajo, my first culture is Navajo, and my English came later.

I served the Native American Church of North America for twelve years as its President and for eight years as its executive officer. As president I incorporated and established Native American Church Chapters in the USA, Canada, and Mexico, as well as working with the United States Congress in the passage of the American Indian Religious Freedom Act and its 1994 Amendment, which guaranteed forever the right of American Indians to use the sacred peyote in our worship. In this endeavor I led a peaceful march on the United States Supreme Court in Washington DC for the religious freedom of all indigenous peoples. I am a retired tribal employee and worked as an administrator of various social service programs for the Navajo tribe, and I am a former elected official of the Navajo tribal council and legislature. Also I served on many Native American programs throughout the United States, Canada, and Mexico, and as president and a member of school boards in both the U.S. and Mexico. I was chairman of the board of the Migrant Farm Workers of America and strove to improve the working conditions, living conditions, and wages of migrant workers. I attended the University of New Mexico and I am a United States Army veteran. Recently, I was honored by the Maya Indians of Guatemala, Central America, as a "Spiritual Leader of America." I am a Navajo Medicine Man.

Foreword

With reference to Charles Langley, in the spring of 2003 I got to know him through Eddie Tso, Program Director of the Office of Dine´ Culture, Language and Community Services of the Navajo Nation. I have confidence and trust that everything he experienced through his visitation with different spiritual leaders is true and accurate. As I read the book I was somewhat surprised that the Medicine Men trusted him to take part in some areas of the divining and healing process. It does not happen very often among the Navajos that a white man is allowed to take part in this kind of thing. But, then, there was always something different about him.

There are many cultures in the Southwest United States where many tribes still practice the ancient Indian ceremonials and rituals with the sacred herbs and prayers of their ancestors. As I travel throughout the United States, Canada, Mexico, and South America, I find it is the Southwest Indians of the United States, to this day, who hold most strongly to their ancient ways and languages. Charles Langley was deeply interested in this and I suppose that is why he decided to do what he did. I admire him for getting down to the grass roots level of our Navajo people—it is not an easy thing for a white man to do, let alone an Englishman from London. It is also a very brave thing for him to do. No one should underestimate the power of Navajo witchcraft and although he denies it, I think he must have been pretty scared at times: because _no one_ can come face to face with Navajo witchcraft and not be scared. I was also amused at his dogged determination to try to bring scientific principals to bear on our ancient practices. I think most Indians would wish him the best of luck with that one! Few will think he is likely to succeed and most of us will trust that in time he will learn better.

As a book for general readers about an important part of our Navajo culture I think this is as good and accurate account as we are likely to see. I agree with him when he says that some non-Indian readers may find it difficult to believe some of the things he describes. But none of it will come as any surprise to Navajos, because these things go on around here ALL THE TIME.

I trust that as you read this book you will understand that it came from the sacred heart of our Navajo Nation, its people, its Medicine Men, and our ancient traditions. I thoroughly endorse this book and I hope you enjoy reading it as much as I did.

Emerson Jackson, Sr., Navajo Elder
Navajo Indian Nation,
Window Rock, Arizona

CHAPTER ONE

Lucky Day

B Y THE TIME I WASHED UP in the United States, I had reached that stage in life where a man less lucky than me might have found himself slipping towards a graceless old age.

Instead, I packed in my job, waved a cheery farewell to the sad man paid to worry about my pension, and one mild May morning set out to wander through the world. That I enjoyed my share of good fortune during this journey is beyond dispute, but I was never luckier than the day I drove into Albuquerque, New Mexico.

I had come that way after a series of unlikely coincidences— if coincidences they be—had sent me hundreds of miles north from Breaux Bridge, Louisana, in search of the Navajo Indian reservation. My task was simple enough. As I passed the reservation on my way to San Francisco, I was to deliver a boot full of presents from folks in Louisiana to some Navajo veterans of World War II. As it turned out, there was nothing simple about it.

Driving west from Amarillo, Texas, on a sunny spring day through a flat and featureless scrub desert, what looked like enormous fluffy white sheep lying down in a field began to appear in the distance. Eventually, a small flock of the creatures dotted the horizon, until closer inspection revealed them to be the snow capped peaks of far off hills.

I was driving on Route 66, the old Road of Dreams. Now re-named the I-40, it is still the only major east-west highway in what remains of the Wild West, and it crosses the desert straight as a speeding bullet to the heart of Albuquerque. The final approach to the city is made through a narrow, winding pass in the snow-covered hills, and once through the gap, the city of Albuquerque, the valley of the Rio Grande, and the distant peak of Mount Taylor appear so suddenly they could have been magicked into existence.

I'd intended to stop for the night in the picturesque old Span-ish part of Albuquerque, which dates from the 1700s, but some-how became lost and found myself outside a Wal-Mart superstore just off Central Avenue. There, seated on a low stone wall by a bus stop, was a young man whose bored and blank expression told the story of bus passengers the world over.

"How do I get to the Old Town?" I shouted to him through the car's open window. He looked at me curiously and for a mo-ment I thought he hadn't understood my English accent. Then his face lit up.

"I'm going that way. Gimme a ride to I-40 West and I'll show you," he volunteered. It was the same I-40 that I had just left, but I figured that if he knew the way, that was fine by me. So I leaned across the seat and opened the door.

"OK," I said. "Jump in."

He threw a small holdall onto the back seat of my fast little Mercury Cougar and climbed in beside me. A long, lean, dark-skinned man in his early twenties, he was obviously an Indian, al-though he was wearing a white cowboy hat, dark jeans, and an old denim shirt. As we drove he introduced himself as Reuben Waneke.

"I'm a Navajo," he said proudly. "Know what that means?"

"Sure I do. You're an Indian," I said.

"That's right, man. Don't ever call us Native Americans. Jeez, the names people hang on us. *Native American* sounds like some fat pizza-eater from Chicago. Do you know what the word Navajo really means?" Reuben demanded.

"No," I admitted. I was about to explain that I was from England and could not be expected to know, but he did not wait to hear.

"It don't mean nothin'!" he grimaced in disgust. "It don't mean nothin' in Spanish, it don't mean nothin' in English and it don't mean nothin' in the Navajo language, either."

"Then why do people call you Navajos?" I asked.

"We're not called Navajos, we're called Diné," he said, emphasizing the word Diné, which he pronounced *Dee*-NAY. "Diné means 'The People' and that's our real name. But sometime, a long time ago so they say, our scouts met the first Spanish people comin' up from Mexico. The Spanish asked who they were and our people told 'em they was scouts. Our word for scout sounds a bit like "navajo" if you say it quick, and the name stuck. Only the story ain't true," Reuben added darkly.

"How do you know it's not true?" I asked.

"Think about it, man!" he shouted, sounding cross.

Reuben took off his hat to reveal a long ponytail of jet black hair, which had been folded over several times into a tight bun at the back of his head and tied with a band of thick white cotton. After wiping round the inside of his hat a couple of times with his bare hand, he threw it into the back to join his bag.

I wasn't in the mood for guessing games. "Tell me. It'll be quicker," I assured him.

"'Cause if it was the first time any of 'em met, how could the Spanish ask the question if they didn't speak the Diné language? And how could our people have answered if they didn't speak Spanish?" he cried triumphantly.

He was right, of course, and I couldn't help laughing at the thought of the mutual incomprehension of the Spanish conquistadors and the Navajo scouts.

"What're you laughing at?" Reuben asked brusquely.

"It sounds funny, that's all," I said.

"It wasn't funny for us," he said grumpily. "We was prey to Mexican slavers and white settlers for three hundred years after that." For a while he sat in silence until, to change the subject, I asked where he was going.

"To the reservation," he said briefly.

"Is it this way?" I asked, naively pointing along the smart, tree lined, suburban avenue of single-story adobe houses through which we were travelling.

"No. Not this way. This is the way to I-40. When I get to I-40 West I can hitchhike," he said.

"Are you going to the reservation to see your family?"

"No," he said. Then, becoming serious, he added, "I'm going because I wanna learn the ways of my people."

"What do you mean?"

"I've spent too long in the city. Too long among the white people," Reuben said. "If you're born an Indian sooner or later you have to make a decision. Either you're going be an Indian, or you're going be a white man. And I'm going be an Indian."

"I thought you said you were an Indian." I replied, feeling puzzled.

"*Of course* I'm an Indian," Reuben replied crossly. "I mean I'm going back to the reservation to study and learn to become a Medicine Man, instead of working in a lumber yard."

I blurted out, "A Medicine Man? Like in films?" and immediately wished I hadn't.

Now Reuben was laughing. "Like one of those guys dancing around inside a teepee shakin' a rattle and praying to a dead buffalo's head? No way! That's not being a Medicine Man, that's being a film actor!"

He laughed some more and when he quietened down I asked, "What does a Medicine Man do?"

He gave me an odd look. "Everything," he said.

"Like what?"

"I ain't supposed to tell."

"Why not?" I asked.

"It's secret. Medicine Man ain't supposed to tell no one. Specially not no *bilagáana*," he insisted.

"A *bila* . . . what?" I'd never heard the word before.

"*Bilagáana*," Reuben repeated. "That means white man in our Diné language."

For some reason I found myself laughing again.

"Now what's funny?" Reuben demanded. "Man, you sure find some strange things to laugh at."

Actually, I hadn't the slightest idea why I was laughing. Perhaps it was because I found myself feeling strangely intrigued by this fierce young man. He was fit and strong and although not well educated so far as I could tell, there was something about him. A purposefulness that caught my interest. So I pressed him further.

"You must be able to tell me something about Medicine Men," I insisted. "It can't *all* be a secret. People must have some idea of what a Medicine Man does."

Reuben thought for a while before asking, "You're not American, right?"

"I'm from England."

"That's not like being an American?"

"It's not the same thing at all."

"But you're white and you speak English," he said suspiciously.

"True. But I'm not an American."

"Which part of England are you from?"

"London."

"Wow, that's cool. Which part?"

"North London."

"Is it right that London is bigger than Albuquerque?"

"A lot bigger."

"How much bigger?"

"About thirty or forty times bigger I'd say."

Reuben whistled through his teeth. "Man! And I ain't seen nowhere bigger than Albuquerque," he admitted. "I guess they must have a lot of Medicine Men in London."

"No," I said, surprised by the question. "Not one."

He looked shocked. "You're puttin' me on!"

"I'm telling you the truth," I assured him.

"I don't understand." he said slowly, as if searching for the right words. "You people must have Medicine Men."

"No. We don't have them at all."

"But who looks after you?" Reuben persisted. "I mean, who looks after you spiritually?"

"No one," I said.

"Man, that London must be one hell of a bad place," he said and sat shaking his head and staring blankly through the windscreen, as if such a thing was beyond his comprehension. After a while he asked, "Don't the English people want to know about the other world?"

"What other world?"

"Where the spirits live," he said simply.

"I expect some people want to know," I told him. "But I don't think they know how to go about it."

"You've got to have a Medicine Man to guide you along the spirit way," Reuben said. "It's bad for the people in London if they've got no Medicine Man."

"You could be right," I said. "It can be a bad place at times."

"What about priests?" he asked. "Don't you have priests in London? Don't they look after people's spirits?"

I was about to explain that in a big city, where people have many pressures and demands upon them, it is difficult to look after the body, let alone the spirit, but he interrupted me.

"I guess they don't believe that Christian stuff no more," he said. "Two thousand years waiting around for someone who never turns up is long enough to wait for anyone."

"That could account for it," I agreed.

Reuben nodded. "They taught us Christian stuff at school and tried to make sure we didn't learn our Indian traditions. They tried to make us think the ways of my people were bad and the Medicine Men were fooling us. But the more those missionaries talked, the more I realised it was the Christians that was trying to fool us, and it was the Medicine Men who knew the truth my people have known since time began. Those missionaries never told us about all the massacres, all the murders, all the ruin they'd brought on my people in the name of Christ. They wanted to keep all that hidden. And they wondered why I never went to church! As soon as I was old enough I knew I wanted to walk the same road the Medicine Men walk. I knew that was the way I had to go and to walk in that Holy Way. Not the Anglo way, not the white man's way, but in the Indian way. Turns out it's not an easy thing to do," he said, looking thoughtful.

Perhaps I should explain that for many years I worked as a journalist, until eventually I found office life too claustrophobic. Since then life had been a dream and my wanderings had taken me across half the globe. Unfortunately, on the day I met Reuben it looked as if the dream was about to end. The money had run out and in a few days I would have to drive west on the I-40 for a thousand miles to San Francisco to link up with friends. Then, after a few days' junketing, it would be time to take the plane back to London and back to whatever constituted normal life. I didn't want to go, but with my bank balance rolling its eyes like a steer in a slaughterhouse, there wasn't much choice.

The pain of knowing the dream was over had been nagging away at me like an aching tooth for several weeks. Constantly going through my mind were ways to avoid it, but so far I had failed to come up with anything convincing and at this late stage it was unlikely that I could. Marrying a rich woman, discovering a gold mine, or tunnelling into the Bank of America were all objectives it seemed unlikely could be attained by next Tuesday. The problem kept revolving endlessly at the back of my mind, even as I pulled in at an underpass to let Reuben out on to the slip road to the I-40. While he twisted round to rummage in the back seat for his bag and hat, I sat listening to the traffic thunder by overhead and wondered if there was any escape for me. It was at that moment that an idea popped into my head.

I'll never know what prompted it. Perhaps spring was in the air and I was feeling the sap rise. Or perhaps the Diné spirits were already at work on me. At any rate, whatever Reuben was up to sounded a lot more exciting than merely delivering presents, and I heard myself volunteering to take him to the reservation.

"I'll take you to the door if you'll tell me more about Medicine Men and what they do," I offered.

His surprise at my offer, as I was soon to discover, was that while my idea of an Indian reservation was of some kind of park outside the city with a few teepees on it, Reuben knew perfectly well that his destination was many hours' drive away in a remote corner of a slab of territory the size of the Republic of Ireland. While I thought I was driving him a few miles along the road, he knew we were on our way to a semi-autonomous, self-governing nation within the United States that is home to 160,000 Navajo Indians. A territory so vast it straddles the three states of New Mexico, Arizona, and Utah and in the north reaches up to the border of Colorado.

Of course, if I'd paid attention to the map I would have known. On the other hand, if I'd read the map closely, I would not have taken him, and the history I am about to relate would never have happened.

I started to get a clue when, two and a half hours later, we crossed the state line from New Mexico into Arizona and shortly after that left the last bit of tarmac behind.

We bumped slowly along a series of increasingly narrower and rougher dirt tracks, each of which led deeper and deeper into a juniper forest that stretched from horizon to horizon. To an Englishman the word "forest" conjures visions of tall trees, sun-dappled glades, cooling streams and panting harts. But this forest was situated on the northern fringes of the Chihuahua Desert, a desert so enormous it stretches all the way to Mexico, where it consists mostly of sand and cacti. However, on the northern fringe where we were, enough rain falls to allow the growth of stunted juniper trees, interspersed by the occasional piñon pine, beneath whose gnarled and knotted boughs grows a spiky undergrowth of sagebrush and prickly pears. Wherein lurk mountain lions, bears, wolves, coyotes, rattlesnakes, black widow spiders and any number of ways of instant death—or so Reuben assured me. Overhead buzzards circled endlessly.

At the time it seemed to me the greatest danger lay not in the snakes and bears, but in the state of the roads. My low-slung little car was not designed for off-road driving and I had to creep along at twenty miles per hour to keep the exhaust pipe in place. Even at that speed the car frequently rattled and shook so violently I thought my teeth would fall out. Occasionally a truck shot past, leaving me blinded and coughing in a cloud of red dust, but for the most part we saw no one. Along the way Reuben told me a lot of things about Navajo life, and in return learnt a fair bit about my life on Fleet Street. But when it came to the subject of Medicine Men he proved to be a master of circumlocution and I heard nothing of substance.

I had been driving for hours, half of it bumping along the tracks, and by now it was almost dark and I was beginning to wonder how much farther we had to go. Then, as we crested one particularly bone-jarring rise, Reuben called out for me to stop. He stepped out of the car and stood peering into the gathering gloom for a several moments before climbing back in and pointing straight ahead.

"It's up there," he said.

We drove for another mile in the yellow glow of the headlights before he again told me to stop.

"There," he said, pointing to the side of the road. "We have to go that way."

At a right angle to the track I could just make out two thin, rutted tyre marks leading due west into the desert. There was no road, no track. Only the tyre marks.

"I can't get my car up there," I told him. "It's just desert."

He seemed to appreciate the point. "Then we'll have to walk," he said.

Reaching into the back for his holdall and hat, he opened the door, climbed out, and stood waiting for me to follow. At first I was reluctant. I had no idea where I was or where I had been, and still less of where I was going. The sun was about to go down and I doubted I could find my way through the maze of tracks back to the main road in the dark. In this isolated place, the possibility that Reuben might be a serial axe murderer suddenly didn't seem funny.

"There's nowhere to leave the car," I objected, aware that my voice sounded plaintive.

"Leave it here," Reuben replied, pointing to the side of the track.

"Here? What if someone steals it?"

"Man, there's nobody gonna steal your car. There's no one for miles around *to* steal your car. Leave it and let's get going," he said, sounding bored.

I hesitated. "I'm not sure. . . ."

"You want to know about Medicine Men?"

I wasn't so sure about that anymore either. But I said "yes," if only to maintain appearances.

"You'll find one over there," Reuben said, pointing along the tyre tracks and into the void.

Still sitting in the driver's seat, I looked through the passenger window and saw that the tracks disappeared over the brow of a low desert hill. It was probably an illusion, but against the red dust of the desert floor, they seemed to glow in the half-light as if beckoning me on.

"Over there?" I asked, pointing and trying not to sound scared.

"Sure," said Reuben nonchalantly.

"What would a Medicine Man be doing over there?"

"Medicine," he replied. Ask a silly question, as they say.

As I locked the car, the last thing I noticed was the dashboard clock telling me that my act of charity had now taken seven hours, while the trip meter told me we had covered 327 miles. Whatever else I was going to do that night, I was not going to sleep in the comfortable motel room in Old Spanish Albuquerque with the king-size bed I had promised myself. As we set out on foot following the thin line of the tyre tracks across the desert, the sun dipped below the horizon. As it went down, the sky turned to a blazing red. After a while the fire in the sky faded to a pale iridescent blue, into which a new moon rose. Thin as a sickle blade and white as mistletoe berries, the moon seemed to float effortlessly straight up from below the horizon to hang alone in the pale sky. After a while a big, bright star came out to join it and the two floated together over the black hump of a distant mesa. Then, one by one, all the stars in creation came out to join them, until the desert night looked like a snowstorm of white, sparkling light. Shining through the unpolluted air, the stars looked so big and bright, it seemed almost possible to reach up and pluck them from the sky.

If the stars appeared close there was no disputing that the cacti and juniper bushes were even closer. Junipers are bushes that probably wanted to be trees, but gave up for a lack of rain. As a result they are rarely much more than about twelve feet high and although they do not have spikes, they do have lots of spiky branches and a genius for sticking them in one's chest and face. In the dark they are a menace.

I cursed as I bumped into the first of many overhanging branches and soon my unsuitable city clothes were ripped and torn. Once I stubbed my foot on a prickly pear cactus and the needle-sharp spines penetrated the soft patent leather of my shoe and went into my toes. The pain was so fierce and sudden I was convinced I'd been bitten by a rattlesnake and, in fear of my life, hopped around clutching my injured foot until Reuben, laughing, showed me what had really happened.

My shoe had come off in the commotion and he picked it up, flicked on a cigarette lighter, and by its hissing flame showed me the prickles jutting out of the toe.

"It's nothin' man, just a prickly pear," he assured me. "It ain't gonna eat you, you're supposed to eat it!" and he laughed fit to burst. To complete my misery I walked into a particularly spiky juniper branch and cut my head. Like all scalp wounds it bled freely and I had nothing to wipe away the blood save the front of my shirt.

After more than an hour's walking Reuben stopped and pointed. Far away there was a faint light shining. "That's it," he said, and we set off again.

By this time the heat of the day had evaporated and, despite the vigorous exercise I was forced to undergo, I was shivering in the cold night air. Any light should have been a welcome sight, but this light seemed to flick on and off with an irregularity that made me feel uneasy. Only when we drew near was I able to determine the cause of the flickering. The light was coming from inside a rickety lean-to shed, and as we walked, the ever-changing angle of our vision to the irregular gaps between the timbers, caused the light to appear to flash on and off at with an irritating and unsettling irregularity.

"It's a *chaha'oh*," Reuben said, when I asked him what the structure was.

"A what?"

He paused for a moment before replying. "It means, like, a 'shade house.' I don't know the exact words in English."

"But what's a shade house?" I wanted to know.

"It's a Navajo thing," he replied, and more than that I could not get from him.

There was no door in the shade house, just a gap in the wall; inside we found five Indian men seated on the ground eating the remains of a sheep, the bloody fleece of which lay close by. They had roasted their meal over a fire in the center of the floor, but the fire had burnt low and the light we had seen came from a single oil lamp standing on top of an upended wooden box. The shade house proved to be made of thin branches leaned vertically against a square timber frame. It was roofed with smaller branches that still had a few leaves attached to them. The men scarcely looked up as we came in, but they silently made room for us

around the fire. Reuben said something in Navajo, which I took
to be an introduction, and then we were offered roast mutton, tortilla bread, and coffee from an enamel jug kept warming among
the embers.

Reuben took a jack-knife from his pocket and cut pieces of
fatty roast from the remains, which he wrapped in the thick, white
tortilla bread to make sandwiches. It was the best mutton I had
ever tasted and, being tired and hungry, I soon took the knife and
began to help myself freely. While I ate I had a chance to inspect
our hosts. They were all dressed in working gear of heavy denims,
big boots, and dark-coloured shirts and jackets. They seemed to
know Reuben and were friendly enough towards me, but apart
from the occasional word in Navajo they stayed silent while we
ate.

After a while two women appeared, bringing more platefuls of
fresh Navajo tortilla. The women were elderly and wore what I
would later learn was traditional Navajo *biil*-dress of calf-length
pleated skirts with brightly coloured velveteen tops. They, at least,
seemed surprised by my presence but they said nothing and, after
delivering the bread, went away again. A little later one of them
returned with a plastic bowl of cold water and an old cloth for me
to wash off the blood from the cut on my head. Which I did as
best I could.

Through the many gaps in the walls I watched the women go
towards the square outline of a house that was just visible in the
moonlight, about 100 yards away. No light came from the house
and the women went back and forth in complete silence. When I
had finished eating I thanked my hosts for the food, to which they
merely nodded politely, and we sat in silence once more.

After a while one of the men rose and went outside and returned shortly with a bundle of dried juniper twigs. Kneeling beside the fire, he pushed the ends of the twigs into the hot embers
and blew until they burst into flame. He carried them outside,
shielding the flames with his hand as he went, and through the
gaps I saw him light another fire about fifty yards away from the

shade house. Leaving a good-size blaze behind him he came back inside and silently sat down again.

Eventually, I could bear it no longer and tugged at Reuben's sleeve. "What's going on?" I whispered.

"We're waiting for the *hastaałi*," he whispered back.

"The what?"

"*Hastaałi*. It means Medicine Man in our language. When he comes you'll have to go."

I was somewhat taken aback. "Where will I go?"

"Go in the house," he told me.

"Will they let me in?"

"Sure."

"But I want to watch."

"You can't. White men upset the spirits. White men make the Medicine weak."

"You're going to do Medicine *here*?"

"Yes," Reuben confirmed.

"In this shack?"

"In this *shade house*."

Somehow I thought Medicine would be done in a special place, a magic place; not in a lean-to that looked as if it might fall down at the first breath of wind. Overhearing us, one of the men leaned forward and spoke in stilted and heavily accented English. He was about sixty years old and his deep brown face was heavily lined and weather beaten. His hair hung down his back in a long black plait and he wore a tatty old blue baseball cap.

"Medicine Man maybe let you stay," he said, smiling a little. "Maybe say 'yes,' maybe 'no.' Navajo people friends of *bilagáana* people. Medicine Man decide." I nodded my thanks.

Soon after, I heard the sound of an old truck wheezing its way along the track over which we had walked. A pair of pale yellow headlights came into view and a minute later the vehicle came to a stop outside the shade house. I heard the doors open and then bang shut and a few moments later two Indians came in. One was short and stout and about sixty. He was roughly dressed and walked with a slight stoop, yet there was an inner brightness about him that set him apart from the normal run of men. His companion was even shorter and looked no more than twenty. He had big round eyes set in a round cheeky face, above which hung a shock of unruly black hair that flapped about in every direction, giving him the air of a comedian.

"This is the *hastaałi*," Reuben hissed, pointing at the older man. "And the other's his apprentice—what I want to be."

As the two entered, the scene sprang to life. The men jumped up to greet them and everyone shook hands. They even shook mine. Logs were thrown on the fire, sending flames leaping into the air and conversation buzzed all around. But as the talk was in Navajo I had not the slightest idea what was being said. The women came hurrying from the house with more fresh bread and coffee and the Medicine Man and his apprentice sat on the ground and were invited to help themselves to the mutton.

After they had eaten, the pair left the fireside and moved a few yards back from the fire to a new position, where they sat cross-legged. The apprentice was on the Medicine Man's right while the rest of the company, including the women who now joined us, seated themselves on the ground in a semi-circle facing them. I could see it was a formal occasion because the women had donned heavy necklaces and bracelets of jade and turquoise to go with their *biil*.

Remaining where I was by the fire I watched as the Medicine Man opened a narrow oblong wooden box and took out what I guessed from its size must be an eagle feather. Next he produced a wooden whistle a bit like a child's recorder but much shorter, some pouches made of white animal skin, and a large piece of crystal the size of a man's fist. Unfortunately, at that moment someone remembered me. Something was said in Navajo and I saw the apprentice lean over to his master and speak softly into his ear. The Medicine Man nodded and a few moments later Reuben came over and whispered, "They want you to go."

"OK," I replied. "I understand." I remained polite, although to be honest I was not pleased and wanted to stay.

"Go to the house and sleep there. I'll come for you in the morning," Reuben said.

"You're going to be here all night!"

"It's possible. So make yourself comfortable, okay, man? The people in the house will show you where to sleep."

I thanked him and had already stood up and had turned to go when the Medicine Man called me back. I could not understand his words, but there was no mistaking his meaning: he motioned for me to come forward and sit down beside him. Then he leaned towards Reuben and asked some questions at which Reuben looked extremely surprised.

"He wants to know if you're a Medicine Man," Reuben explained.

"You know we don't have Medicine Men in London," I reminded him.

The Medicine Man knew enough English to understand that one and broke in. "You Canadian?" he asked. He pronounced it "Can-a-Dan."

"I'm from England," I replied.

"England-London?" the Medicine Man paused for a moment. Then asked again, "Can-a-Dan-London?"

I'd forgotten there was a town called London in Canada and ended the confusion by assuring him I was from "England-London." At this he smiled and said something in Navajo at which the apprentice, Reuben, and everyone else laughed. Then he nodded and motioned for me to sit next to Reuben, who by this time looked so amazed I thought springs were about to come out of his head.

"Man, he must like you," Reuben whispered when I had taken my place cross-legged on the earth floor beside him. "This ain't normal, not normal at all."

"What did he say?" I whispered back, wondering why everyone had laughed.

"He said the Crees live in Canada and they're our friends. And there are Navajos living in Canada, so why not in London," Reuben answered.

"Why is that funny?"

"He's saying you're like a Navajo."

"But I'm not."

"That's why it's funny," Reuben assured me. Then becoming serious for a moment, he whispered, "Maybe he's seen something inside you that he likes. Medicine Men can do that. They look inside and see things people don't know are there."

I would have liked to know more but at that moment the Medicine Man called the gathering to order. There was just time before conversation drew to a close for Reuben to whisper, "If you'd been American he wouldn't have let you stay, that's for sure." The Medicine Man now began to talk at length in Navajo. At times he seemed to be praying, at times he seemed to be addressing individuals. When he had finished, the man who had lit the fire outside the shade house went outside again, carrying a shovel. He returned a minute or so later with the shovel full of glowing charcoal that he emptied carefully on the ground in front of the Medicine Man. Altogether he brought in four loads of hot coals and when he had finished, the Medicine Man opened one of his skin bags and threw a few pinches of something onto the ashes where it spluttered and smoked, filling the air with a strange fragrance.

I sniffed at the air and hissed softly to Reuben, "What's that?"

"Cedar," he whispered. "To purify the air." Then he motioned to me to be quiet again.

The Medicine Man took a piece of wood and shaped the glowing charcoal into a five-pointed star. One of the points was aimed directly at him and at the tip of this point he placed his large crystal. He peered intently into the crystal, and also into the coals, while all the time continuing to throw cedar on them. Now and again he would point with a black drumstick at something in the coals and invite those nearest to take a look for themselves. I had no idea what they were looking at until, in what Reuben later told me was a dramatic departure from the normal course of events, the Medicine Man called me to the fire.

"He says there are many bad things in this fire," Reuben began to translate. "He asks, can you see the snake in the fire?"

I looked into the coals, where the Medicine Man was pointing and there was indeed what looked like a small snake nestling among the glowing embers. I nodded and the Medicine Man looked pleased and said something to Reuben.

"Snakes are a bad sign and he says it's unusual that you can see it. Most white men can't see anything in the fire," Reuben said. Then the Medicine Man pointed again.

"He asks if you can see the bear?" I could, and what's more it looked very like a bear. There was no struggle to interpret these shapes, they were as clear as photographs. The bear even had black ash hanging off it, giving it a ruffled appearance like the real coat of the black bear that lives in those parts. Then the Medicine Man pointed once more into the fire, but this time I could see nothing and looked blankly at Reuben.

"You would have to be a Navajo to understand what he's pointing at now," Reuben said. Following the line of the Medicine Man's drumstick with his finger, Reuben showed me a small piece of charcoal that had a strange double humped shape, with one hump smaller than the other.

The Medicine Man was talking and clearly expected Reuben to translate. Nevertheless, I had the strong impression that even with his powerful say so, Reuben was not at all comfortable about explaining to a white man what this was about.

"That's what he's looking for," Reuben said.

"What is it?" I asked.

"It's a curse," Reuben said through clenched teeth.

With that my lesson was over and we returned to our places while the Medicine Man stood up and, taking two of the men with him, went outside and began to walk around the shade house blowing his whistle.

"What's this curse?" I asked Reuben.

"These people have been cursed by witches," he explained. He sounded glum.

"What people?"

"The people here."

"These people!" I was amazed. They didn't look cursed, they looked perfectly normal.

"They own the house," Reuben said. I thought he was going to stop there, but after a second or two he shrugging resignedly, as if deciding that he might as well tell me what was going on after all, and explained. "Things are going badly and the Medicine Man has come here to lift the curse."

"But why would someone want to curse these people?"

Reuben replied with one word. "Jealousy."

I did not understand at the time—how could I?—that among the Navajo a curse is a physical object and not a form of words uttered with bell, book, and candle as among us Anglo-Saxons. A Navajo curse usually consists of various taboo items and "witching" objects that are wrapped up in a bundle and buried close by the victim's home. In some instances they can even be hidden miles away.

"The job of the Medicine Man is to find the curse, destroy it, and send the evil back tenfold to those who sent it," Reuben explained.

"Why does everyone keep looking at the fire?" I wanted to know.

"It is in the fire that the spirits show the Medicine Man what's afflicting the family. The snake and the bear are bad signs. When the spirits have shown the Medicine Man the bad things that are going on, they show him where to find the witch curse so he can destroy the evil," Reuben said.

"Have they gone outside to find the curse?" I asked.

"Sort of," Reuben agreed, adding, "but it may not be here, and if it isn't they may have to go miles to find it."

As he spoke, the Medicine Man and his two companions came in again and resumed their seats. There was more conversation in

Navajo and then the Medicine Man and the same two men once more went out into the night. After a few moments I heard the sound of truck doors opening and closing and an engine starting. There was a slight crunch as the ancient clutch was let in and then the truck wheezed away across the desert.

When he was sure they had gone Reuben relaxed a little. "They took the truck," he said. "This curse must be a long way off."

"And if he can't find it?"

Reuben barely suppressed a laugh. "You think anything can be hidden from the spirits? Man, you're crazy! With the spirits to guide him the Medicine Man *always* finds the curse."

"Why doesn't he take his apprentice?" I asked, looking over at the younger man who had remained seated and was accepting a doughnut and more coffee from one of the women.

"It's his job to look after the Medicine Man's equipment," Reuben told me, pointing to the box and the skin bags that lay on the ground. "He can only leave those with someone he trusts for fear the witches might get to them."

"Are there a lot of witches among the Navajo people?"

"Sure. Anyone here could be a witch. You can never be certain."

"Why can't the Medicine Man get rid of them?"

"Why can't the Christians get rid of evil?" he retorted.

"Good question," I agreed.

I waited to see what would happen next. But by now it was well after midnight and, exhausted from the day's journey, I soon nodded off. Reuben jogged me awake a few times, but I couldn't help falling back to sleep. Finally, he elbowed me hard in the ribs and accused me of snoring. "It's rude to fall asleep in a ceremony," he said. "Go into the house and get some rest."

I wanted to stay but as I was unable to guarantee wakefulness, I decided it was probably wiser to head for the house. As I moved towards the door of the shade house, one of the men gave me a blanket: a traditional-looking, brightly-coloured, woolen Navajo blanket with a weave so thick it could hold water. Wrapping it round my shoulders I stepped out into the night to find the temperature had dropped below freezing. That part of the reservation is nearly seven thousand feet above sea level and at that time of year, the beginning of April—or *T'aachil*, the Month of Buds, as the Navajo call it—the temperature dips sharply at night. I was glad of the blanket as I made my way in almost complete darkness towards the house. I intended to go inside and lie down but, as I stepped onto the rather rickety wooden veranda, curiosity got the better of me and despite my tiredness, I found a spot in the shadows and settled down to watch. But there was nothing for me to see and, eventually, I dozed off.

I awoke to find myself shivering violently and my teeth chattering like castanets. The sickle moon had long ago set and low clouds had come over to obscure the stars. It was so dark I really did have trouble seeing my hand in front of my face, and despite the blanket, I was so cold that at first I could hardly move. As I could neither see nor move, I tried listening instead. This rapidly became an alarming experience because I was unused to the silence of the desert after the city's bustle and roar. Soon I began to hear things, and what I heard was not pleasant. The intense darkness of the night produced in me the notion that every rustle in the underbrush—each breath of breeze through the dry twigs of the juniper bushes—must be Indians creeping up on me. I had been right all along: Reuben really *was* a serial axe murderer and, what was worse, he had axe murderer friends! The whole trip was obviously a put-up job to lure me to this lonely place and steal my car, dispatch me with cruel blows, and no doubt dismember my bleeding corpse with a chainsaw and feed me to the coyotes. No one knew I was on the reservation and there was no one to report me missing. My friends in California would miss me eventually, but it could be weeks before anyone came to look for me. How could I have fallen for it?

I briefly considered escaping into the desert, but the fear of running over a steep cliff in the dark, or into the jaws of a mountain lion or a nest of rattlesnakes was too much. Instead, I placed my back firmly against the timber wall of the house and prepared to sell myself dearly. However, no sooner had this desperate plan been adopted than the sound of a distant engine broke upon my ears, followed by the pale, glowing lights of the Medicine Man's truck. The vehicle rolled to a halt beside the shade house and I heard the doors open and bang shut again. Then I saw a spark, and a flame, and a new fire was lit outside the shade house. Doubtless to hide the evidence by burning my body! A few moments later flashlights were turned on and I knew at any minute they would come for me. As my paranoia reached fever pitch, there was a loud click and the door of the house opened behind me. A dark hooded figure stepped out on to the veranda, holding something large and black in one hand that was pointed straight at me. My only defense was to screw myself into the smallest possible bundle, thereby reducing the target area in the hope the inevitable bullet would miss. But nothing happened.

Then a woman's voice asked solicitously in English, "Have you been out here all night? You must be freezing." When I opened my eyes I saw that her "hood" was a blanket pulled over her head against the cold, and the large black thing in her hand was not a gun, but a mug full of hot, steaming, coffee she was offering to me. Coffee did not seem like a prelude to murder, so I thanked her and after greedily gulping down some of the hot, sweet, liquid asked, "What are they doing in the shade house now?"

"You mean the fire?" she replied. "They're burning the witch curse."

"Why are they burning it?"

"To destroy the evil."

"Can I go and have a look?" I still could not see her face in the dark, but her reply was kindly enough. "Sure, you can go and look. And when they're done, tell them to come inside because breakfast will be ready soon." She added this last matter-of-factly, as if burning witch curses was an everyday event.

I rose stiffly and, still clutching my coffee, made my way towards the shade house. There I found the Medicine Man, Reuben, and the other men gathered round the blaze. On seeing me the Medicine Man opened a paper bag he was holding and reaching inside pulled something out. A flashlight flicked on and in its beam I saw he was holding an object about six inches long and maybe two across. Thin, and tapering at one end, it was roughly the size and shape of an old fashioned wooden tent peg. I noticed at once that at the thick end it had two humps, a big one and a small one, exactly like the object I had been shown in the fire.

"That's the curse," Reuben told me. "Only the Medicine Man is allowed to touch it; if anyone else tries it will harm him bad. They found it a few miles away under a tree."

The curse and the Medicine Man's hand were both covered in a strange gray powder.

"It's wood ash," Reuben said when I asked about the powder. "The ash neutralises the evil. So they fill the bag with ash and put the curse inside to make it safe."

Some sort of twine had been wrapped round the curse and only when the Medicine Man had untied it, did I realise that what he was holding was not a single object but a bound bundle. As he took it apart the witch bundle proved to contain two pieces of wood that had been tied together and then wrapped in cloth. The whole thing had then been bound around with string. The Medicine Man pulled the two sticks apart and showed around the inside surfaces, which were crudely etched with drawings of people, lightning bolts, and other things I could not make out.

Reuben whispered, "It's a lightning curse. It was hidden in a tree on a hill a few miles off. The tree had already been struck by lightning and if it's been struck once it'll be struck again. You white men say lightning never strikes twice in the same place, but that's not true. Lightning attracts more lightning, and if that tree had been struck again with the curse still hidden in it, the lady of this house would have been killed."

"The lightning would have killed her?" I asked, trying to hide the disbelief in my voice.

"Yes," said Reuben. "The curse was directed at her and would have transmitted the shock of the lightning to her and she would have died. The white doctors would have put it down to a heart attack or a stroke or something, but we Navajos know better."

"But how? How exactly would it have killed her?" I wanted to know.

"I can't tell you how," Reuben said, his mouth set firmly. "In fact, I don't even know for sure. But take it from me, that's what would have happened." While Reuben was speaking, the Medicine Man picked up the piece of cloth in which the curse had been wrapped and shook it. Two fresh objects fell out and lay in the red dust where they were picked out by several flashlights. I saw that one was a stone arrowhead and the other a piece of broken stick with more strange etchings on it. The sight of them brought an audible intake of breath from the assembled Navajos.

"Something broken and something sharp. That's what they curse with," Reuben said softly in my ear, and for the first time he sounded scared. "Looks like we were just in time."

Quickly the Medicine Man scooped everything back into the ash-filled bag and handed it to one of the men. More juniper branches were thrown on the fire and when it was blazing fiercely the bag of ash containing the pieces of the curse was thrown into the flames.

"Did you notice from what direction they threw the bag into the fire?" Reuben asked, as we sat watching the flames consume it. I confessed that I had not.

"From the east," he said. "Always from the east. It's the most powerful direction against evil because the sun rises in the east, and brings warmth, light, and life."

Half an hour later the sun did come up and turned the desert into a kaleidoscope of colour. I had never seen the sunrise in a desert before. The dull earth and the sky were transformed into a riot of blues, reds, purples, yellows, golds and colours of every brilliance and hue. The dust of the desert floor turned from red to brown, to gray and even to pink, while the juniper bushes and cacti shone green in the early sunlight. The sun looked so yellow and bright, and rose so purposefully through a cloudless sky, that it was as if a living creature took to the sky. I was so taken with the beauty of the desert morning, I quite forgot that I was supposed to call everyone in for breakfast. It was only when one of the women appeared on the veranda to find out what was keeping us all, that I remembered and apologised sheepishly.

"I can't answer your questions," Reuben said over breakfast of more roast mutton and tortillas. "Anyway," he said, "even if I did, you don't know enough about Navajos to understand what you're being told. But I will tell you that everyone was pleased by the way you behaved last night."

"What did I do?" I asked, puzzled.

"You shut up and did what you were told," Reuben said. "That's unusual for a white man around here," he added. Later, after breakfast, Reuben walked me to my car. "I'm really grateful for the lift, man," he said, clapping me on the shoulder. "Let's keep in touch." He gave me his mobile phone number.

That morning I found my way back to Albuquerque and then eventually managed to deliver the presents to the veterans before driving to San Francisco where my friends were waiting for me. Despite their splendid hospitality in a huge house overlooking the Bay, my mind returned repeatedly to Reuben, the Medicine Man, and the Navajos. I wondered time and again how on earth the Medicine Man could find a curse the size of a tent peg in a desert bigger than some European countries, in the dark. Clearly it was a trick: it *had* to have been.

However, I could not help being impressed by the sincerity of all the people taking part. They had all seemed down-to-earth and honest—and while they might appear uneducated in a Western sense, I had the impression that they knew a few things that I did not. Looking back, I think it was their simple sincerity that put the hook in me.

After a wonderful few weeks, my friends poured me on to a plane back to England. Back to the big house in north London with its four bedrooms, two bathrooms, and the self-contained flat in the loft for stroppy-teenage-kids-if-you-have-them. There were plans for another bathroom and bedroom somewhere in the vastness of the house, I can't exactly remember where. As the kitchen was bigger than some people's flats I lived mostly in there, leaving only to buy take-aways. I slept on the sofa in the front room, as I could rarely summon the energy to walk upstairs to bed.

I began to realised I could no longer stomach London. The roads were so crowded it could take five minutes to get out of my street and onto the main road, while in New Mexico and Arizona I could drive a hundred miles at night and never see another vehicle. On the station platforms I saw thousands of anxious-looking people coming and going from work in the rain. Hating what they were doing, hating the way they were wasting their lives, despising themselves for it, they kept doing the same thing over and over again because they did not know what else to do. For a time it looked as if I was about to rejoin them.

I tried to work in newspapers again but somehow the motivation had gone. Someone suggested I get another job and I laughed in his face: it was like telling a restless tiger to move to another part of the cage. There was a growing realisation that I could no longer go on doing the things I had always done.

Looking back there is no doubt a voice was calling to me from out of the desert. It was as if, on that night with Reuben, a veil had lifted just enough for me to glimpse a new world. A world as utterly unknown to me, or my people, as the Americas had been to Columbus and his people. I knew enough to know that to explore it would be difficult, demanding, and possibly dangerous. But something deep within me said that not to at least attempt it would be even more dangerous and undoubtedly ruinous for my spirit.

One day I woke up, opened the ridiculously expensive curtains that were a legacy of a failed marriage, let in the gray day, and knew I couldn't stand it anymore. I still had Reuben's mobile phone number and so I rang it.

"*Ya'at'eeh*," he greeted me in Navajo.

"I'm in England," I said.

"Ah-ha." He didn't sound too impressed.

"I hate it."

"So why are you there?"

"I don't know.

"Why are you calling me?"

"I don't know. . . ."

"Yes, you do."

"I want to know more about Medicine."

There was a pause.

"You ain't gonna learn nothin' over there in England man," Reuben said.

"What can I do?

"Come back here," he said as if it were the most obvious thing in the world. I was broke but during the course of the day I hocked myself to my eyeballs, bought a plane ticket to Phoenix, Arizona, and within thirty hours I was back on the reservation.

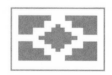

CHAPTER TWO

The Skin-Walker

FOR THE NEXT TWO WEEKS Reuben escorted me to the remoter parts of Navajo territory and displayed me to various Medicine Men. None of whom—predictably enough—would have anything to do with me. Until, eventually, we found Blue Horse. A well respected Medicine Man in the southern part of the reservation, Blue Horse was a small, round man aged over sixty (how much over, it was impossible to determine). As a young man he had served in the U.S. Marines and he maintained an air of authority. He reluctantly agreed to see me and, having seen me, even more reluctantly agreed to let me accompany him to a couple of ceremonies.

"Only once, *maybe* twice, that's all," Blue Horse warned. "Don't think this means you can come all the time. A lot of Navajo people don't want no *bilagáana* around for these things. The white man makes it all go wrong, all the power goes out of it."

By this time the idea of being allowed to attend one, let alone two, ceremonies seemed like something from the wider side of wonderful. It may not seem much, but it felt as if the first key to a door of many locks had been placed in my hands. But the joy was short-lived. I waited to be called to Blue Horse's side, but somehow months went by and it never happened.

During this period I enrolled at the University of New Mexico in Albuquerque with the idea of taking part-time courses in anthropology. I had the vague idea that my studies might fit well with anything I learnt about the Navajo and their ancient Medicine practices.

Finally, when I'd reached the point where I thought I would never again see that strange new world I had glimpsed but once, fate, or perhaps it was the spirits, lifted the curtain once more and enabled me to take my first stumbling steps into the ancient world of the Navajo Medicine Men.

I was sitting in the shade of a cottonwood tree near the entrance to the Canyon de Chelly, trying to memorise a list of Navajo words, when an Indian woman emerged from the red sandstone mouth of the canyon. She was riding a small, wiry, brown mustang and leading a second horse on a long rein.

Splashing through the crystal waters of the shallow river that flowed from the canyon mouth, she came to a halt a few yards in front of me and without dismounting, introduced herself in Navajo: "Ya'at'eeh. Shi Renata yinishye. Haash yinilye?"

"Shi Charles yinishye," I replied.

"Haadish nighan?" She asked.

"London, England di shighan," I told her.

"Please to meet you, Charles. I'm Renata," she said, switching into English. "I wanted to be sure you were the right man. It's not wise to go picking up strange males around here." She slid smiling from her horse.

"You speak good Navajo," she said.

As a matter of fact I spoke terrible Navajo and not much of it either. What she meant was that she was surprised to find a white man, particularly an Englishman, could speak Navajo at all.

"Diné bizaad ayóo shił nanitł' ah," I confessed. "The Navajo language is very difficult for me."

This was hardly surprising when one remembers that the Navajo language is so complex it was used as a code during the Second World War and for many years after. Full of glottal stops, strange half clicks made as if calling a horse, and irregularly changing verbs and post-positions, Navajo can defy years of study. During the Pacific War even such formidable code breakers as the Japanese were unable to make sense of messages broadcast in plain, ordinary Navajo.

Renata, however, had a different view. "English ain't exactly easy either," she said. "But we have to do our best with it." She paused for a moment to take a good look at me. "So *you're* the sponsor," she said.

"I suppose I am," I said.

A few months earlier when it began to look as if I would never link up with Blue Horse, I had tried a different tack and set off to find anyone who would talk to me about Medicine. At first I'd drawn a big fat zero but I kept at it because even if I didn't find anyone, at least my search gave me the chance to travel across more of the vast and very beautiful Navajo reservation than most visitors ever see.

One day my travels took me to Chinle, a small town deep in the reservation, where I had gone in search of a retired Medicine Men who was rumoured to be friendly to whites. He may well have been, but by the time I arrived he had been dead for several months.

My journey had been wasted and Chinle, a town of almost third world bleakness, was a place I couldn't leave fast enough. However, I was hungry and thirsty and decided to stay long enough to devour a burger and a coffee. Dodging the drunks begging near the Mustang petrol station, and stepping over the dead dogs littering the curbside, I crossed the road into the car park of a shopping center, only to be hit by a sudden dust storm. Blinded by the dust, my eyes streaming with tears, I dove for shelter into the nearest doorway. This turned out to be the entrance to the local supermarket and as I staggered inside, sightless as Samson, I collided with a tiny Navajo granny and sent her flying into a stack of empty plastic pallets used for bread. This poor woman was so slight of build that even with both eyes wide open I might easily have overlooked her.

I helped her to her feet with one hand, while trying to wipe the dust from my eyes with the other. Naturally, I tried to apologise profusely, but she spoke not a word of English and in the panic of the moment I could not remember the Navajo way to say "I'm sorry." Fortunately, one of the shop girls came over and translated an apology for me. During this the elderly woman shyly hid her face beneath her traditional head scarf and nodded politely. Only when I'd finished speaking did she say something in Navajo, at which the shop girl screamed and rushed to the upturned stack of pallets. Throwing brown plastic pallets left and right, she emerged after a few moments with what I thought was a bundle of washing, but which turned out to be a baby.

"It's her great-granddaughter," the girl explained. "The baby's called Shah." And without further ado she thrust the child into my arms and went back to her till.

Indian babies don't cry a lot—certainly not so much, in my experience, as their white counterparts—and this one was no exception. Despite having been rudely knocked from her great-grandmother's arms and deposited in a stack of bread pallets, the child still cooed to herself contentedly.

Despite the delights of Navajo babies, I was wondering what to do with her—and her great-grandmother—when the rest of the family began to arrive. First came the elderly woman's husband, Mr. Begay, who like his wife spoke no English, and shortly behind came their granddaughter and her husband, whose child I was holding. The granddaughter Michelle, a stunning-looking woman of twenty-five, worked as a computer engineer in Phoenix, Arizona, where her husband, also Navajo, was a pilot.

I explained what had happened and to demonstrate no harm had been done tickled the baby and made her laugh. At this the older Begays reacted so strongly I thought I must at have been mistaken for a well-known child molester and quickly handed the baby to its mother. Mr. and Mrs. Begay were waving their arms about and pointing at me and speaking loudly in Navajo to their grandson-in-law. Soon they were surrounded by a small crowd of bystanders, who looked at them and then at me and laughed and smiled and clapped their hands.

The mystery was soon explained when Michelle, told me, "You made the baby laugh for the first time, and by Navajo tradition when a baby laughs for the first time we have to hold a ceremony. My grandparents are extremely traditional people."

"That's very nice," I said. "I'm glad to have been of service."

Michelle pulled a face that was a cross between embarrassment and forbearance. "According to tradition it's the person who makes the baby laugh who has to sponsor the ceremony," she explained. "My grandparents are saying it's you who must sponsor the ceremony for Shah."

"Me!" I was astonished. "Are you sure that was the first time your baby's ever laughed?"

"Quite sure," she said.

"But I wouldn't know what to do. I'm from England." I explained.

At that moment her husband came over and introduced himself. His name was Josh. "Don't worry," he said, handing me his card. "It's an old tradition and the old folks feel strongly about it, but you won't have to sponsor a ceremony. It's expensive and complicated and I don't expect a complete stranger to get burdened with it. I'll sort it out."

They had turned to go when I called them back. "It would be an honour for me to sponsor the ceremony for Shah," I told them. "Please let me help."

When this was translated the old people looked very happy, although the young parents looked a little uneasy.

Over the next several days, after a series of phone calls, it was agreed that I would indeed be the official sponsor of the ceremony and the parents would share the cost with me.

"At the First Laugh Ceremony the idea is that it's the baby who's holding the party and giving away food and presents," Michelle explained. "The more she gives away the more generous a person she will grow up to be and the more people will like her.

The thought is that she'll grow up to be like the sponsor of the ceremony, so the sponsor has to prove himself to be very generous as well."

In the end the costs were not that great and baby Shah contented herself with providing a good lunch and giving away lots of brown paper goody bags filled with cake, biscuits, and little toys.

I assumed the ceremony would be held at Josh and Michelle's home in Phoenix but then late in the day I learned the great-grandparents were insisting the First Laugh Ceremony be held at their home. I knew the Begays lived deep inside the Canyon de Chelly, but I had no idea where. So it was decided that Renata, who was Michelle's aunt, would pick me up and take me there.

Now that we'd met, Renata seemed a pleasant lady, jolly and rather round, like many Navajo women, but I had rarely seen a woman wearing so much make-up. She was simply plastered in it.

I'd been expecting to be picked up in a truck, the usual mode of transport in the area, and had not the slightest idea at that stage why my "lift" had turned up on a horse. Nobody had enlightened me to the fact that there are no roads into the canyon and the only sure way of getting about is on horseback. I suppose Renata's make-up went some way to distracting me from any any suspicions I might have had, so the first inkling that something was wrong came when Renata remounted and hauled on the leading rein to bring the spare horse alongside me.

"Get on," she said.

"But where's the truck?" I asked in astonishment.

"There's no truck. There are no roads," she replied, sounding equally astonished at the question.

I looked at the thin, deep brown mustang before me and gulped. "But I can't ride. I've never been on a horse in my life," I told her.

Renata affected a complete lack of concern. "Get on. You'll soon learn," she assured me. So, with a good deal of trepidation,

I put one foot in the stirrup and began hauling myself into the saddle.

"No! Left foot in the stirrup!" Renata shouted. I switched feet.

"No! Go round to the other side of the horse or you'll get on backwards! Always mount your horse from the left side," she yelled, adding for good measure, "The horse's left, not yours!" Remembering to stay clear of the rear hooves, I walked round to the other side telling myself to be grateful these Indians no longer rode bareback, and somehow managed to scramble aboard.

"He's an old horse so he won't give you any trouble," Renata said, riding close and patting my steed soothingly, although it was me who could have done with soothing. Then she slipped the leading rein, coiled it and put it in her saddlebag, and without another word turned and set off into the wild and cavernous canyon. Obediently, my horse turned and followed, which was as well because had he chosen to do otherwise, I knew of no way to compel him.

The Canyon de Chelly (pronounced *Canyon der Shay*)— with its companion the Canyon Del Morte—the Canyon of Death—and various attendant side canyons make up an area of about 180 square miles of utterly wild and desolate scrub lands into which no roads, electricity, or modernity of any kind has yet penetrated. In the interior are bears, mountain lions, wild horses, and a few Navajos, who mainly live there during the summer to tend small family farms, much as they did before the white man ever came to their territory.

Near its mouth the canyon is about a mile wide and the walls are quite low. As we travelled further into the interior, however, the walls of red sandstone grew steadily narrower and higher, until they towered a thousand feet or more above us. It was still early in the year, but the canyon trapped the heat, and as the day wore on the temperature began to rise. Combine that with a large, hot, horse between my legs, and I was soon running with sweat and feeling uncomfortable in the hard American saddle. My steed turned out to be called War Arrow, an aggressive name that, fortunately for me, he failed to live up to and plodded obediently along behind Renata. At first we saw no signs of human activity and little sign of wildlife. A hawk circled lazily overhead, occasionally a lizard skittered across the path and little flocks of quail strutted among the undergrowth, the white crests of the males giving these timid birds an almost military air.

The only excitement came when we crossed the path of a small herd of wild mustangs grazing among the cottonwoods and Russian vines. The lead stallion came forward to warn us off. Angrily shaking his head and mane, he stood between his herd and us, whinnying and pawing the ground aggressively. Whether it was us or our horses he objected to I don't know, but Renata changed course to give him a wide berth. As she did so, she called over her shoulder, "If he comes after us, you fight him off and I'll make a run for it."

I spent several minutes wondering how one fought off the outraged leader of a herd of wild mustangs until eventually I decided she was making a joke.

Occasionally, Renata would stop to point out a landmark, or to pass me her water bottle, or slap on some more lipstick, but mostly we travelled wordlessly. I was lost in the silent grandeur and majesty of the canyon's vastness. Dazzled by the vibrant contrast of colours between the pale sand of the floor, the dark red of the sandstone walls, and the deep blue gash of sky overhead, I didn't feel like talking, and the further we went the deeper the silence became. Soon the only sound was the soft *thrub-thrub* of unshod horses' feet on the sandy floor.

We had been riding for some hours when, rounding a bend, we came upon the stunning sight of an abandoned city built high up in a gigantic split in the canyon wall. Buildings three stories high stood white and shining five hundred feet above the ground, so fresh and new in appearance I thought people must still occupy them.

"Anasazi built it," Renata told me when I asked. "Anasazi were the people who lived here in the canyon. The name means 'Enemies of Our Ancestors' in our language. 'Stay away from those places,' my grandfather told me. 'The spirits of the Old Ones live there and if you go among their houses and disturb them they'll come after you and haunt you,' so my grandfather said. Because of what he told me I've never been up there, and I never will."

We dismounted and Renata led the horses to a nearby stream to drink, while I stood looking in awe at the abandoned city. At first I couldn't see any way to climb the sheer cliff face in which it was set, let alone a way to carry up thousands of tons of building materials. The mystery was solved when Renata returned with the horses and pointed out a series of handholds that ran diagonally up the face. They were so small they were almost impossible to see at a distance, which was probably the idea. One can only stand in wonder at a people who had no draft animals and no wheel, and so had to carry on their backs every bit of mud, stone, and timber needed to build their city on the side of a sheer cliff hundreds of feet high. In addition, they had to carry up their daily requirements of food, water, and wood for their fires. It was a stunning achievement.

"I suppose they built their homes up there for defense," I remarked, but Renata shook her head.

"Not really," she said. "That was part of it, sure, but another reason is that those buildings are held together by mud. The heavy rain storms we have around here would dissolve them if they weren't built into a split in the cliff where the rain can't reach them."

"It seems to have worked," I said. "They must be hundreds of years old."

Renata pulled a face, "Those clever men at your university say maybe a thousand years old. Some say older, some say not so old. I don't think they know at all."

"When did the Navajos reach the Canyon de Chelly?" I asked.

"We've been here since the world began," she replied.

"The history books say the Navajos migrated from the north about five hundred years ago," I told her.

Renata laughed. "I read that too. I think the white people say these things so they can pretend they got here first and give themselves another excuse to steal our land." So saying, she remounted, and we set off again. A few miles farther on we came across a series of strange carvings on the canyon wall. Some seemed to be of men, some of animals, some snakes, and some were shapeless things that appeared neither human nor animal. Bringing War Arrow to a halt—he and I had now reached a sort of understanding—I asked Renata what they were.

"They're the work of the Medicine Men of old," she said reverently. "Some of the figures I can explain and some I can't."

I pointed to one of a man who appeared to be giving the kiss-of-life to a fallen deer. Renata laughed at my interpretation.

"That one shows a deer that was hunted for a girl's puberty ceremony," she explained. "The deer had to be killed without shedding blood, so the people chased it on foot until it collapsed with exhaustion. The picture is showing the moment when the Medicine Man bent over it and blew corn pollen down its throat until it suffocated. That way no blood was spilt in its killing and the hide was very valuable."

I asked if deer were still killed in this way but she did not seem terribly sure.

"We still hold the puberty ceremony and the Medicine Man brings the deer hide with him, so I guess people only need to kill a deer in that way once in a long while when a hide has worn out," she explained. "Like everything else, ceremonies change with the times. In the puberty ceremony we Navajo girls have to prove we know how to make use of corn, because corn has always been sacred to us as well as being our food. As part of the puberty ceremony girls have to grind a twenty-five pound bag of corn into flour, like their mothers and grandmothers before them, just to prove they can do it. For my puberty ceremony I had to grind the corn between two stones in the traditional way and it took me two and a half days. Now the girls use an electric grinder and it takes them fifteen minutes!" She snorted, making clear her disapproval of this modern affectation.

Next she pointed out the long, sinuous outline of a snake carved into the rock. "That's the symbol of the Snake Clan of the Hopi Indians. The Navajos fought them for this canyon and the Hopi went away. Now they live about 140 miles west from here. Those shapes that look like arrows are really lightning signs and those spirals are signs for the sun," she said, pointing to the universal shape that seems to have signified the sun to ancient peoples all over the world.

High up the cliff face, at a point it seemed impossible for anyone to climb without ropes and pitons, there were other carvings. One was of a man on a horse wearing a distinctive Spanish helmet and carrying a lance.

"The wall is like a newspaper and people came here to record what they saw in dreams and visions and sometimes in reality," Renata explained. "That picture is of the first white man the Indians here ever saw. He's clearly Spanish and the picture says 'Strangers have come into our land. If you see them, this is what they look like.'"

There was another, altogether different figure that caught my attention. It looked like a stick man with a big sail-like shirt billowing out in front of him. It looked so strange that I asked Renata for an explanation. But she became suddenly reluctant. "Come on. We'd better get going or we'll be late," she said, and urged her horse forward again.

We had not been going again for long when a large four-wheel-drive Toyota pick-up truck came tearing along behind us using the bed of the river as a road. As it went by in a cloud of sand and spray, Renata raised her hand and waved. There were at least fifteen Indians in the back of the truck, and I could just make out

Josh, Michelle, and baby Shah, among others, packed into the cab.

"I didn't know you could get a truck up here," I said to Renata, feeling rather put out, as well as saddle sore.

"You can if the river's not too deep," she conceded. "It's low now because we've not had much rain this winter. In the summer it's even drier and people often drive into the canyon along the river."

"Why couldn't we go in the truck?" I complained, looking longingly after the pickup.

"We've only got one truck and there's no room," she explained.

For a couple more hours we plodded on until, rounding a giant spur of rock, without warning the canyon—which had been steadily narrowing up till then—opened into a huge, sun-filled amphitheatre which, at my best guess was probably a couple of miles wide. Surrounded by the canyon's high red walls, it was a truly spectacular spot in a place of already overwhelming natural beauty. The amphitheatre contained within it a fertile plain, green with grass and crisscrossed by little streams that sparkled in the sunshine as they tumbled over beds of white stones. Bright green sprouts of Indian corn were already poking through the red soil where Navajo farmers had carefully planted them by hand. Beneath groves of cottonwoods, small herds of sheep, cattle, and horses grazed contentedly.

A few minutes later a strange, single-story octagonal structure with a domed roof made of earth hove into view among some scattered clumps of junipers. This strange-looking building turned out to be a traditional eight-sided Navajo log cabin called a *hooghan*. The word is pronounced "hoo-garn" in Navajo, usually truncated to "hogan" in English and pronounced "hoe-gan" as if it is an Irish surname. As the only source of timber in the area is the stunted junipers, Navajo builders resorted to building homes with several short walls instead of four long ones. When the walls are finished, the gaps between the logs are packed with mud to make the structure weatherproof and then the roof is added. This last is made of interlocking timbers, put together in a traditional design without a single nail, and is enormously strong. It has to be, because several tons of earth are then piled on top to waterproof it, and it is this great pile of earth that gives the house its distinctive, dome-like appearance. The result is a home both spacious and comfortable, and so well insulated that while it is warm and cozy in winter, in summer it is refreshingly cool inside. The door of a hogan always faces east to catch the rising sun and in the days before clocks, people judged the time of day by how far round their hogan the sun had travelled.

This particular hogan was the Begay family home and old Mr. and Mrs. Begay were standing outside waiting to greet us. Mrs. Begay was wearing her traditional *biil*, as well as some pieces of fine turquoise jewellery so improbably large they could have come from a rockery.

Once inside, the hogan appeared more round than multisided and there was far more headroom than I'd supposed. The floor was made of earth and in the middle was a stove fashioned from an old fifty gallon oil drum. A crooked chimney, made from old tin cans slotted together, took the smoke from the stove out through a hole in the roof.

The rest of the family, having long ago arrived in the truck, were anxious to get on and so, when the horses had been turned out to graze, baby Shah's First Laugh Ceremony got underway. I did not understand much of what was going on, but enjoyed the food, coffee, and soft drinks. There was no alcohol because alcohol is such a plague to Indians that traditional people like the Begays would never permit it in their house or on their land. Still less would they proffer it at a traditional ceremony for their great-grandchild.

When the moment came for baby Shah to give away the goody bags we'd prepared for her, everyone had to stand in line and hold out their left hand. Michelle then popped a peanut-size lump of rock salt into each hand and we all had to swallow it before getting a goody bag.

"Why salt?" I asked Renata, still grimacing from the effort of getting it down. "And why the left hand?"

"I'm actually not sure," she said. "You've got to remember our ceremonies go back to the Ice Age, maybe even before that. That's a long time for anyone to remember exactly why things are done in a certain way!" She laughed, before adding, "My mother will know, so let's ask her."

Old Mrs. Begay knew they answer all right, but did not have any English to convey it. So Renata translated for me as the old lady explained:

"At the beginning of all things, before there were people, the world was full of monsters. Then the *Diyin Dine'é*—the Navajo creator gods—created Changing Woman so the monsters could be overcome. Changing Woman gave birth to twins called Monster Slayer and Born for Water and one day they met Salt Woman. Salt Woman was happy to see the twins and the twins laughed, so Salt Woman gave Changing Woman salt for their First Laugh ceremony. Just as salt brings out the taste in food, salt brings out the best in life, and so we give salt in memory of Salt Woman, Changing Woman, and the twins, because it was given at the first First Laugh ceremony ever known." She paused before adding, "Some say it was White Shell Woman who had the first baby that laughed and salt was given to the *Diyin Dine'é* when they came to visit the baby. I don't know which is right, maybe both are right, but either way you can see why we give salt. And why in the left hand? It's because we Navajos hold things in our left hands to protect us from evil. By taking the salt in the left hand, we are protecting ourselves from evil things." It was slightly reminiscent of the old English tradition after spilling salt, of taking a pinch in the left hand and throwing it over the right shoulder in order to "hit the devil in the eye."

The party was a great success and when it was over and it was time to go home the family, who apparently all had urgent appointments somewhere else, piled into the truck and set off along the riverbed back to Chinle. There was no room for me, so I was left standing at the door of the hogan waving goodbye. The sun was already setting and the temperature falling, and I didn't relish the thought of another six hours on War Arrow. In fact, I was still wondering how I would manage to get home that night when Renata announced that I wasn't.

"The horses are tired and in any case we'll never get back to Chinle before dark," she said. "So we'll have to stay here for the night."

Mr. and Mrs. Begay curtained off a corner of the hogan for their daughter, while I was invited to bed down on the earthen floor beside the stove. There was no electricity, and once the family's two oil lamps were extinguished, the only light came from the flickering glow of the oil drum stove. After kicking off my shoes and socks, I lay down in my clothes and wrapped myself in the two blankets my hosts had kindly provided. Dead tired from the journey, and full of food from the party, the last thing I remember before falling into a deep sleep was the sweet smell of burning juniper wood.

I was dreaming that War Arrow had locked me in a stable and was hammering nails into the door with his hoof, when I awoke with a start thinking someone was knocking on the hogan door. Propping myself up on one elbow, I listened sleepily for a few moments before deciding it was only a dream and lying down to sleep again. My eyes had closed and I was drifting happily away, when suddenly: Bang! Bang! BANG! There were three heavy knocks on the door. There was no mistake this time; someone was trying to get in.

Hoping the others were still sleeping, I rose, put my shoes on, and padded silently across the soft earth floor. The stove had burnt down and it was pitch black inside the hogan, except for a single shaft of moonlight coming through the hole in the roof where the chimney went out. By this feeble light I found the old-fashioned wooden door latch and lifted it. It made hardly a sound and I had already begun to ease the door open when, behind me, I heard Renata call out, "Charles, don't open the door!"

It was too late.

At that moment a gust of wind snatched the latch from my hand and with a crash the door flew wide open. Behind me I heard Renata call urgently for me to shut the door and, thinking she was worried about drafts, I stepped outside and closed the door behind me. There was nobody there.

It was fortunate I had been sleeping in my clothes, because the temperature outside had plummeted and a chill wind was blowing. Reasoning that anyone knocking on the door in such a remote spot must be in trouble, I set off to walk round the hogan. Dark clouds scudded across the sky but, thankfully, the moon was well up, filling the canyon with its cold, clear light. With my eyes already adjusted to the dark, I was sure that I would see anyone who had perhaps been injured and collapsed nearby.

I'd almost completed a circuit of the building and had seen nothing, when I detected a movement in the shadow of a large juniper bush about fifty metres away. I turned towards it and then, unsure if I had seen anything or not, stopped and waited. For a few moments nothing happened. Then came the quick thud of heavy hooves and a crackle of snapping twigs, as something started in the underbrush. A few seconds later a large shadow detached itself from the juniper bush and began to move awkwardly across the landscape. Avoiding the moonlight it moved furtively from one clump of dark bushes to another. Whatever it was, it was a big animal and even though I could not see it clearly in the shadows, I could see it was moving so clumsily that I thought it must be injured. Its gait appeared awkward and at times it seemed to be staggering sideways, its movements crablike as if its legs were not working properly.

I'm often accused of being a city boy, although that is not really accurate. Long nights under the stars are nothing unusual to me and I've hunted by day and by night. Even when poor light and distance make it difficult to tell one animal from another, species can almost always be distinguished by the way they move. The bodily movements of a deer could never be mistaken for those of a cow or a pony, for instance, although they are all of relatively similar size. A fox moves in a quite different way to a dog, and a wild duck and a partridge both fly fast, but their passages through the air are so distinct that one could never be mistaken for the other by even a relatively inexperienced eye.

All that not withstanding, for the life of me I couldn't figure out what kind of creature this was. Its movements were unlike anything I'd ever seen. Then, for an instant, the creature passed through a patch of bright moonlight and I saw that it was a deer. The animal carried its head at an odd angle, its neck stretched forward as far as it could go and its head raised straight up. It had no antlers and its huge eyes were tilted in their sockets staring back towards me. Its nostrils were flared and its mouth open wide and panting as if in a state of panic. A second later the moon went behind a cloud and when it came out again the animal had vanished. Naturally, I didn't think a deer would be knocking on the door of a hogan in the small hours, so I continued my search for a while longer but, finding nothing, I returned to the hogan.

Inside, an oil lamp had been lit and after I'd closed the door behind me, it took a few seconds for my eyes to adjust to the brightness. When they did I saw the old people in their nightclothes sitting on the ground, moaning with fear, and holding their heads in their hands. Renata, who was doing her best to comfort them, looked up as I came in and with a look of desperation on her face held her hands out, palms up, in a silent, angry "WHY?" Not understanding, I started to tell her about the knocking on the door, but she cut me short.

"Don't you know never to open the door when something knocks like that in the night?!" she demanded.

"Someone might have been hurt," I told her.

"The only person gonna get hurt is you," she scoffed. "Don't you know that was a *yee naaldlooshii* knocking on the door?"

I didn't recognise the word and must have look blank because Renata shouted in English. "The *yee naaldlooshii!* The skin-walker! Don't you know what a skin-walker is?" She looked terrified.

I knew enough to know that a skin-walker was the most feared of all Navajo *Ch'iint'ii*, or Evil Ones. By day he often poses as a respectable Medicine Man, but at night transforms himself into the shape of an animal to go swiftly across the countryside doing evil. Only the most powerful Medicine Men have the knowledge to accomplish this shape-shifting. And the creature is all the more feared because no one knows which of the apparently respectable Medicine Men in the community is secretly a skin-walker.

"You must never, never, never open the door when a skin-walker knocks," Renata was shouting. "If you open the door the evil will get in and once through the door we will never get it out again!"

While she was speaking the old people were crying out loudly in Navajo.

"They're trying to tell you about the skin-walkers around here," Renata said.

"OK," I said. "But first let's all calm down a little."

After making sure the door was secure I threw some logs into the stove and got a blaze going so that I could make fresh coffee. Only after coffee had been served, and some sort of calm restored, did I ask Renata to translate what the old people were trying to tell me.

This is their story, which I wrote down shortly afterwards.

"A few years ago an old Medicine Man lay dying. He was a well-respected man. We knew him and thought well of him, as did everyone in this area. As he lay on his deathbed he called his family to him and confessed that he was a skin-walker. He told them he wanted to confess and put right all the evil he had done. The family was horrified; they had no idea, and neither had anyone else. It is not unheard of for skin-walkers to sometimes recant when they are dying, believing that if they confess they can save their lives.

"Before the family could do anything, other skin-walkers heard the old man was dying and began to gather around the house. They each wanted a piece of his body, because skin-walkers use body parts to make their spells, and pieces of a dead skin-walker are more powerful than pieces of an ordinary body. As the night wore on there was a constant rustling around the house as the skin-walkers gathered in the shadows, waiting for the death and a chance to pluck out parts of the body.

"Before he died the old man made a full confession of all the evil he had done and his relatives were shocked. Many of them realised they had been among his victims and that he had harmed them out of envy and jealousy. His confession did him no good, however, and he died before the sun came up. Normally the family would have carried him outside to die because, according to our traditions, if someone dies in a house no one is allowed to enter it again and it has to be burnt along with all its contents. With all those skin-walkers waiting for them, the family didn't dare go outside and so, after the old man's death, they had to burn their home. That turned out to be the old man's last act of evil and it cost them a great deal of money. Eventually they had to move away to Phoenix and get jobs to survive, although they were loath to leave the land they loved so much.

"The old man was buried according to Navajo custom and the family took great care to conceal his grave. But the skin-walkers discovered it and when the family went to look, they found the grave desecrated and the body bled of every drop of blood. Even the urine had been drained from the corpse and taken away to make evil spells.

"When the news got out it made people realise there were many more skin-walkers in this area than we ever imagined. Even worse, now that they had the body parts of another skin-walker, they were more powerful than ever. In the old days we would have gone to a Medicine Man and asked for help. But now we're afraid because we no longer know who is a good Medicine Man and who has sold his soul to the *Ch'iint'ii'*."

By now it was dawn and, exhausted with the effort, and probably relieved to have unburdened themselves, the old couple fell asleep. For myself, I did not believe in skin-walkers and was more concerned that someone might still be lying injured outside. So I invited Renata to come and search with me. At first she was reluctant, but as the dawn light strengthened and the night's terrors receded, she agreed to accompany me and we again searched the area and found nothing. Then, as we were returning to the hogan, we passed the spot where I had seen the deer and casually mentioned the creature's odd movements and appearance. Renata was horrified.

"It must have been the skin-walker," she gasped, grabbing my arm.

"No, no, it was just a deer," I insisted

"You don't understand! These people can do anything. If you'd gone near it, it would have killed you," she cried.

I reasoned the creature's tracks would prove it was only a deer and lay her fears to rest. But when I suggested tracking the animal, Renata would have none of it, arguing that even to track it was to invite evil consequences. Eventually, and only after much persuasion, she agreed to accompany me, although for the strangest of reasons: "I wouldn't dare go if you was a Navajo," she said. "I'm only going because you're a white man and white men are difficult to witch."

I was puzzled by this remark and would have asked more, but she already seemed nervous enough as we approached the juniper bushes, and I didn't want to make things worse.

We soon found the tracks and they were obviously the hoof prints of a deer, known as a "slot." Deer tracks are absolutely distinct and cannot be mistaken for anything else. However, I had to admit these slots looked decidedly odd. Instead of following one another they were at all sorts of odd angles and widely spread, as if the deer had been running with its legs spread apart. At times the animal appeared to have been moving sideways, which I have never observed a wild deer to do.

For all this, and the strange way I had seen it acting in the moonlight, Renata had a ready explanation. "If you turned yourself into a deer, you'd find it difficult to move like a deer at first," she pointed out. "The body of a deer and the body of a man are different and it takes some getting used to. That's why, when they turn themselves into animals, they move in a strange way. That's how you know it's a skin-walker and not a real animal."

After about a hundred yards, and not far from where I had last seen it, the deer tracks suddenly stopped. I cast around but could find no further trace of the creature.

"This must be where he turned himself back into a man," Renata said in a hushed tone.

"No," I told her. "This is where the ground gets rocky. Look, it's too hard for prints." I stamped my heel into the ground to show her that it made no mark, but she was not persuaded.

"He deliberately picked this spot to change back into a man," she persisted. "So that he didn't leave any footprints for us to follow." We searched for another hour, after which I was reasonably certain there was no one lying injured in the vicinity, and we walked back to the hogan. On the way Renata confided that her parents had been pestered for several nights by this strange banging on the door.

"Skin-walkers bang on your door to let you know they're there. Then they go around the house casting evil spells. But you mustn't open the door or go outside in case the evil gets in. And if you see one, that's even worse," she said. "My mother and father sort of hoped that a white man in the house it would scare it away for a few days, but no such luck."

Seizing my chance, I asked. "Why would a white man scare it off?"

"Because most of you guys don't believe this stuff. That's why it's so difficult to witch you and that's one of the few things that might scare a skin-walker," she said.

My private explanation was that the deer was injured or sick. Disorientated and in pain it had banged into the side of the hogan in the dark and, when I came out, gathered the last of its strength to stagger away into the darkness. By now it was probably lying dead in a thicket somewhere. To humour Renata and her parents I kept quiet about my theory, and on the surface went along with their more traditional explanation.

We would have rounded up the horses and started for Chinle immediately after the search was over, but the weather had turned cold and windy and was threatening rain. So instead we sat around the stove keeping warm and drinking coffee while Renata talked about skin-walkers. The picture I got was that they were bad and powerful, but good Medicine Men could overcome them—if they knew what they were doing.

"Surely you can find a Medicine Man to come and cast some spells to make it go away?" I suggested.

Renata shook her head. "These days fewer people are following our traditions and it's becoming difficult to find a Medicine Man who knows how to deal with the *yee naaldlooshii*. In any case we can't ask a Medicine Man around here after what's happened, we wouldn't know who to trust. We need a good Medicine Man from far off, but we don't know anyone."

It was then that I remembered Blue Horse. As far as I knew he was a good man and he lived at least 150 miles away.

"I do," I piped up cheerfully, although if I had known what was to follow I might well have kept quiet. "I know a really good Medicine Man who lives miles from here." And I told her who he was.

I used the Navajo form of his name and she smiled at my pronunciation. I said *billee*, which sounds like the English name Billy, but with a long *ee* at the end, and means literally "his horse" And followed it with the best stab I could make at *dootł'izh*, the

Navajo for blue. The whole name literally means "His Horse is Blue."

"I think you mean *biłįį dootł'izh*," she chided me gently. "But despite your pronunciation I *have* heard of Blue Horse. He's famous among the Navajo people." Then, slowly, a look of surprise spread across her face and she turned to look at me most quizzically. "How do *you* know the famous *biłįį dootł'izh?*" she demanded. It was the first time I had ever heard he was famous. So I told her.

"A white Medicine Man!" she cried when I had finished my story, clapping her hands to her head in mock horror. Then, turning serious again, she added, "It really would help if he could come here. It would help a lot."

Later that day Renata and I saddled up the horses and rode for two and a half hours to reach the canyon rim. The path was so steep and narrow that at several places we had to dismount and lead the sweating and panting mustangs by their reins. At some particularly narrow points, especially where the drop of hundreds of feet into the canyon was steepest, piles of rocks several feet high had been deliberately placed across the path and we took some hair-raising risks to get round them.

"These are from the old days when the canyon was a hold-out for the Navajos," Renata explained when I asked about the stone obstructions. "The people would hide in the canyon and the warriors would fight our enemies from behind these rocks to keep them out."

Eventually, dog tired and bathed in sweat, we made it to the top where, mercifully, my mobile phone picked up a weak signal and I was able to call Reuben.

Two hours later he rang back. "Blue Horse will come," he said. "Expect him towards evening, three days from now."

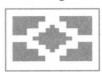

CHAPTER THREE

Blue Horse

WHATEVER IT WAS DID NOT return the next night, nor the night after, and even if it had, in deference to my hosts' wishes I would have taken no action.

Renata attributed this non-appearance to my presence. "See, all you need is one good white man and they run off scared," she joked. "It knows it can't get you."

Most of the three days waiting for Blue Horse were spent improving my Navajo and taking long rides on War Arrow through the stunningly beautiful canyon. It was a measure of my growing confidence in the saddle that he and I would sometimes be out exploring for hours. In the evenings, tired out and full of mutton stew and fry bread (a kind of deep-fried tortilla), I curled up on the floor next to the stove and slept like the dead.

While out riding I came upon a strange carving etched into the canyon wall. It was of a horse with its rein stretched across a carving of the sun. Many people do not know that before the Spanish invaded Mexico in 1519 there were no horses in the Americas. Indians walked everywhere and used dogs as pack animals. When the horse finally reached the tribes in the late 1700s and early 1800s, many believed it was some kind of "magic-dog" and in some Indian languages that is exactly what it is called.

The carving seemed to imply some kind of magic and so that evening I asked Renata about it and she told me the story of how the horse came to the Navajo people.

"According to our traditions it was the Sun that created the horse," she began. "The sun moulded it and breathed his spirit into it, which is why the horse is so beautiful and why its coat shines so bright. But the Sun was not satisfied and said to himself, 'this new creature I have made needs to have eyes that are bright and can see far into the distance.' So he reached into the sky and plucked two stars and put them into the horse for its eyes. Then he found white stones from the stream and put them in the creature's mouth so it would have strong, white, teeth.

"In the beginning the Sun created only four horses. There was a white horse for the East, because in our world white is the colour of the dawn. There was a blue horse for the West, because that's where the sun sinks into the deep blue of the night; a yellow horse for the South, because the South is the direction where the bright yellow sun is most to be found; and a black horse for the North because the north is dark and cold.

"When the Sun had made these four horses, he said to himself, 'I need to make sure this new animal is fast and strong.' So he spoke to Lightning and said, 'Lightning, strike this new creature I have made so he will move swiftly and kick hard at his enemies.' So Lightning struck the horse and that is why the horse moves so fast and kicks so hard. At first these were the only horses, but after a while Changing Woman saw the Sun and his four horses and wanted one for herself. The Sun gave her the White Horse of the dawn and from this she bred many other horses and gave them to the Navajos.

"Horses have many uses, some you might not think of for yourself. Horses are good to eat and in the old days, when a horse died, the Navajos ate the meat, which was very good, so they say. The horse can also protect you from illness, and if you kill one and eat it in the autumn you will never get sick during the winter, so the old people say. Horses are good companions because they are big so they can protect you, and strong so they can carry you from danger. For all these reasons we Navajos revere the horse and are taught that you must never mistreat one or kill one without good reason.

"At least, that is what we were taught in the old days, but now people often mistreat them. This is against our traditions and it makes me sad that some no longer honour the ways of our people." When she had finished, Renata recited a few lines of Navajo poetry about the beauty of the horse:

> My feet are made of mirage,
> My bridle of strings of the sun.
> My mane is like the white lightning,
> My tail is a long black rain.
> My eyes are big spreading stars,
> My teeth are of white stone.
> My belly is white as dawn light,
> My heart of everlasting garnet.

While we were waiting, Renata also taught me about the deep, central symbolism of the hogan in everyday life. "Everything in the Navajo world is male or female and so there are male hogans and female hogans. Naturally, female hogans are the biggest, most accommodating, and usually the most solidly built," giggled Renata, who herself was not exactly the slimmest woman I have ever met. "The male hogan is probably the original type. It's smaller and cruder, very easy to erect," she added, finishing with a perfect Freudian slip.

"The word hogan means, literally 'place home' and there are three main types," she continued. "The one you see most nowadays is the female type, which usually has six or eight sides. Small ones have six sides, big ones eight sides, but it's always six or eight, and never any other number. The door always faces east so the first rays of the sun strike the entrance every morning as a blessing. The story of the Navajo people's creation tells how First Man and

First Woman built the first hogan and covered the entrance with four layers: pale dawn, blue sky, evening twilight, and deep darkness. If you think about it, these are the same layers that pass over the entrance today.

"The hogan was the first thing that was ever built upon the earth and First Man and First Woman made it for us to copy. They made it so that it has a man's side, that's on the left as you come in, and a woman's side, which is on the right. It doesn't mean a man can't sit on the woman's side, or a woman on the man's side, particularly if she's sitting with her husband. But, in general, the women will sit on their side and the men on their side, which is how it was meant to be. The hogan is a very complicated thing and when you come to understand it, you'll see that although it's small, it contains a code by which the entire universe can be understood."

She pointed to the four main poles. "The four poles hold up the hogan and stand at the four cardinal points. This is to remind us of the four sacred mountains that stand at the east, south, west and north of our land." To Navajos it is the east, not the north, which is the most important direction and it is from the east that all other directions are reckoned. "The four mountains mark the borders of our territory and hold up the sky, as the four poles hold up the roof of the hogan. If the four mountains should fall, then so will the sky, just as the hogan will fall if the main poles fail.

"The poles also represent four important woman spirits: Earth Woman, Mountain Woman, Water Woman, and Corn Woman, and each one has a colour and a precious stone or shell that goes with it. The east is represented by the dawn and white shell; the south by blue sky and turquoise; the west by yellow twilight and the abalone shell; and the north is the land of cold and darkness and is represented by black jet stone. When you entered my mother's house you probably saw what you thought was an old oil drum acting as a stove. To us it's not an oil drum or a stove. To us it's the North Star burning bright in the center of our homes. As the North Star is the one fixed and unmoving point in the sky around which all the other stars revolve, so the fire is the point around which everything revolves in our homes.

"When I was born my mother was wearing a special juniper berry necklace to give her protection. She gave birth to me squatting, while she hung by her hands from the two ends of a specially woven sash women used to make in those days. The sash was attached to the roof and represented the rainbow. It was on the rainbow that First Man made his journey through life, kind of like a magic carpet." She laughed. "So the idea is that your mother holds the beginning and end of your life in her hands, and your life is brought together and made whole through her, by the act of her giving birth to you.

"In those days we still did things in the old way and so a hole was dug underneath where my mother hung from the sash. That was so the afterbirth would fall into it. As I fell from my mother, the midwife caught me in a sheepskin, and then cut the cord with a stone arrowhead. White women are taught that the first thing they must do for their babies is to suckle them. But the first thing my mother did was to turn my face to the fire. There wasn't even the stove in our hogan in those days. Instead there was an open fire of juniper logs burning in the center of the floor, right there where the stove is now. My mother turned my face to it so that, from the moment I took breath, the Fire God would enter me and I would know that the center of the universe lay in the center of our home. I would have done the same for my children, but it's difficult when you live in a trailer with central heating." She laughed again.

"After this my grandmother massaged all my limbs to bring life into them and then I was given back to my mother, so that she could shake my little hand and welcome me into the world. Soon after she took my first stool and smeared it on her face. That's to show the baby it is welcome and, no matter what it does, it will always be welcome with its mother. These days Navajo mothers buy diapers from the supermarket like anyone else, but you'll rarely hear her criticise her baby when she changes it. You won't hear her say anything like 'Ugh! This is gross.' Not a properly brought up Navajo girl anyway. That is not our way and our children are welcome to us whatever they do.

"As she smeared herself my mother recited an old chant:

Little girl, little girl, you come
Riding a pearl white horse.
You are welcome here. Welcome.

"If I'd been a boy she'd have said, 'Little boy, little boy you come riding a turquoise horse.' You Anglos have blue for boys and pink for girls, but we have white for girls because White Shell Woman gave birth to her first baby on *Sisnaajini* — that's Mount Blanca in Colorado to you white people — which marks the traditional eastern boundary of our land. Turquoise is for boys, because turquoise is the colour of our Father Sky.

"We are not allowed to destroy any of our body tissues, so the afterbirth was not burnt in some horrible, smelly, hospital incinerator like white women have to put up with. We always bury the afterbirth in a special place and in a special way. It is treated with herbs and charms and buried here on our sacred Navajo land. In that way part of us remains here in our land forever and so, wherever we go in the world, it will draw us back here to our homes."

Later, Renata spoke to her mother, and together they showed me the sash she had hung from when giving birth. It was made of thick, woven cotton, rather like the belt judo and karate fighters wear, but wider and softer and immensely strong. It had been in their family for more than 100 years.

As more Navajos become doctors and nurses, these traditional practices have been reintroduced into modern health centers on the reservation. Mothers can now choose to give birth while hanging from a sash in the labour ward. However, thanks to the hefty proportions of some Navajo ladies — even before they get pregnant — a specially reinforced beam has been installed to take the strain.

"When you enter a hogan you always walk to the left, keeping the fire on your right," Renata continued. "That way you travel around the hogan in the same direction the sun travels around the Earth. That's the Holy Way to walk. As you move around the inside of the hogan there are many things to remind you of your place in the universe. The roof is the sky, and the sky is our Father. The floor is of earth, and the earth is our Mother. And in the center, the stove the burns bright as the North Star to guide us to our families and our homes."

That evening, I found myself standing alone watching the stars come out. I don't usually think of myself as an exile, but all Renata's talk of home had made me think of my own. It was comforting to know that the same stars that shone on me were shining on my children so far away.

Towards the end of the third day Blue Horse appeared as promised, speeding along the riverbed in a four-wheel-drive truck and a cloud of mud and spray. On his head he sported his trademark white Stetson hat, to which he had attached a hatband of Indian beadwork and an eagle feather. A Navajo full-blood—as he often liked to remind me—he had a full head of jet black hair and wore a diamond earring in one ear, as well as several large rings of silver and turquoise upon his fingers.

"It's good to see you again, Charles," he said, descending from the truck and shaking hands. But of Reuben, there was no sign.

"He ran out of money and had to go to work," Blue Horse explained, before turning to Renata and the Begays—the rest of the conversation was in Navajo.

It was one thing to have Renata speak to me slowly and painstakingly so-that-I-might-u-n-d-e-r-s-t-a-n-d, and an entirely different experience listening to people speaking to each other in their everyday language. The only bit I could understand was when Blue Horse asked Renata, "*Díkwíish niná,áhai?*"—meaning "how old is he?" To which she replied, "*Naadiin naaki.*"— "twenty two." As they clearly were not talking about me, I took no further notice.

What I did not realise at the time was that my understanding of the situation in which I now found myself was a good deal less than I imagined. I thought the elderly Begays believed they were being haunted by a skin-walker sent by an evil Medicine Man, and that Blue Horse had come to lift the curse. I had not yet learnt that in this, as in so many matters concerning the Navajo, most of what was going on was hidden beneath the impenetrable cloak of a culture far, far, older than my own. The visible part of any business was always considerably less than the tip of an extremely large iceberg, and discovering what was really going on in those early days was often a matter of chance for me.

On the other hand, I have to admit I had not taken much trouble to find out, and for that I had only myself to blame. I am ashamed to admit that at the time what most interested me was the ceremonies, chants, charms and magic spells by which I fondly imagined Blue Horse would deal with the witchcraft. I was far more excited by the privilege of being allowed to witness this than I was concerned for the welfare of a badly frightened family. I did not believe in skin-walkers or witches, and at heart believed it was silly for anyone else to do so, and, for that reason, I failed to take their distress seriously. It was the typical delusion of which white men are so often guilty and I excuse myself today only by pleading that, at the time, I was too ignorant to know otherwise. I have learnt better since.

To compound the fault, I also did not realise that the person who had really been witched was not old Mrs. Begay, or old Mr. Begay, or even Renata. The person at the center of all this haunting turned out to be Renata's son Juan, who lived in Albuquerque, and of whose existence I was entirely ignorant.

A few hours later I was drinking coffee outside the hogan when a second truck unexpectedly appeared and parked beside Blue Horse's. From inside the hogan I heard Renata say to Blue Horse in Navajo, "my son," and a few seconds later a young man stepped out. Renata hurried forward and hurled herself upon the youth, who disappeared under an avalanche of motherly hugs and kisses.

Juan was a graceful six-footer, darkly good looking, with fashionably cut jet black hair and a diamond stud in one ear. As we shook hands I noticed his fingers were long and finely manicured. After the formalities, Renata insisted on taking him into the hogan to ply him with food and coffee, while Blue Horse took me for a walk.

"You're going to have to help me tonight," he began. "Reuben couldn't come and I need another man to help with the ceremony. It should be a Navajo man, but I couldn't find anyone, so you'll have to do."

"Why ought it be a Navajo man?" I asked. I was not much pleased at being relegated to the status of a barrel-scraping.

"A man has to be properly introduced to the spirits so they can get to know him and recognise him, if he is to take part in Medicine" he explained. "The spirits don't know you, and that's a disadvantage."

"Does it matter?" I asked.

"Very much," Blue Horse told me earnestly. "You have to be acceptable to the spirits or they won't help you."

"Would any Navajo man be acceptable?" I wanted to know.

"Not any Navajo man," he conceded. "A bad man, a sinful man, would be no use at all. But mostly a Navajo man would do. An Indian from another tribe would probably be ok, but most anyone would do better than a white man."

"What about Old Man Begay?" I suggested, still feeling a bit slighted, but also wanting the best result for my new friends.

"He's a member of the family. He's much too close to be of any use in a business like this," he told me.

"Couldn't you introduce me to the spirits now?" I asked, as if being introduced to the spirits was like being introduced to someone's friends in a bar.

"No, I can't," he said, giving me a scathing look. "We have to hold a special ceremony for you and it can't be done now. For tonight it won't matter because you don't have to do much. I'll explain to the spirits about you, so if you get things wrong they'll understand."

"What do I have to do?"

"I'll tell you when the time comes," he said.

I wanted to ask more questions but Blue Horse had other things he wanted to discuss and asked if I knew the cause of the haunting.

"All I know is that Renata's family is being troubled by a skinwalker," I said.

"Did she tell you why?"

"No," I admitted.

"I didn't think she would," he said, seeming uneasy for a moment before continuing. "It's all right for me to tell you what I'm going to tell you because you're going to assist me tonight. But be sure that you keep it to yourself."

He went on to outline a complicated land dispute between Renata's family and a rival family named Bennally who lived not far away. Apparently the two families had been warring over land, influence, water, cattle, sheep, and just about everything else since long before the white man appeared in the Southwest. The only change in recent times was that the two sides generally stopped short of killing each other—although, often, not by much.

"Then young Juan goes and gets mixed up with one of the Bennally girls," Blue Horse said. "Not only that, but it's Old Man Bennally's favourite granddaughter and, boy, is he not happy! The girl's father wanted to go after Juan with a gun, but Old Man Bennally said 'No, the white man will lock you up or kill *you* with the death penalty if you do. They're just kids. Give it time and they'll break up anyway.' But they didn't. Renata didn't like what was going on any more than the Bennallys. But when she saw her son was in love with on this girl she put out peace feelers, but Old Man Bennally wouldn't buy it.

"Nobody dared to do anything while the kids were together. They were scared in case they stampeded 'em into running off to Vegas and getting married and no one wanted that. After a while, though, her family began to put on the pressure and tried to get Juan fired from his job. Then they tried to send the girl away to school in Oregon. She wouldn't go and Juan hung on to his job, but eventually the pressure began to tell. There's a limit to how long an eighteen-year-old girl can keep going when her mother and sisters are refusing to talk to her. Finally, about six months back, the kids broke up and that's when all this bad stuff started. That's when they witched Juan so he started drinking and taking drugs and things, and then this skin-walker business started," Blue Horse finished gravely.

"But who witched him?" I said, still not fully understanding.

"The girlfriend's relatives. Who else?" he replied, as if stating the blindingly obvious.

"They did it themselves?"

"Of course not, they hired someone to do it for them."

"Who?" I asked.

"I don't know," he said, sounding a bit exasperated. "That's something I'm going to find out tonight."

"But surely," I said, you don't need witches to explain Juan's drinking and taking drugs. Surely he's upset about the girl."

"Then who sent the skin-walker?" Blue Horse countered. "His mother told me the thing's been banging on Juan's door at his apartment in Albuquerque too. It banged all night and he was scared stiff. In the morning he opened the door and found the metal screen was still locked in place. How does anyone bang on a door when the outer screen's locked? Tell me that?"

I had no idea.

"Juan's got a good job, a government job, working in the Motor Vehicle Department," Blue Horse continued. "He was doing well, but now he gets in late, he shows up hung-over and misses days at work. That's what happens when people witch you. They're trying to get him fired from his job."

"Did Renata tell you all this?" I asked.

"A Medicine Man has to know these things to work a cure," he said.

As evening drew on and the appointed hour for the ceremony drew closer, a kind of lethargy seemed to settle on the Navajos. Claiming he was tired from the journey, Blue Horse stretched out full length on the men's side of the hogan and fell asleep. The elderly Begays retired to a corner and lay with their heads propped against the wall, occasionally speaking to each other in whispers. Renata sat cross-legged on the women's side, staring vacantly at the ceiling while Juan sat on the floor staring at the stove. Occasionally, the boy would lift his hand to his face as if thinking of something unpleasant, until eventually he lay down as if to sleep. I too must have dozed off. When Blue Horse roused me it was dark.

"It's time," he whispered. "Get up. Light the lamps and the stove."

I went outside to get some wood and found the weather was changing fast. Black clouds scudded across the sky. A chill wind had begun to blow, ruffling the junipers and stirring up the undergrowth. Tin cans rolled about clattering against stones, while bits of cardboard and paper took flight. The cattle sought shelter under the canyon wall and it began to rain.

I had lit both oil lamps and was attending to the stove, when the door burst open and Renata came in. The storm had broken outside and she was wet through and there was snow on her clothes. She had been outside to light the sacred fire from which Blue Horse would take hot coals to divine the source of the evil afflicting the family. She'd had a hard job of it.

"It kept going out," she said irritably. "I got it going eventually, but it's not a good sign." She looked at Blue Horse, but if he showed any concern I did not detect it. Instead, he nodded almost absentmindedly, and sat himself down on the west side of the hogan in what is known as the Seat of Honour. In this position he was facing the door, and therefore the east, and the powerful rising sun.

Everyone else began to take their place in a circle around him. Blue Horse motioned for me to sit in the traditional right hand place of the Medicine Man's assistant. Renata sat on his left, in the traditional place reserved for the sponsor of a ceremony, and her parents were seated to her left, with her father nearest to her. Juan took a position sitting between his mother and Blue Horse.

Proceedings began with Renata giving Blue Horse a bundle of used dollar notes, which he slipped it into his top pocket with barely a nod. I don't know how much it was, but it looked about $120. It had never occurred to me that the Medicine Man needed to be paid like anyone else, although strictly speaking, it was a donation not a payment. When I came to understand how demanding the work can be, I was amazed Medicine Men sometimes worked for much less.

When all was ready Blue Horse called us to order. "It's important that we walk in a Holy Way in this hogan," he said. "Follow me and we'll do things the old way, the proper way."

So saying, he formed us into a single file behind him, with Juan—who from now on was regarded as the patient—immediately behind him. After Juan came Renata, who as sponsor of the meeting was very important in the hierarchy of the proceedings; behind her came her parents; and I tagged along in the rear. Blue Horse led us clockwise, strictly speaking "sunwise," round the hogan. When we came to the door, to my surprise, he opened it and led us out into the driving sleet and rain. Heads bowed, we paraded round the woodpile, which is regarded as holy because it feeds the light of the fire within the home, before going back into the hogan to walk sunwise once more, dripping to our places.

Once we were settled Blue Horse began slowly to unpack his Medicine equipment, or *jish*. He kept this in a highly polished oblong cedar wood box, which was about eighteen inches long and four inches wide, and decorated with shiny brass hinges and fittings. Sitting cross-legged on the floor and speaking conversationally in Navajo all the time, he took out some small bags of soft white doe hide, decorated with bright blue and red beadwork, and placed them on the ground beside him.

Next he produced a small piece of woolen rug woven with traditional Navajo designs, which he carefully unrolled before placing it on the floor in front of him. From his box he took an eagle feather and laid it on the weaving. This was followed by a drumstick made of dark black wood I could not identify, a small silver cup, which he filled with water, and a fan of brightly coloured feathers, all of which he laid on the little woven rug. When everything was arranged to his satisfaction, he spread a large red and white bandana on the ground and placed several stone arrowheads and a pair of large stone spearheads upon it. As big as my hand and made of black obsidian, the spearheads glittered wickedly in the lamplight. Finally, he produced a huge silver crystal, which, after a perfunctory polish, he also placed on the little rug.

This done, he leaned back to admire his handiwork before reaching into the box once more for a battered brown leather tobacco pouch and a sheaf of corn leaf cigarette papers. These corn leaf "papers" are something never seen in England. They are made from the outer leaves of the corn cob, which are gathered and dried until they become yellow like the colour of old paper, then cut and trimmed to a convenient square size. In order to be pliable, the dry corn leaves must be wetted. This he achieved by putting them in his mouth and gently chewing and licking them. When he judged his paper was sufficiently wetted, Blue Horse took it from his mouth and began to hand roll a cigarette using wonderfully aromatic Indian tobacco, which smelt of sweet herbs and honey. It was while he was still rolling his cigarette that he decided to send me out with an iron shovel to fetch the embers from the sacred fire.

The storm wind was blowing hard and it was raining, sleeting, snowing, and blacker than hell outside the hogan. Renata had lit the fire no more than fifty yards from the door, but it was so dark only a chance flare-up showed me the spot where it burned among the flailing junipers. As fast as I could I scooped up a shovelful of charcoal and ashes and, dripping wet and freezing cold, hurried back to the hogan. Once through the door I walked careful in the Holy Way, keeping the stove on my right, round to Blue Horse who pointed to a spot a few feet in front of him. But when I emptied the contents of the shovel he was not pleased.

"It's all ash," he complained, poking at it despairingly with his drumstick. "Ash is no good, I need charcoal. Go out and try again."

So off I went out into the cold, cold storm once more. After blundering around for a while, I found the fire and determined to bring him the biggest, hottest pieces of charcoal I could find. On the way back, the wind fanned the fistsize lumps of charcoal until they burst into flames and the snow and sleet hissed wickedly as they fell into the blaze. By the time I re-entered the hogan, the shovel load was an inferno but, once again, when I proudly displayed my efforts to Blue Horse his face dropped like a stone.

"It's no good if they're still burning. And those are much too big!" he told me, looking cross. "I need lots of small, glowing charcoal, not great big lumps on fire. Take them away, they're no good at all."

I set off again into the teeth of the storm, carrying the still-blazing coals with me. At least they helped light the way. I put them back in the fire, smashed them up with the shovel, made sure they were no longer flaming, and picked up a good quantity to take back. By this time I was so cold and wet I was probably in the first stages of hypothermia. Rain and snow were dripping off my hair and ears and down my nose, and I was miserable and shivering violently when I backed carefully through the door once more. This time I took the precaution of holding up the coals for Blue Horse's inspection before emptying the shovel. To my intense relief he nodded his approval and all might have been well, had I not tried to be helpful and scrape the coals into a neat pile for him.

"Stop!" Blue Horse yelled in horror. "The charcoal has to be left exactly as it falls or I can't read it." Panicking, I poked at the pile with the shovel, trying to put it back the way it was. "Leave it alone!" Blue Horse yelled. "Look at the mess you've made!"

It was no use, I'd wrecked it and he sent me out once more into the storm. As I closed the door behind me, I heard him mutter surely the Navajo equivalent of "you can't get decent staff these days."

By now it was a nightmare outside. The storm had increased in intensity, the wind was howling and blowing stinging ice crystals straight into my eyes, and the branches of the junipers whipped around dangerously, frequently hitting me on the face and back. I had been back and forth three times, but it was now so dark that, only a few feet from the hogan, I could no longer recognise the way. I had carried off so much fire that it had ceased flaming. I had no torch and it was only by chance I found the small patch of red, glowing dully, low down among the dripping bushes. On the way back I became so disorientated I could not find the hogan. Thankfully, a momentary break in the clouds revealed the angular corner of the roof; a straight dark line against the waving sea of junipers. Gratefully, I made my way towards it, found the door, and staggered inside. This time I managed to do everything right and was rewarded by being allowed to return soggily to my seat.

Sitting before the glowing coals Blue Horse at long last was able to light his roll-up from a special fire-stick that he placed in the ashes until the tip became red hot. Then he smoked for a while before passing round the cigarette for everyone to take a puff. The Navajos smoked in a way I had never seen anyone smoke before. They blew smoke up and down and to each side of them. Then they blew more smoke into their hands and patted the smoke all over themselves. Renata even opened the top buttons of her blouse and blew smoke down her amble bosom. I had no idea what they were doing, but decided the best course was to copy what everyone else did. So when at last the roll-up came to me, I took an almighty drag, only to find the tobacco was so strong my throat felt as if it was being scoured with wire wool.

Coughing fit to burst, my eyes streaming with tears, it was half a minute before I recovered enough to pass the cigarette back to Blue Horse. He said nothing, but took it and sat puffing away thoughtfully. Staring into the fire and nodding to himself as if to say, "I knew it was a mistake to let this white idiot come along!"

After a while he spoke. "We do this with the smoke to bless ourselves. To us the tobacco is holy and pleasing to the Great Spirit. Bless yourself with the smoke, like this." So saying, he cupped smoke in each hand and patted it all over himself, starting with his feet and finishing with his head. Then he handed the cigarette back to me.

I did my best and he seemed satisfied enough because he said nothing more and instead bent forward and, taking a stick from his *jish*, he shaped the charcoal into a five pointed star, with one of the points aimed directly at himself. Then he set his crystal at the tip of this point and sat peering intently into it for a few moments. Next he opened the largest of the white doe hide pouches and threw a couple of pinches of dried cedar fronds onto the fire. As the fragrant smoke rose from the embers he took his eagle feather and wafted the smoke over Juan in a gesture I took to be a blessing. Then he wafted the cedar smoke over everyone else in the hogan and began to pray.

The prayer went on for a while and, when it concluded Blue Horse tapped me gently with his drumstick, then silently pointed to the fire. While we had been praying, one of the largest coals had taken on the shape of a snake's head; a bad omen indeed among the Navajo. How this happened I don't know. All I can say is there was no snake's head before he began praying. If there had been, I would have noticed as, before bowing my head in prayer, I had been looking into the fire hoping to see something.

I should again emphasise that all the many shapes and creatures I saw in the fire that night were crystal clear. It was not a case of squinting, standing on my head, or using a lot of imagination.

The snake's head was huge and unmistakable, right down to the zigzag markings on its head that showed it was a rattlesnake. There was even a little forked tongue of flame flicking in and out of its mouth. Next to the snake was something that looked like a man dressed in a shaggy bearskin, and next to him was the figure of a bear that seemed to be wearing a wolf skin over its head. Also nearby was a gray, fluffy piece of ash about four inches long that looked for all the world like a tree trunk burnt by a forest fire.

Blue Horse leaned over to me and whispered, "Can you see?"

"Yes," I whispered back.

"Tell me what you see." So I did, and he seemed pleased.

"That's very good," he nodded. "Not many white people can see in the fire, so I had to be sure. If I told you what I could see, you might have repeated it back to me, and then I wouldn't have known for sure if you were really seeing for yourself or not."

"What do these shapes mean?" I asked.

Blue Horse shook his head. "It's very bad. Much worse than I thought. The snake's not a rattlesnake, by the way. It's a bull snake. The bull snake copies the rattlesnake and has the same markings. Its bite isn't poisonous, but it's a lot more deadly. A man bitten by a bull snake is more likely to die than a man bitten by a rattler, because the bull snake will poison his soul. The snake's bad enough, but the man and the bear with the wolf cloak, they're skin-walkers. To get all three together is terrible and the tree you can see hasn't been burnt in a forest fire, it's been struck by lightning. Never go near a tree struck by lightning, the Old People used to say, because it's filled with evil. Never use wood from a lightning tree to make your fire, for it will surely make you sick and you may die."

While we were talking I saw something else appear in the embers. It was the stick man with the big sail-like shirt billowing out in front of him that Renata had refused to discuss when I found it carved on the canyon wall.

"It's an evil spirit," Blue Horse said when I asked about it, but he would say no more.

With the preliminaries over Blue Horse got down to business and what followed next was, thankfully for me, mostly in English. This was because Juan, like many younger Navajos, could not speak his own language very well. Later, Renata told me her biggest regret as a mother was not teaching her children to speak Navajo properly.

Blue Horse began his questioning gently enough. "Juan, have you been near a tree that's been struck by lightning?" he asked.

"No," replied Juan.

"Not at all, or not recently?" Blue Horse persisted.

The young man hesitated. "Not really," he said, sounding a little sulky.

"Not really?" Blue Horse repeated. "Does that mean yes or no?"

Juan shifted uncomfortably and glanced at his mother, who nodded at him encouragingly.

Finally, he admitted, "One day, not long ago, I met some Navajos camping out on the reservation. They invited me to sit down with them and after a while they asked me to put some wood on the fire. I did as they asked, but I remember thinking the wood looked like it had already been burned and scorched."

"As if from a tree struck by lightning?" asked Blue Horse, at which Juan nodded unhappily.

Blue Horse asked several more questions, but he received no clear answers. Then, after more prayers and more cedar, he tapped me again with his drumstick, and pointed at a large piece of charcoal in the fire. The side turned towards us was not burning and stood out black against the hot red glow of the other coals.

"What do you make of that?" he asked me quietly. I didn't know. I thought it looked rather like a large slab of rock that might have fallen across a path in one of the canyon's narrow defiles and blocked the way.

Blue Horse smiled when I told him. "Very good," he said. Then, pointing to Juan, he whispered confidentially, "He's hiding things from us. Probably he's trying to protect the girl. The things he doesn't want us to know are hidden behind that rock you see. But he's going to have to tell us before we can help him."

"How can you make him do that?" I asked.

"You'll see," he said, sounding extremely confident, and reaching once more into his Medicine box, he produced a small box made of birch bark. From this he took two small, dark-coloured, feathers. Each was about the length of my little finger and I watched curiously as from inside the little box, he took an even smaller box, also of birch bark, which he opened to reveal a lump of dry black earth. He took a feather in his right hand and moistened the tip of the quill in his mouth before rubbing it gently on the block of dry earth. Using the quill as a pen, he carefully drew a thin black line under his right eye. When he had finished, he returned the feather to its box and repeated the process, this time placing the other feather in his left hand to draw a line under his left eye.

"These are the feathers of a woodpecker," he explained. "We Navajos call it the Hammer Bird and we invoke its help in this way to give us greater vision. The Hammer Bird goes bang-bang-banging away until he gets to what he wants. So I call upon the Hammer Bird to sharpen my vision when I have a difficult problem to divine."

Looking once more into the fire he paused for a few seconds, rather like a lawyer pausing to refresh his memory from his brief before turning again to the main witness.

"Have you been near any snakes?" he asked.

Juan looked like he was about to say no, but glancing over at his mother he decided to come clean.

"Maybe," he admitted softly. "The men I met were cooking some stew over the fire. After I finished putting on the logs they asked me to eat with them. I don't know what was in the stew, but it wasn't anything I'd tasted before. As I was leaving I saw a bull snake skin on the ground near the edge of their camp. I don't know, but maybe they'd killed a snake and put it in the stew."

By now Renata was looking as if the end of the world was nigh and she covered her face with hands.

"To eat a bull snake is as bad as being bitten by one," Blue Horse whispered to me. "This is very serious."

He directed my attention back to the fire. Deep in the heart of the glowing coals, a large gray owl had appeared next to the rock I thought was forming a blockage.

"Juan, tell me about the owl," Blue Horse said.

"Do I have to?" Juan asked, and I could hear the panic in his voice.

"Tell him, Juan!" Renata burst out. She sounded terrified.

Blue Horse gestured to her to keep silent. "Come on," he encouraged Juan gently. "It can't do any harm to tell us now."

Juan cleared his throat. "I was worried about the snake," he said. "I knew it was wrong to eat a snake, but I didn't know what to do about it. I wasn't even sure it was snake that I'd eaten. I was on my way to Window Rock and the road goes by the cemetery where my *cheii* [grandfather] is buried. I thought 'I'll stop at my *cheii's* grave and ask him what to do.' But when I got there I couldn't remember which grave it was, so I walked up and down among the rows of graves looking for it. While I was looking I heard a noise in the bushes and a big bird hopped out. It was gray like an owl, but it was bigger and there was something weird about it. I don't know what it was, but it wasn't like any owl I'd ever seen before.

"I thought it must have hurt itself because it didn't seem able to fly right and just hopped around. But whenever I went towards it the bird hopped away some more. So I kept following it, until it disappeared into a big bush and I heard it fly away. I was about to walk back and start looking for my *cheii's* grave again when I saw some bones under the bush where the owl had been. They were big bones, human bones, I think, and very white like they'd been out in the sun for a long time. I thought animals must have dug them up and it didn't seem right to leave them there. So I picked them up and started walking back to the car thinking may be I could give them to a Medicine Man and he would know what to do. I didn't see anyone until I was nearly back at the car and then I met a man walking towards me. He asked me why I had the bones, so I told him I'd found them under a bush.

"The man said, 'You know it's taboo to touch the bones of the dead. I'm a Medicine Man. Give them to me and I'll take care of them.' So I gave him the bones and drove home."

I thought he'd finished but, after a short pause, Juan suddenly burst into tears and began shouting, "Ever since then I can't sleep at night. If I go to sleep I dream about the bones. They come chasing after me and beat me all over my head and body. Bad things happen to me. Sometimes I can't stop drinking and I don't know what to do!"

After this outburst there was complete silence in the hogan for a few moments. Then Renata began quietly to weep, while the older Begays began talking in whispers to each other. The whispers grew louder and suddenly Renata, Blue Horse, and Juan all began to talk rapidly at once and mostly in Navajo. I couldn't understand a word.

It took some time for things to calm down, but when order was restored Blue Horse turned to me and quickly explained. "The boy's been trapped by witchcraft. The men he met on the reservation were bad Medicine Men. They made him touch wood from a tree struck by lightning. Then they fed him snake to poison him, and when he drove away they put a thought into his head that he should go to his *cheii*'s grave. The owl was a skinwalker and it led him to the bones on purpose. Juan knows that Navajos aren't allowed to touch parts of a dead body, but the Evil Ones put him in a position where he had to take the bones in case they were his grandfather's. Remember, he said he heard the owl fly away? Impossible! The flight of an owl is silent. Of course, it wasn't an owl and that's why it made a noise. While he was picking up the bones it flew back and turned itself into a man again and walked to meet him. They set a clever trap for him, without a doubt. By getting him to handle the bones, and getting the bones back again after he'd touched them, they gained even greater power over him," Blue Horse concluded.

"Is there anything you can do?" I asked, wondering what on earth anyone *could* do in such circumstances.

"I need to find out who did this and send the evil back to them," Blue Horse replied.

"I thought you said the girl's relatives were responsible?"

"They're behind it, but they must have paid a bad Medicine Man to do the evil for them. I have to find out who he is and then send the evil back to them all," he told me.

From this point the ceremony took on a new direction. Blue Horse began a series of long prayers during which much cedar and other herbs were thrown upon the fire. Again and again Blue Horse prayed. The stove burnt out, and the oil lamps burnt down, while outside the storm raged with unabated fury. With the stove out it was no longer remotely warm in the hogan, but I noticed the back of Blue Horse's shirt was soaked with sweat, and big drops dotted his forehead and ran down his face and neck. Prayer followed prayer, while cedar, sage, and sweet grass were thrown into the fire, their scent rising to the spirits to please and placate them.

By midnight the only light in the hogan came from the sole surviving oil lamp, whose guttering flame cast deep and eerie shadows on the walls and roof. The charcoal had burnt down to a dome of red-hot coals, which in the dark seemed to pulsate in time to the rhythm of my heart. Whether this was an illusion, or not, I am unable to say.

At last his prayers were finished and Blue Horse directed my attention once more to the fire. The "rock" blocking the way was still there, and although it was smaller than before, to my eyes it had somehow grown blacker and more forbidding than before. Telling me to watch the rock carefully Blue Horse took out an eagle bone whistle and blew three short blasts. A few seconds later the rock fell to one side and in the space it left behind, there arose immediately the clear and unmistakable image of a man.

If possible, this apparition was more clearly defined than any I had seen that night. It sat in the heart of the fire in a striking pose just below where the mound of charcoal rose to its peak. Unmoving, and slightly turned to his right, the man in the fire had a face that was both stern and unyielding. Obviously an Indian, his face was so perfectly clear that if I saw him in the street today I would recognise him. He was clutching an Indian blanket around his shoulders, and appeared to be sitting on the side of a steep slope. I realized at once that not only was this the Medicine Man who had witched Juan, but that Blue Horse knew who he was. He said nothing, but his eyes held mine for a second and he nodded the slightest of nods. Then he began to pray again.

Stripping off his T-shirt, he threw it behind him and sat before the fire invoking the spirits, his great barrel chest heaving and panting with the effort. Rivers of sweat ran off him and as I watched it began to dawn on me that Blue Horse was doing a lot more than praying. What he was really about was wrestling with his enemy for possession of Juan's soul. I was aware also that, whatever else was going on, no trickery was involved. I had brought the coals in myself and placed them on the floor.

How long Blue Horse continued to battle with his rival, I cannot say. Certainly it went on for a long time. Then, without warning, Blue Horse's efforts seemed to rise to a peak. His prayers grew louder and his whole body seemed to tense and expand like a weight-lifter going for the final, winning heave. Once more he raised his sacred eagle bone whistle to his lips and sounded three shrill blasts. A few seconds later, as I looked at the fire, I saw the mound of pulsating, glowing, charcoal collapse in on itself, taking the image of the evil Medicine Man down with it. When the fire settled again, there was no sign of him at all. A few seconds later Blue Horse ceased his prayers and, panting from the effort, turned to me with a look of triumph on his face. "My Medicine is strong," he said gravely, pointing to the newly collapsed fire. There was nothing I could do but agree.

Renata began to weep again. There were a few more prayers, a last scattering of cedar, and then it was all over. A little food was served to our exhausted group, but nothing much was said, and soon I fell into a dreamless sleep.

I was woken at dawn by the clatter of Renata lighting the stove to make breakfast. Juan had to leave early to get back to work and when his hastily made meal was over, Renata walked him to his truck. They had been gone only a few minutes when I heard a penetrating scream from Renata.

Blue Horse and I ran out of the hogan to find Juan with the iron spade I used to bring in the coals, chopping wildly at something on the ground, while Renata stood with her face to the wall of the hogan shrieking. While I ran to Renata, Blue Horse hurried to Juan. Shortly afterwards he called me over to look at the remains of the largest snake I had ever seen.

"It's a bull snake," he said, stirring the remains with the spade. "Big evil."

The snake was well over six feet long, despite missing its head and a few other chopped-off chunks.

"What are we going to do?" wailed Renata, when she came to look. "And just when I thought we were winning!"

Of course, I had no idea what was going on, but when Blue Horse asked me to carry the dead snake down to the steam and toss it in, I did as I was asked. He explained later that running water was a good a neutralizer of witchcraft and evil. When I returned Juan was standing with his arm round his mother to comfort her and telling Blue Horse, "I saw something hanging down underneath the engine like a piece of loose hose. When I looked closer I saw it was the bull snake trying to get into the engine compartment, so I ran and got the spade. Bull snakes are usually pretty timid but this one started coming after me. I hit it with the spade and that's when it went crazy and tried to bite me. Mom was screaming and the snake was really going at me. I was so scared I chopped and chopped until I chopped its head off."

When he had finished his tale Blue Horse walked to Juan's truck, lifted the bonnet, and invited us all to look inside. Among the grease and grime was a big, wide trail where the snake had crawled around the engine.

"You were wrong about one thing, Juan," Blue Horse told him. "The snake wasn't trying to get into your engine, it was coming out. It had done the evil it was sent to do and was trying to escape. It came after you when you chased it because it knew we would find out what it had done and undo its work. It was a last, desperate attempt to get the evil into you and make sure you die. Those people who witched you, they know we brought down their man last night and we're too strong for them. So they sent the snake to fix your truck and if you had tried to drive it something bad would have happen to you for sure. They nearly got away with it too," he added, shaking his head thoughtfully.

Clutching her son's arm, Renata peered into the engine compartment. "What did it do? What did it do to the truck?" she asked, holding back tears.

Blue Horse began to search inside the engine compartment and after a few moments gave a grunt and held up something. It was a little white bone about the size of the end digit of a man's finger, but to what creature it belonged I could not say. Carved upon it was a sort of face, with two obvious eyes and a mouth.

"It's an evil sign," Blue Horse said, not that Renata or Juan needed to be told. "A curse."

Renata's voice shook as she spoke, "A Medicine Man must have given it to the snake to put there. I'm so scared now, I don't know what to do."

Nodding, Blue Horse agreed, "This is how they do it. This is the evil we are facing." Then, to comfort Renata, he added, "But I'll fix it, you'll see."

He sent me into the house with instructions to find a little bag and put some more ash from the stove into it. When I returned he dropped the bone into it, along with three or four more he had by this time found in the vehicle, and told me to light a fire at some distance to the hogan and burn the bag and its contents. This I did, but when I went to rejoin them, I quickly realised I was no longer wanted.

"Matters are too serious to have you around," Blue Horse explained.

"Personally, I don't mind, but the old people are very traditional. They like you but they think it's not good to have a white man here when we're doing this serious stuff. They were OK about last night, but after this business with the snake, they'd prefer it if you went away for a while."

There was nothing to do but saddle up the long-suffering War Arrow and explore the side canyons for a few hours. While I was away, Blue Horse carried out some kind of ceremony to purify Juan's truck, but I don't know the specifics of what he did. All I know is that when I returned everyone looked a lot happier. Blue Horse told Renata, "Give it four days and you'll get a sign that the evil has gone back to them."

"What kind of sign?" she asked.

"I can't say for sure, but when it comes you'll know. It won't be something you could mistake for anything else," he assured her.

Juan looked worried and asked, "Does the evil really have to go back to them. Isn't there another way?"

"No," Blue Horse told him firmly. "There is no other way." Which did not seem to comfort the young man much.

"He's worried about the girl," Blue Horse confided to me later. "He's scared she'll get hurt, but he doesn't need to worry. It'll be OK."

While I was out riding I had done a lot of thinking, and after Blue Horse had gone, I did a lot more. At first I thought the whole business was extremely convincing. I could see no trickery by which a man, or any other creature, could be made to appear so clearly in a fire. Or that a fire could be brought to collapse so dramatically at will. Doubtless I was influenced by the fact that I carried the charcoal in myself and no one else had touched it during the vital period. However, it is extremely difficult for the Western mind to let go of its roots, and my belief in science, backed by a long spell as a national newspaper journalist, has given me a profound disinclination to believe anything for which I can't produce the facts to back up my belief. It had to be a trick, surely? Or, if not a trick, a coincidence.

Bull snakes—and other kinds of snakes—frequently seek the warmth of an engine compartment to curl up in, especially on a cold night. The little bones with a face on could easily have been slipped down Blue Horse's sleeve, and people see things in fires all the time. After all, if enough people light enough fires, some of them are bound to produce burning coals that look like snakes and Indian Medicine Men. In a similar way, once in a while one of the trillions of clouds that float across the sky is bound to look like Elvis. When this happens, fascinating though it may be, it means absolutely nothing at all. I concluded that, extraordinary though the events had been, they were nothing more than a few million-to-one chances.

Instead of going home, I spent the next few days mulling these events over, exploring the canyons, and enjoying the hospitality of my new friends. Then, four days later, and just as predicted, Renata received the sign Blue Horse had promised her. Or, at least, that's how she chose to see it.

On the fourth day we heard that Juan's former girlfriend had rolled the family's $30,000 dollar pick-up truck on a rough reservation road. While the girl was unharmed, the vehicle was totaled. Few Indian vehicles are insured for more than third party damage and so the loss was a severe financial blow to the Bennally family.

Renata was triumphant when she heard and danced round the stove waving a wooden spoon and chanting, "Thirty thousand dollars! Thirty thousand dollars!" Blue Horse had more than earned his pay, she told me.

I have to admit that, as I rode out of the canyon for the last time a few days later, this event did prompt me to wonder how many million-to-one chances could reasonably be expected to turn up in one small place in one short time? But, as I could not answer the question, I put it aside.

Later, I learnt that Renata's euphoria had evaporated after a few days, when she learnt that Juan had been to visit the Bennally girl in hospital. She turned positively vengeful when she found out he had taken the girl home to his flat to convalesce. But, when the couple married six months later, she had mellowed enough to attend the wedding. Incidentally, Juan's bad dreams and bad behaviour also disappeared. His family attributed this to Blue Horse lifting the curse. Although the influence of a very sweet girl might well have had something to do with it.

CHAPTER FOUR

Cursed of Suburbia

I T WAS SOME WEEKS BEFORE Blue Horse agreed to see
me again. I spoke to him on the telephone a few times to emphasise I was anxious to experience more, but without much result. He did not say yes, he did not say no. In fact, when I analysed
our conversations he often seemed to have said nothing at all.

"Haven't you enough to do?" he demanded irritably one day.
"Why do you want to follow a poor Indian about?"

"I thought I might learn something," I said congenially.

"Learn!" he sounded shocked by the idea. "If you want to
learn something go and learn to be a doctor. Then you can work
in a hospital and make a lot of money. I've been a Medicine Man
for nearly forty years and I hardly know a thing. There are Medicine Men among the Diné who are very old and know a lot more
than me. One day I might know a thing or two like them, but not
yet."

Despite this kind of rebuff, and there were many of them,
early one morning the telephone rang at my bedside and I picked
it up to find Blue Horse calling *me*. It was still dark outside and I
was more than half asleep. "Meet me at the Flying J on I-40 West
in a couple of hours," he said. I started to ask why, but the phone
went dead at the other end.

The Flying J is a busy truck stop a few miles west of Albuquerque, which day and night heaves with truckers and travellers pouring in from all parts of the United States. In the crowded café I found Blue Horse sitting alone eating breakfast, his white Stetson hat with the feather lying on the table in front of him. He was in an ebullient mood as he shovelled bacon, sausages, eggs, and hashbrowns into his mouth and washed them down with great gulps of black coffee.

"So the *bilagáana* from England wants to watch me play tricks?" was his opening salvo. "You think I do conjuring tricks? You think Navajo people are so stupid they get fooled easily? You think the Medicine Man can do the same trick for thousands of years and nobody's gonna notice?" He paused for a second to reach for a plate containing a mountain of toast and two pots of jam.

"I never said they were tricks," I replied defensively.

"You don't say, but that's what you think," he countered, opening a jam pot and taking out a massive dollop on the end of his knife.

He was, of course, quite right. I still could not figure out what had happened that night in the hogan at Canyon de Chelly, but I was damned if I was going to believe in magic.

"I've got an open mind," I assured him.

"Open mind? An open mind is for the man who knows nothing," Blue Horse hurled back contemptuously. "Every white man thinks he sees tricks. They come to a ceremony and say 'Very good, very clever. The spirits must be helping you, there's no other explanation.' Then they go home and say to the other *bilagáana* people, 'Those Indians do tricks. Those Medicine Men fool people and cheat them. The Indian people aren't clever enough to see through it, so it's a good job us white people are so clever and we know everything so we can't be fooled!' Isn't that right? Isn't that what they say?" he demanded.

"I've never said any such thing," I told him. "And I've never heard anyone say that." Both were true, but as I still had only an extremely small number of acquaintances in the area, admittedly the subject had never come up.

"If you ask those people how the trick was done they can't tell you," Blue Horse continued as if I had never spoken. "They keep saying 'It must be a trick, it must be a trick!' over and over again. They are like children who think if they say something enough times it will come true, but they'll never know the truth because they never take the trouble to find out."

I was still reaching for some suitable defense to this onslaught when, to my utter surprise, he suddenly added, "It doesn't matter to me what you think. If you want to come and watch me, you can come and watch. I've nothing to hide. You'll find out we Diné people know a few things, we know about your country of England and some of us have been there. We even have a name for your country and in our language we call it *Tóta'*, which means Between the Waters, because your land lies between three seas." He meant the Atlantic, the North Sea and the English Channel. "Isn't that right?" He laughed and slapped the last portion of jam on his last piece of toast and swallowed it in two bites.

"OK," I said. "Let me come and watch. Let me ask lots of stupid questions and let me learn." Too late I realised I'd done it again!

"*Learn?*" he said. "Ain't never known a white man want to learn anything. The white man only wants to teach everyone else what to do and make 'em do what the white man says. Particularly us poor Indians. They tell me I have to go to church, they tell me I have to go to school, they tell me Medicine Men are devil worshippers and I should get a job instead. But *learn*? White man learn from Indian people?" He laughed out loud. "That's a new one!"

When he had finished laughing he fell silent for a few moments and sat looking at me steadily from across the table. "Ain't never seen a white man like you before," he said, shaking his head, and this time his eyes found mine and held my gaze. Almost as if hypnotized, I felt the bustling truck stop and café begin to fall away. It became impossible to move my head, or any part of my body, and my eyes were riveted to his. Though surrounded by people using mobile phones, watching a big TV screen, and ordering hamburgers, it was as if we two began to move away from them and towards a separate plane of being in which we were still part of, yet apart from, the everyday world. I could see our fellow diners sitting around us, but I was no longer among them. The clatter of the cafe's huge dining room faded and within seconds all such activity appeared to be taking place behind a thick gauze curtain through which I could make out only the fuzzy outlines of the world to which I normally belonged.

Whether Blue Horse was hypnotizing me, or simply overwhelming me with his considerable personality, I could not say. The Navajos and Apaches firmly believe the Medicine Man's spirit can leave his body and enter that of another to examine it from inside. In the fuzzy other-world I now occupied I was unsure exactly what was going on.

Then, as suddenly as Blue Horse's invasion of my psyche had started, it stopped, and things snapped back to normal. The return to normality was so sudden that the first thing I heard was the mundane sound of Blue Horse ordering coffee for us both, and soon I was tucking into a breakfast of bacon, sausages, refried beans, and toast. He made no comment about the examination I had been subjected to, if indeed it was such. When I had finished eating, Blue Horse indicated that it was time to leave.

"Where are we going?" I asked.

He drove ahead in his truck and I followed in the silver cougar, which I had reclaimed upon my return to the States. I expected him to head west, out of town and back towards Indian territory. To my surprise he turned east and headed into central Albuquerque. After a drive of no more than twenty minutes, we pulled up outside a suburban house on the north side of town.

Several vehicles, none of them particularly old or new, stood outside the house and inside the family was waiting for us. They were Navajos who lived in town and made jewellery for a living.

They had become moderately prosperous through this business and their prosperity, they believed, had excited someone's jealousy and resulted in them being witched.

Inside the house Blue Horse talked to the family for a while and from what they said it seemed the witching centered on two members of the family, adult children in their mid-twenties, brother and sister.

The siblings looked rather more raddled than people of their age should and the brother looked as if he might have a bad hangover.

"We've started to have a lot of bad luck," the brother explained. He was a typical looking Navajo, of about five foot eight inches in height, with a big barrel chest, and short, strong arms and legs. He may once have been good looking, but his face was puffy now and his eyes bloodshot.

"We've got a place outside town where we keep horses, but just about everyone who's gone riding recently has fallen off," he said. "We haven't had any serious injuries yet, but if it keeps happening someone's going to get hurt bad. And two of our horses collided at the gallop and both were injured. You should have seen the size of the vet's bill! Then my sister fell through the porch and hurt her leg."

The sister was a small, stout woman with beautiful long, straight black hair that shimmered and shone all the way down to the small of her back. As her brother spoke she nodded and patted her leg to show where it hurt.

"At about the same time we met a stranger at a pow-wow where we were selling jewellery," she said, taking up the story. "He asked us for a ride but once we took him to where he wanted to go he refused to get out of our van and we were forced to drive around with him. He drank a lot and became drunk and abusive and we think he must have been either a witch or an evil spirit, sent to put a curse on us. Maybe he wasn't really drunk, maybe he was pretending, but when he wouldn't leave the van we had to bring him to our home. We think that when he was here he took something of ours and used it to mix with his witchcraft and increase the power of his cursing," she concluded, and she looked badly scared.

The brother added that they owned a trailer, which he used as a jewellery workshop, and also slept there sometimes. "Lately, I've been hearing strange noises, kind of like a woman moaning," he said. Dropping his voice slightly, so the younger members of the family would not hear, he added. "I can't tell whether it's, like, well, you know, sexual moaning, or if she's in pain or something. I can hear it coming from somewhere inside the trailer. It's not loud, but it goes on all night and I'm worried about the kid being in there if something's going on," he confessed, indicating a boy of about five.

I couldn't work out if it was his or his sister's child. But whomever he belonged to, the boy had apparently been suffering bad nightmares every night for a month while sleeping in the trailer.

Later, when he and I were alone outside the house, the brother confided, "I like to drink and so does she," he said, indicating his sister. "I play music. I'm a good musician. I have a little recording studio in the trailer and we take people back there to drink with us and play music. We invite lots of people, we don't mind who, as long as they're good company. But we don't always know the people that come, sometimes we've only met them that night. They use our trailer, they walk around the place. We can't watch them all the time and someone could have had the chance to witch us. There's plenty of women come back with me too. There's a thing in Navajo called Prostitute Way, where you have one woman after another. But it leads to disaster. Let me tell you, you can't get happy if you have that many women, but you can't find one who's right for you either, man, and eventually it all blows up in your face."

It occurred to me that things in England weren't so different.

The brother paused for a few moments to light a cigarette before continuing, "My sister's the same. She drinks a lot and there's been a lot of men. One after the other and sometimes she has more than one at a time in the trailer. It's not doing either of us any good and the truth is that neither of us are really like that. The way we're acting sometimes is not the way we want to. It's the witching that's making us drink and be promiscuous and go carrying on. That's how people try to destroy us in our society, and the worst thing is that it's probably family who is doing this to us. Cousins, people like that. . . ." He paused for a moment. Then, after making sure no one could overhear us, added softly. "Maybe people even closer than that. Like . . . family." And he nodded towards the house.

I went to get a portable fireplace that Blue Horse kept in the back of his truck. It was made from the base of a fifty-gallon oil drum and was about two feet in diameter. Filled with sand and supported on three short metal legs about three inches high, it was used for carrying in and out of people's living rooms when there was nowhere else to put the red hot charcoal he needed for his divining. At one time all Navajos lived in traditional hogans with earth floors. But since people began moving into town, a way has had to be found to place a fire in the center of the house without damaging the carpet. Technology moves with the times even for Medicine Men, and Blue Horse's travelling fireplace was a brilliant solution to the problem.

It was a pretty heavy piece of kit and I was glad of the brother's help. We brought it into the living room and placed it in the center of the room, on a special cloth we spread to guard the carpet from flying sparks. A sacred fire had already been lit in the family's backyard and when all was ready, the brother went out and returned with a shovel full of smoking charcoal, which he placed in the center of the fireplace.

It was the family's grandmother who had asked Blue Horse to come and after speaking to her for a while he began the ceremony. I sat cross-legged on the floor to his right while the family, including the young children aged from about four to eight years old, gathered all around us.

Blue Horse threw some dried cedar on the coals and as the aromatic smoke rose to fill the room, invited us to waft the smoke over ourselves with our hands in a traditional Navajo blessing. Talking to the family all the time in Navajo, he carefully took his *jish* from his medicine bag and laid each instrument gently on the small piece of woven blanket he carried expressly for the purpose. When he had laid out his eagle feather, drumstick, whistle, crystal, and spear and arrowheads of flint and obsidian, he took up his tobacco pouch and began to roll the ceremonial cigarette using the dried corn husk. When this was done he produced a "fire stick," which is a piece of soft wood—these days balsa is often used although it is not native to the Navajo—and to my delight he asked me to light it, specifying that it must be done from the east side of the fire.

Because of their low density, these fire sticks seldom burst into flame and instead glow red hot like the cigarette lighter in a car. Lighting one can be more difficult than it sounds, especially when—as it proved in this case—the fire stick is not a good one. I huffed and puffed and blew with increasing desperation on the coals, until I was sweating and my face was covered with specks of ash. It was embarrassing, making heavy weather of something so seemingly simple in front of people who knew how it should be done properly. Eventually, I managed to get the thing lit and handed it to Blue Horse, who calmly lit his ceremonial cigarette and handed the fire stick back to me. As it was still very much alight, and smoking heavily, this placed me in somewhat of a quandary. I could not hold the burning fire stick all through the ceremony, nor could I put it down on the carpet while it was still alight. Blue Horse saved the day by producing another piece of wood, this time a piece of hard wood about the length and breadth of a school ruler, but triple its thickness. I was able to safely prop the fire stick against it, and watched with satisfaction as it burnt itself out after a few minutes.

The ceremonial cigarette, or "the smoke" as it is more generally known, was passed round for everyone to bless themselves with the tobacco smoke. Even the older children were encouraged to take a puff, and a relative blew smoke over those too little to safely hold something burning. While this was being done the family asked Blue Horse to bless various items that they put before him. These included two bags full of jewellery they had made and—and I sometimes wish I'd thought of this—an Income Tax bill!

So far most of the conversation had been in Navajo, but the Income Tax problem was complicated and as most of the terms were in English, the family slipped back into that language while discussing it. It appeared that one of the sons had been expecting a $2,500 rebate, but this had suddenly been withdrawn when the Internal Revenue Service refused to believe one of the little girls in the house was really his daughter. Not only was the rebate being withdrawn, but the tax man was demanding an additional $1,400 in unpaid taxes.

"Can you get my money back?" the son asked, handing the document to Blue Horse.

"You see?" Blue Horse whispered to me in English. "It's his money and now the jealous people are trying to take his money away from him."

"But it's the tax man," I whispered back. "He needs to fill in a form and appeal."

Blue Horse looked astonished at my naiveté. "That won't do any good. He's been witched. He'd have got the money straight away if he hadn't been." Tut-tutting to himself, he turned to the family and solemnly assured them, "I'll do my best."

He threw more cedar on the fire and looked into the coals just as he had done at the Canyon de Chelly. I looked too, but could see nothing except a ridge of oddly broken coals in the center. This ridge looked strange and artificial and while I thought it was probably meaningful, I had no idea what it might mean. Blue Horse also seemed puzzled, and after a while he tapped me lightly on the hand and pointed to the ridge with his drumstick.

"Do you know what that ridge means?" he asked.

"No," I confessed. "I've no idea."

"When you see a ridge like that, it represents the family's unity and progress through life. The fact that it's broken shows that they're being attacked. Unfortunately, at this stage I'm not sure how, or by who," he confided.

"Can you find out?" I asked.

"Oh, yes," he said, sounding surprised by the question. "I'll find out. Don't you worry."

He threw more sweet-smelling cedar on the fire and continued to gently question the family, until someone mentioned the trailer. He had not been present when the brother spoke to me about it and, as I had no idea it might be important, I had not thought to mention it. Now he became animated.

"Where did you get this trailer?" he asked.

"It came from one of the Pueblos," the brother answered. "We've had it for a couple of years, but we've only just repaired it enough to be able to sleep and work in it."

"Where is it?" Blue Horse demanded, leaping up.

"A couple of miles away," the brother told him, by now looking thoroughly alarmed.

"We must go there at once. There's no time to lose," Blue Horse told him, quickly picking up his *jish* and moving towards the door.

Among the vehicles the family owned was a minibus and soon everybody, except for the children and their granny, had clambered aboard. Before we left, Blue Horse asked for a strong paper bag into which he put a couple of shovelfuls of cold ash from the wood-burning stove in the family's front room.

Pueblo is a Spanish word meaning "village" that is generally applied to certain tribes living in the Rio Grande Valley and the Southwest U.S. that traditionally reside in villages of adobe houses.

"Pueblo Indians are full of witchcraft. No wonder these people are having trouble if they bought a trailer from one of the Pueblo tribes," Blue Horse confided as we were getting into the minibus. Then, handing me the bag of ashes, he added, "Keep that safe, we're going to need it."

The first night I had been on the reservation with Reuben, the Medicine Man had used a bag full of ash to neutralise the power of the curse he found. I supposed Blue Horse was doing the same, so I asked, "Is it because the ash has been sterilised by being burnt in the fire that it neutralises the witchcraft when it touches a curse?"

This stumped him. Navajo was his first language and he did not understanding words like "neutralise" and "sterilise." Later, the difficulty in language between us led to some odd mix-ups, but for the moment he simply repeated, "It makes it safe," and left it at that.

Producing two flint arrowheads from his *jish* he gave one each to the siblings.

"You two keep an arrowhead in your left hand all the time and hold it tight. That'll stop any evil power from hurting you," he said, handing them out.

"Which hand did he say?" the sister asked her mother.

"You put it in your left hand and keep it there, girlie," her mother told her firmly.

We drove for a while until we reached a part of Albuquerque known locally as the War Zone. Albuquerque is not in my experience a violent place but, like any big city, there are parts that are distinctly less friendly than others. We stopped outside a rundown trailer park surrounded by a metal fence patched with razor wire. Mean-looking dogs and even meaner-looking young thugs eyed us as we pulled up. Broken-down vehicles, overturned rubbish bins, and the foul ammonia-like smell of methamphetamine production from an illegal drug factory added to the general air of decay.

Inside, the trailer was huge. But it was scruffy and ill-kept. There were stains on the ceiling and walls where water dripped through in bad weather. The family insisted they were slowly doing it up, so heaven knows what it must have been like before.

The brother proudly showed me his jewellery workshop and the little recording studio he had built in one of the rooms. In the living area, where the siblings apparently entertained, there was a seedy old green carpet and some furniture that had seen much better days. There were two air vents in the floor for channelling the air conditioning in summer and the heat in winter. The sister mentioned that she had found an "old dirty magazine" stuffed down the air-conditioning duct.

"Like Playboy?" Blue Horse asked.

"Much worse than that," said the sister, looking embarrassed. "Really dirty. I threw it away."

Immediately Blue Horse dropped to his knees and pulled out the air vent grill. He pushed his arm inside the duct until it disappeared up to his shoulder and felt around, but he found nothing. Removing his arm he told the brother, "Get me a piece of wire. Or a coat hanger. Something I can use as a hook."

A wire coat hanger was quickly produced and Blue Horse pulled it out into one long wire before doubling it back on itself at one end to form a rough hook. With this new tool he fished around once more inside the vent and succeeded in raking out all sorts of rubbish, including a great deal of fluff and bits of fabric, but found nothing of any significance.

Still on his knees, he turned his attention to the second vent. After a while he gave a grunt of satisfaction and pulled out three dirty and discoloured pennies. Each of them had been deliberately battered around the edges. He held them in the palm of his hand to examine them and then stood up and gestured to me to come to his side.

"Open that bag so I can get some ash," he said.

I held up the bag and he dipped his hand inside, took a large pinch of fine gray ash and dusted the coins with a thin layer. Next he blew on them to remove any excess before holding them up for inspection.

"Look at this," he said.

I saw the image of a woman on the face of one of the coins, outlined in the fine grain of the ash in much the same way finger-prints show when treated with fine powder. The image was too small to see much detail, but it was undoubtedly the figure of a woman wearing a long dress.

"It's been painted on the coin in sheep's grease," Blue Horse said. Then, dropping his voice, he whispered in my ear, "It's the sister. It's a bad sign."

Laying the coins carefully on a small table, and warning everyone to keep away from them, he once more dropped to his knees and began to rake around inside the vent. This time he came up with a flint arrowhead and four wafer-thin pieces of wood. Putting the arrow-head to one side, he examined the pieces of wood carefully. After a while he discarded two of the pieces, then fitted the remaining two together before holding them up to the light for us all to examine.

Peering carefully, I could see the rough drawing of a human arm stretching across the two pieces.

"It's a drawing made on a single piece of wood that's been de-liberately broken," Blue Horse explained. Pointing to the arrow-head he added, in words reminiscent of what Reuben had said to me at that first Medicine ceremony, "Something broken, some-thing sharp. That's what they use for a witching."

Once more he began to search the vent and this time ex-tracted two pieces of torn paper and a thin strip of plastic. One piece of paper was torn from a magazine advertisement and printed on it was the rough blue outline of a house. The other had been torn from a pornographic magazine and contained a few lines of text.

Placing them in the palm of his hand, Blue Horse pointed to the piece of plastic. "This was used for holding them all together," he said. "The bundle tore open when I pulled it out. Can you see the house? It represents this family's house, so the evil will know where to go when the curse is laid upon them."

Blue Horse could not read English very well, so he passed me the lines torn from the magazine and asked me to read them aloud. I saw that it was a graphic description of a woman performing fellatio. Apologizing in advance to the ladies present, I did so. A more graphic, hardcore pornographic description of anything it would have been difficult to imagine. I'm no prude, but you would have to go a long way to find something as crude as the descriptions contained in that fragment.

Turning to the brother, Blue Horse told him, "That's the moaning you heard. They cursed you so you would hear their filth."

"Who would do this to us?" the brother asked mournfully. "Who?"

The question went unanswered as Blue Horse placed the fetishes besides the coins on the table. Then he asked to be shown to the bedroom of the little boy who was having nightmares.

"This way," said the brother and led us to the next room. Here Blue Horse ordered everyone to stay outside while he entered the room alone. The siblings and the family crowded into the narrow doorway to watch, pushing me to the back where I could see only by looking over their heads. The room was dirty and rundown, and I noticed a number of holes in the walls and ceiling. There were signs of attempted redecoration, and a paper frieze of toys and teddy bears had been pasted at head height around the room, presumably in an attempt to brighten its depressing appearance.

I saw Blue Horse raise his right arm and begin to feel about with his finger inside one of the small holes in the ceiling. After a few seconds he gave a cry of triumph and pulled out a piece of white plaster about the length and width of the first three fingers of a man's hand. Excitedly he brought it over to show us and we all saw that, crudely drawn on one side, was a face with staring eyes and an evil smile. Stuck to the plaster were hairs that Blue Horse identified as those of a deer. It was another witchcraft fetish, he said, and placed it in the bag of ash I still held clutched in one hand. After this he led everyone outside and began to walk round the trailer praying and blowing on his Medicine Man's whistle. It was late in the afternoon, but the sun was still well up and shining strongly. At one point he stopped and turned towards the sun to address it directly in Navajo.

"I'm talking to the Sun," he told me. "That's the source of light. I'm asking him to help lift the darkness here." When he had finished he blew three or four blasts on his whistle.

When he had done, we went inside again, and Blue Horse asked me for the paper bag of ash. Carefully, for he was the only one allowed to touch them, he picked up the witching objects and placed them inside the bag. Then he shook the bag vigorously to make sure everything inside was well covered in ash. Only then was the bag handed back to me for safekeeping.

Apparently we had now finished at the trailer and, mission accomplished, we climbed back into the minibus. I can't pretend I wasn't glad to get out of the place.

As we drove away Blue Horse ordered, "Keep that bag closed tight, Charles. Put your foot on it. We don't want anything bad getting out."

I kept my foot on the bag until we arrived once more at the family's home. Still clutching the bag closed, I was about to enter the house when Blue Horse barred my way with a strong arm.

"Don't bring the bag inside!" he warned. "Even though it's in the ash, the evil is still present. It would be dangerous to bring the evil into the house and it would only be helping the people who are witching this family." Instead, I was told to walk round the outside of the house to the backyard and put the bag under a tree. I placed a large stone on top to keep it shut. Back inside, everyone was sitting cross-legged around the portable fireplace and soon more hot charcoal was brought in.

"I'm going to give a general blessing to the house and everyone in it," Blue Horse announced. "After that we will consign to the fire the evil that has been done to you."

So saying, he threw more cedar on the fire, then stood up and with his eagle feather in hand, wafted the sweet-smelling smoke all over the family and about the room. When he had finished he sat down and looked into the fire for a few moments. Once more he tapped me with his drumstick and pointed. This time my hair really did stand on end. There in the fire was the bad face he had pulled from the ceiling! Yet I knew for sure that the plaster face we had found was in the bag of ash I'd carefully placed under the tree outside. Once more, as at Canyon de Chelly, the image was crystal clear. There was no doubt it was the same face from the ceiling.

"How did that get there?" I gasped.

"The fire is showing us that we have found the true evil and that we have contained it within our power," Blue Horse assured me with quiet satisfaction.

Later, when I was sent into the yard to burn the bag holding the witch objects, the face was still visible in the fire in the center of the living room. I was so curious about this that I opened the bag, although I knew I was not supposed to. The piece of plaster with the face on it was still in the bag and there were no burn marks whatsoever. To say I was puzzled would be to put it mildly.

I consigned the bag and its contents to the flames from the east side, as I had been told and made sure everything inside had been well and truly burnt before going back inside. When I sat down at the fireplace again and looked into the fire, the face was no longer visible.

"It went from the fireplace at the moment you put the bag into the flames," Blue Horse told me. "The evil was destroyed at that moment and it no longer exists."

When the ceremony was over I helped Blue Horse place everything back in his truck.

"Are you tired?" he asked.

"Yes," I admitted.

"Now you see what hard work this is," he said, he himself looking weary. "Fighting evil is not easy."

Only then did I realise how tired I actually was. I had been concentrating solidly for more than five hours, three of which had been spent cross-legged on the floor without food or drink. No wonder I was wacked.

Before I burnt the curses Blue Horse had removed the non-flammable items, like the coins and stone arrowhead, and told me to put them in a plastic freezer bag the family had kindly provided. It may have been my imagination, but as I was sealing that bag, the arrowhead seemed to move suddenly of its own volition and I felt its sharp tip jab into my thumb. It failed to penetrate the skin and although it may have been pure imagination, I had the distinct impression it was trying to stab me and draw blood. I told myself not to be so stupid, not to be so cack-handed, and to handle sharp objects with more care. But the incident left me wondering.

"Take those things to the river and throw them in," Blue Horse instructed me, pointing to the freezer bag I carried. "Running water will carry the evil away so it can never come back."

"Like at Canyon de Chelly?" I asked. "When you told me to throw the bull snake in the stream?"

"You learn quick," he said, nodding approvingly.

The next day I drove into Albuquerque and stopped on a bridge over the Rio Grande. Leaning over the bridge I threw the freezer bag into the river, but to my dismay it refused to sink. Instead, it floated along on top of the thick brown silty waters, and for a moment I thought I might be witnessing the triumph of evil over common sense. Then, belatedly, I remembered I'd forgotten to make a hole in the plastic bag to let the air out. As I was wondering if the bag and it's evil cargo might float all the way to the sea, it sank slowly and reluctantly beneath the waters.

"No, you should not have made a hole in the bag," Blue Horse chided me a few days later when I told him what had happened. "If you had done that the evil would have escaped and found its way back to the family. The bag floated because of the evil inside it, not because of any air inside it. Even if you had opened the bag and tipped everything into the river, that stone arrowhead would still have floated for a while. That's because at first the evil tries to save itself by finding a way out of the river. But it can't survive for long in fresh running water and after a while the purity of water overwhelms it and it is carried away."

I asked, "I don't understand how the face you found in the trailer, the face I put in the bag, the face I burnt outside in the yard, also appeared in the fire inside the house?" I thought he would give me a serious explanation, but he only laughed.

"You have a lot to learn, my *bilagáana* friend," he said. "A big, big lot to learn." And, despite my prompting, he would say no more.

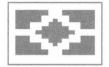

CHAPTER FIVE

The Sweat

WHEN THE UNIVERSITY TERM ENDED in mid-May I decided not to return to England, although for lack of money I would have been well advised to do so. Instead, I went to stay at Blue Horse's home near the southern boundary of the reservation in Arizona.

"What happened to the brother and sister after you removed the curses?" I asked one day.

"I don't know," Blue Horse confessed. "I was supposed to go over and do another ceremony for them but they didn't call me."

"I didn't know you were planning another ceremony."

"Part of the family live north of here and they wanted me to do the same at their house because they'd been witched as well. I said I would, but I didn't hear from them. Maybe they couldn't afford it, I don't know," he added.

"Does that often happen?" I asked.

"What?"

"That you don't get to hear what happens afterwards."

"Sometimes I hear, sometimes I don't," he said simply.

So I never found out whether our de-witching had done any good or not. I only hope it did.

When I say I went to "stay" at Blue Horse's home, this is stretching the facts slightly. The truth is that I took advantage of a general invitation to "come over any time" to turn up and camp nearby. The grand idea was that if I was on the spot he was more likely to allow me to accompany him on his travels across the reservation to do Medicine. However, it didn't work out that way: while Blue Horse went about his business as usual, he left me behind.

"Sure I'll take you with me," he would say avuncularly, whenever I broached the subject.

"Maybe I could go tomorrow?" I would suggest.

He would think about this for a few moments, rubbing his jaw as if chewing a particularly knotty problem, before replying, "Hmmm, not tomorrow. I'm going to visit a very traditional family tomorrow. Maybe another day."

I soon came to realise that "traditional family" was code for "don't want any whites around."

Despite these rebuffs, and there were many of them, Blue Horse and his family were kindness itself, and allowed me to pitch my little green tent beneath a stand of junipers not far from their neat wooden house. Blue Horse and his wife shared their home with several relatives and, as he appeared to have endless relatives who all came and went more or less at will, I became accustomed to seeing new faces almost daily. So many new faces that I quickly came to understand the wisdom of the Navajo habit of calling every man grandfather, father, brother, son, or grandson and all women grandmother, mother, sister, daughter, or granddaughter, depending on age or clan. It was much easier than to trying to remember all their names. Periodically, I was invited into the house to eat with the family and use the shower but, despite this personal kindness, my ambitions to find out more about Medicine advanced not one iota. To make matters worse, shortly before leaving Albuquerque I had received a phone call from Reuben.

"Man, you'll never guess what!" he began.

"You're right, I won't," I said. "You'd better tell me."

"I've got a Medicine Man. I've got a real, big time Medicine Man!" he yelled excitedly down the phone.

"What do you mean 'you've got him?'"

"We're attached." He said.

"At the hip?"

"No," he laughed. "Like I'm his bag carrier. I do the driving for him. I clean up after him and that kind of thing. You have to make yourself useful to get a big time Medicine Man like him to take notice of you and show you the Medicine Road. If he likes me, and I think he does, I could become a real apprentice!" His voice positively vibrated with excitement.

I was pleased for him, of course, but could not help feeling that I was being upstaged and my determination to succeed grew stronger. For the moment, however, there was nothing to do except sit under the junipers, swat away the flies, and hope Blue Horse would eventually yield.

Blue Horse's wife *Baa'*, whose name means "Warrior Woman," was tall and slim and aristocratic by descent and nature. She was possessed of great intelligence and dignity and these traits she combined with an indomitable will. These fine parts of her nature had been inherited by her granddaughter *Asdzáán mą'ii dootł'izhí* ("Gray Fox Lady") who was staying with her grandparents, having recently had a baby. *Dootł'izh* is a word in Navajo that can indicate not only blue, but the kind of bluish gray that is often the colour of young foxes. In English, she was called Fox.

Perhaps I should explain that the Navajo are a matriarchy, which means the women are in charge of most matters. Men are expected to do the heavy work and know their place, while land, inheritance, and home passes through the female line in matrilineal descent. Matriarchy and matrilineal descent are an ancient cultural response to the vagaries of inheritance in a world without DNA testing. While a man often cannot be certain he is the father of a child, everyone knows who is the mother, and so inheritance through the female line is by far the most reliable. The Celtic parts of Britain retained matrilineal descent until comparatively recent times.

Among the Navajo this means that when a man marries he often goes to live on the land of his wife's family. There he builds a house for himself and his bride and settles down. He may work the land, herd the family's sheep and cattle, and make a living there, but he often owns nothing and the property remains that of his wife until she dies, when everything passes to her daughters and female relatives. Of course, it is often not quite so simple and in any case things are changing as more people get regular city jobs. But the matriarchy still holds in most areas and Navajo women retain an almost total dominance within the home. As one would expect in a system run by women, while in general the tribe are a pretty prudish lot—you'll wait a long time to see a girl in a short skirt on the reservation—having children out of wedlock is not one of the things they are particularly prudish about.

As it happened Fox had a perfectly decent man to wed, and he had asked her to marry him. It was just that, so far, they hadn't got round to it. So, while he worked in the oil field at Farmington a hundred miles to the north, she stayed with her grandmother, as there was no more room at her mother's house.

Within a matriarchy women are expected, and expect, to do "women's work": the cooking, cleaning, washing, looking after children, and a thousand and one other domestic things. Men, on the other hand, are expected to keep out of the way and do "men's work," such as chopping wood, herding, planting crops, finding a job and, occasionally, hunting. On the few occasions when I tried to help the women in the home—thinking I was being a good guest—I was thoroughly chewed off by *Baa'* and Fox.

"You'll only get in the way," *Baa'* told me crossly one day when I offered to clean the dishes after breakfast. "Go and sit down and I'll bring you some coffee."

"Perhaps I could help with the laundry?" I offered gamely.

"I'm not giving you my underwear!" said Fox, sounding shocked.

"I give you mine," I pointed out.

"That's different!" Fox said crossly. "I'll do my own laundry, thank you."

"Why don't you go outside and sit on the porch," *Baa'* told me pointedly. "You can have your coffee out there." And so I was unceremoniously dismissed. With Blue Horse absent most of the day, and with nothing to read and nothing to do, I was left to contemplate nature.

In the ancient world, Roman philosophers of the Cynic school held that the Book of Nature was the only one a wise man needed read, and that what was provided by nature was all a wise man should have. Some of them took this to such extremes they divested themselves of all their worldly goods, including all their clothes, and wandered the highways and byways of the Roman Empire stark naked. Their rivals of the Stoic school of philosophy agreed with the need to dispose of unnecessary bourgeois affectation, but did not go so far as walk about naked. This led to a narrow doctrinal dispute that prompted the Roman satirist Juvenal to comment that he could tell a Cynic from a Stoic only because the Stoic wore a shirt.

I hung on to my clothes but otherwise came to agree with the ancients that the Book of Nature is the greatest of all, and its pages contain much of what is most missed in our busy modern world. This was the first time I had the leisure to gaze upon this great book, and among the many things I discovered within it was the beauty of northern Arizona and New Mexico Navajo territory, which is frankly stunning.

I enjoyed sleeping out under the stars and the junipers, but my Indian friends became increasingly fretful and feared I might fall foul of a skin-walker.

"It's hard to witch a white man," I reminded them.

"That's because you don't believe in it," Fox said, and there was a hint of accusation in her voice.

"I don't know what to believe," I told her honestly.

"A skin-walker came here once," she said. "Blue Horse was doing a ceremony and I had to go outside for a moment and I saw it. It was standing in the shadows under a tree. I was terrified."

"What did it look like?" I wanted to know, but Fox would not be drawn.

"It looked like nothing else on earth," was all she would say. "Blue Horse went out and dealt with it and it didn't come back."

More than once *Baa'* and Blue Horse invited me to sleep on the sofa in their living room. At first I refused, preferring my own company and feeling in no way afraid of skin-walkers. Then, one morning at about three A.M., I was awoken by an unmistakable clump-clump of hooves. Instantly awake, I automatically reached up to the little net in the crown of the tent where I kept several vital items, including my matches, my torch, and my knife. It was for the knife I felt and as my hand closed over it, I heard the hooves again and a huge shadow crossed the moon and fell upon the tent.

A man lying in a small tent is extremely vulnerable because he cannot stand up if attacked. I did not know what it was outside, but all those stories about skin-walkers must have been getting to me, because I rolled outside like lightning, knife in hand, and leapt to my feet, only to find myself looking at a stray horse. It was hard to say which of us was the more surprised.

During the day the sun beat down mercilessly. By now it was summer in the desert and despite Blue Horse's house being at an altitude of more than six thousand feet, the temperature sometimes reached more than a hundred degrees Fahrenheit during the day. Water is a rare commodity in that part of the world and I had to buy it in gallon plastic containers from a trading post two miles away. By now I was so short of money that, despite the heat, I walked to the trading post and back to save petrol. This meant a strict limit on how much I could carry and, being English, I naturally used most of this precious water (a dollar thirty-five a gallon!) to make even more precious tea.

I did this by boiling a small kettle over a fire of sweet-smelling juniper twigs, removing it from the flames, and throwing in a tea bag. This was left to brew for several minutes after which I added some powdered milk. It had to be powdered milk because I had no fridge and the real stuff went sour in the heat within a few hours. For coffee I smashed up coffee beans between two rocks, put the crushed beans into an old tin can, added water, and boiled it over the fire. The trick to this extempore coffee making is always to use a tin that still has part of the lid attached. When the dark brown, lava-like substance foams up the inside of the tin and threatens to erupt over the edge and douse the fire, one can use the lid to remove the tin from the flames without burning one's fingers or losing the coffee. (Though from personal experience, I can make no promises about the safety of said sharp metal handle.)

The coffee was never finer than one morning when a fierce gust of wind blew sand and bits of juniper bark into it. I had used the last bit of water and, being unwilling to walk all the way to the trading post and back for more, I strained the coffee through an old pair of socks. Delicious!

Each morning I used a little water to wash my face. But there was not enough to waste on extensive ablutions and so the occasional shower I had at the house was probably as welcome to everyone else as it was to me.

One morning I was lying under the shade of the junipers, drinking tea, looking at the cloudless sky, and thinking that if Blue Horse continued to ignore me I might as well start hitchhiking back to England, when a young girl of no more than eight years walked into my camp and stood looking at me shyly. She was a chubby, round faced little girl, who wore owl-like, glasses over her big, dark Indian eyes. On her feet were a pair of pretty pink trainers and she wore a thin cotton dress that did not fit her plump little form at all well. I recognised her as one of Blue Horse's many grandchildren.

Swaying shyly from side to side, with her hands clasped behind her back and looking at her shoes, she announced: "*Acheii biłii dooł' izh*, Grandfather Blue Horse wants you to go sweat with him."

"Now?" I asked, somewhat taken aback.

"Uh-huh," she replied smiling sweetly. Then, before I could say anything else, she turned and skipped away across the desert towards the house.

Puzzled by this sudden and unexpected invitation, I had another cup of tea before picking up my rather grubby towel, and strolling over to the house. There I found Blue Horse sitting at his kitchen table drinking coffee with his trademark white Stetson firmly on his head.

"Come in," he said agreeably. "Have a seat. Have some coffee. Would you like a pastry?" He handed me a mug of coffee and a couple of sweet Danish pastries. After some small talk, during which I finished the pastries, he asked, "You want to go sweat with me?"

"Yes," I said. "I'd like that a lot."

Looking at my grubby towel Blue Horse told me to get a clean one from his bathroom cupboard, then led me outside to a spot not far from his house where his sweat lodge lay.

"Get the rocks together for the fire," he said pleasantly. "I'll be back later."

An Indian sweat is pretty much like a sauna, except that it takes place in a little tent called a sweat lodge. This is a semi permanent domed construction made of flexible branches and covered with hides or thick rugs. A few months earlier I'd taken part in an Indian sweat lodge ceremony with Reuben, and although I'd never had a hand in preparing one, I knew that before it can begin wood must be gathered for a bonfire. The bonfire has to be big enough to heat the heavy stones of volcanic rock used to generate steam, and the rocks need an hour or so to reach the right temperature. It means a lot of work because wood has to be gathered and chopped for the fire, the rocks have to be put in place, and the fire watched while the rocks heat. The lodge has to be properly prepared and cleaned out and the surrounding area swept. Despite all this work, I was glad to be put to use at last and there was little doubt that after weeks in my tent I needed the sauna. Remembering Reuben's words about the necessity of making oneself useful to a Medicine Man, I determined to do a good job and set to with a will.

There are various kinds of sweat lodges among the Indians, including a specific Navajo sweat. In modern times, what is known as the Sioux sweat has become the most popular and widely used among the tribes, and it was this type of sweat lodge Blue Horse had built for himself. The Sioux sweat lodge originated with the Sioux, or Lakota, tribe of the Great Plains. It stands about four feet high and is made of a framework of overlapping willow branches. These branches are put together in a special and sacred way that represent the earth, the sky, the universe, and all living things within it. In the old days buffalo hides were thrown over the framework to seal in the steam, but now a thick canvas or tarpaulin and some heavy rugs are almost universal. In the center of the lodge is a circular pit, about a foot deep and about three feet wide, into which the heated stones are placed. The stones vary in size from about the size of a man's head to the size of his fist. Once they have reached sufficient temperature, they are removed from the fire with the aid of a heavy iron pitchfork and carried a few at a time into the lodge. Once enough have been placed safely in the pit for a "round," that is to say, a sweat period of about fifteen to twenty minutes, the Medicine Man orders the lodge door sealed, and when all is ready he pours water on the red hot rocks to create superheated steam to cleanse the participants.

Inside, the men sit naked, or nearly naked, around the pit as the steam sears over their bodies. If a participant finds the steam excessively hot, which it often is, it is permissible to lie down flat to get out of the worst of it. However, if the lodge is crowded this may not be possible, and it is considered extremely bad form to run outside; an indignity that, so far, I have managed to avoid — although not by much!

A traditional Navajo sweat lodge would have had the pit for the hot stones to one side rather than in the center. Because the participants sweated naked, men and women always sweated separately. Today people generally wear baggy shorts and T-shirts into the sweat and so men and women do sometimes sweat together, although it is more usual to find the men sweating alone. If women join them they are almost always family members and rarely strangers.

Usually there are four rounds in a sweat, and sometimes six. While it is not a rule, each round is often hotter than the last, and sometimes the ceremony ends with the searing "warrior round," which is definitely not for the faint-hearted. During the rounds the Medicine Man leads everyone in prayer and it is open to anyone to pray for as long as he likes for anything he likes. The whole ceremony usually takes between two to four hours, depending on how many take part and how voluble they are, and there is a break between each round of sweating to go outside to drink water and stretch one's legs. When the sweat is over, everyone is deemed purified in body and spirit.

Blue Horse's little dome-shaped sweat lodge, with its covering of heavy white cloth and tarpaulin, lay behind a line of junipers that kept the wind at bay in the winter. About ten yards in front of the east-facing entrance was the fire pit where the stones were heated. I was pleased to see a good layer of charcoal had been left in the bottom from the last sweat, because that would help me get the fire going.

Soon I was busy among the junipers with an axe gathering dead wood for the fire. While I was working, the old thermometer Blue Horse had nailed to a nearby tree rose into the 90s. By the time I'd laboured away for more than an hour, chopping and sawing juniper logs, breaking up wooden pallets, and heaving rocks about, I had worked up a bigger sweat than I would have done sweating inside the lodge!

The result of my efforts was a classic, cone-shaped, Guy Fawkes–style, good old English bonfire. On the top of which— with some considerable difficulty—I'd managed to place some of the volcanic stones. My idea was that as the fire burnt down, the stones would fall into the center and get even hotter. Unfortunately, the big stones would not stay in place and kept rolling off down the steep sides of the bonfire. So I put them at the side of the pit with the idea of throwing them on when the fire had burnt down a little.

All seemed set and I was standing back, mopping my brow and admiring my handiwork, when Blue Horse appeared. I waited for him to express his admiration, but instead, a look of horror crossed his face and he gasped, "This won't work!"

"What's the matter with it?" I asked, stunned.

"It's the wrong shape," he said. "It's shaped like a mountain. You can't build a fire like that for a sweat!"

He looked into the bottom of the pit and held his hands up in exasperation. "You didn't even sweep out the pit!" he cried. "All the old charcoal in the bottom has to be dug out and carried away. We want the new fire to be fresh and new and not tainted with old sins. And *why* aren't the stones on the fire?"

"I tried to put them on, but they rolled off," I confessed.

"Of course they did!" he said, and he held his hand to his head in consternation. "If you build a fire to look like a mountain, of course they won't stay on it. If they think they're on a mountain they'll roll off because that's what stones do on mountains. They start at the top and roll to the bottom. The reason so many rocks are round is so they roll away and see places far off." Hitting stride he continued to lecture me. "Rocks are very curious creatures and once they get the wanderlust on them they can roll for hundreds of miles, thousands probably. If you give them enough time they'll roll right round the world." His story sounded very like a Navajo version of what any geologist would recognise as the phenomenon of rock transportation by rivers, erosion, and glaciers. During this process rocks—some of them extremely large—can be moved hundreds of miles. I'm not suggesting that ancient Navajos had a better understanding of geology than modern scientists. Only that they may have noticed this phenomenon many years before it was recognized by European scientists in the nineteenth century.

"To keep stones in the same place you have to make them comfortable. First you have to build a fire that is flat and square, so they're on an even surface and won't get restless and want to roll around somewhere else. You have to sweep out all the old charcoal because it carries the sins we washed away in the lodge. Everything has to be cleaned up and swept carefully both inside and out before we can start."

"But I've worked so hard," I said, feeling completely deflated.

"It's no good to work hard doing the wrong things," he admonished me. "You'll have to start again."

Shaking his head he sat himself gingerly on an upturned log beneath a shady juniper, and began to roll a cigarette. While I laboured, he sat and smoked his wonderfully aromatic Indian tobacco, pausing only to offer the occasional word of advice. Under his direction I carefully swept out the fire pit and carried away the old charcoal to a dump beside a dry stream bed about sixty yards away. From there, he assured me, the rains would eventually generate a flood that would wash away the charcoal and, with it, the sins of those who had last used the lodge.

Next I began to reconstruct the fire in the shape of a rectangle, with the first layer of wood being laid down with the long logs running north-south and the short ones east-west. A layer of stone was placed on top, then another layer of wood on top of that, and so on.

"Think of a sandwich, Charles," he told me. "It's like making a big sandwich of rock and wood."

The final result was a pyre with five layers of wood, each of which contained within it a layer of neatly placed stones.

"That's better," Blue Horse said, easing himself from his log and nodding contentedly. Then, satisfied with his inspection, he pointed to a plastic bottle of petrol he had brought with him and told me to pour it on the pyre and set it alight. I shook my head and instead asked for his box of matches. Using a handful of dried juniper bark for tinder, I struck a match, lit the tinder, and shoved the lighted tinder deep into the pyre. Wood is so dry in the desert that it catches far more readily than it does in our damp English climate. Within minutes there was an inferno with smoke billowing a hundred feet or more into the clean desert air.

"Is that how you do it in England?" he asked, scratching one ear in puzzlement. "Using just one match?"

"Sure," I lied. "No one in England ever uses more than one match to light anything."

Blue Horse scratched the other ear. "I don't know many Indians who could do that with one match," he conceded.

The single match trick is not much of a trick and I learnt it in the 1st Hertford Sea Scouts when I was a lad. I can look after myself fine in the great outdoors, but as I rarely get the chance to do so these days, Blue Horse was understandably taken aback by any show of field craft on my behalf. But the match trick made me feel that, after working like a slave all morning, I could still pull one back and I felt much better. For a while I continued to stoke the fire, but soon the heat became so fierce it was impossible to get near and I was forced to stand back.

Taking pity on me as I stood there mopping my brow and swigging water to counteract the dehydration, Blue Horse offered me a seat on his log and passed me a fresh roll-up.

"Smoke, my friend," he said. "It's good to start a sweat with a smoke. The Creator, the Great Spirit, likes the smell of tobacco. Smoke and let the smoke be carried up to him, so he'll be pleased with you."

I'm not a smoker, but Blue Horse's tobacco was exceptionally good. It was gathered from wild tobacco plants, and he processed it at home by mixing it with honey, licorice, and sweet herbs. The resulting concoction smelt good enough to eat, although it was so strong in nicotine I formed the opinion that it was probably similar to a heroin hit. Still, I accepted the smoke from him and drew on it for a time, while he took the opportunity to tell me more about the purpose of the sweat.

"To understand the sweat you have to look at everything we use to create it," he began. "Everything we are going to use today has been given to us by the Great Spirit. The rocks, the wood, the fire, the water, the tobacco, they all come from him. I want you to look at those rocks and the wood and the fire and tell me what you think about them?"

Not for the first—or last—time I didn't understand the question, and replied that I didn't think anything about them. This made him roar with laughter.

"Could you sit on the fire like those rocks?" he laughed, pointing to the crackling, smoking logs. He seemed genuinely amused by my display of incomprehension.

"Not likely," I said.

"What about the wood. Could you burn like that?"

"No," I said again, looking at the fire and not understanding at all where he was leading.

"How long do we live, we human men?" Blue Horse continued.

"May be seventy or eighty years," I said.

"Perhaps a hundred, a hundred and ten, a hundred and twenty?" he suggested.

"In a few cases," I conceded.

"Is that a long time?" he asked.

"Yes."

"That's the longest we can live and we think it's a long time, but it's only the wave of a man's hand compared to real time," Blue Horse said. "Look at those rocks. How old do you think they are? Millions of years old? Tens or hundreds of millions of years old? Maybe those smart professors at your university know how old they are, but whether they do or they don't, it doesn't matter to the rocks. It doesn't matter to them either what we do to them. Because they've been around a long, long, time, and during that time they've been through so much, a little thing like heat from our fire doesn't bother them. We put them on the fire, we take them off the fire. We pour cold water on them and we put them back on the fire again. The rocks don't care, they probably don't even notice. But if someone did the same thing to you, you would notice, because to humans the fire is hot and the water is cold. You're a man and you can't stand the fire, not even for one minute, because you've not been around long enough to get hard and tough like a rock. You might think you're tough because you can walk through the desert, but the reason you walk through the desert is to get out of the sun and find water. The rock doesn't have to do that. He can lie in the sun for a few million years without a drop of water and it doesn't worry him. I know you like to jump out of airplanes and come down in your parachute, and that's pretty tough. But the rock doesn't need a parachute. If you throw him out at 30,000 feet it won't do him any harm. Mostly he'll land with a thud and lie there for a few million years as the Great Spirit intended, or maybe he'll go for a roll around and amuse himself for a few million years. Even if he breaks into a thousand pieces he won't care, because it's like him scattering his children over the land. How do you think you get little rocks? Only by big rocks breaking up. But if you or I tried the same thing we couldn't do it and we'd die, because we don't get time to get hard like the rock. We're here on this earth for a moment." He took back the cigarette. "And then we're gone, like this puff of smoke," he said and blew a big puff to the heavens.

"The Old People used to say 'if you want to know how tough the rocks are, go and shout at them. Every time you shout they're going to shout back. You go to the canyon wall and shout all day and those rocks will still be shouting back at you when night comes. It doesn't matter how many times you shout. You can shout as loud and as long as you like, but the rocks will have the last word.' A bit like a woman, I guess," he added laughing.

He fell silent for a while and then, pointing to the juniper bushes, continued, "Look at the wood we're burning and think how old it is. Some of these bushes are hundreds of years old, thousands maybe. We can cut them down, but we can't destroy them because they've been here a lot longer than we have and, like the rocks, they know a thing or two. We burn the wood but we can't destroy it. All that happens is that it turns to smoke and goes back to the Great Spirit. When it goes back to Him it leaves behind ash and the ash is good and rich and helps more bushes to grow. So it doesn't matter how many I cut down and burn, all I'm doing is helping more to grow. That's why the junipers will always be here for us Indians, to give us light for our homes and fire for our cooking stoves, because that's how the Great Spirit intended it.

"Maybe one day the white man will build some machine and chop down all the trees and then there'll be no more junipers for a while. I dare say the white man could do that if he wants and we Indians couldn't stop him. But one day the white man, too, will be gone. When the white man goes the trees will come back and maybe the buffalo will come back too—I hope so. But you and me, my friend, we will never see it, because we come and go from this earth in an instant. Our lives last no longer than the flight of a hummingbird from one twig to another. There's a flash of many colours, a whirling of wings, and a little disturbance in the air, and then it's gone and so are we. The best we can do is to learn a little during the short time we're here, and hope that when we go from this place, we leave a little wiser than when we arrived."

Pausing again, he bent down and picked up a rock in one hand, and a small juniper log in the other. "We can learn from the rocks and the wood, the fire and the water. The rock is very hard and nothing can hurt it. The wood is hard too. Sure, you can chop the wood, but only with the stone, which is harder. In the old days we made axes of stone and now we use axes of steel but it's still hard work, as you know, because you've cut all this wood for the fire. The fire cannot exist without the wood, the wood cannot exist without the water, and the rocks cannot give us steam for the lodge without all the other three. So you see, although all these things are very tough and hard and strong, without each other they're not much use. So we take all these hard, tough, things and bring them into the sweat to help make us clean through their strength and wisdom."

Becoming confidential he leaned closer, and dropping his voice, pointed to the air around us. "All around us there are evil spirits and ghosts waiting to make trouble for us. Yes, right here, now. We can't see them, but they're here listening to us, hearing what we keep in our hearts, and what thoughts we have in our heads. We can't help having bad thoughts, or doing bad deeds from time to time, because we're men and that's how we are. The ghosts and the bad spirits pick up on these bad thoughts and deeds. For them such thoughts are food and drink and when the bad spirits see them forming in us they begin to follow us around like coyotes waiting to feed. They say 'here is a man having evil thoughts. I'll follow him and feast well on his bad thoughts and make trouble for him, so he has more bad thoughts and gets himself into more trouble. That way I will feast even better.'

"Soon the Evil Ones find it easy to follow us wherever we go. Into the country, into the town, anywhere. We can't hide from them because they're following the trail of our bad thoughts. We become like carrion and leave a trail of stench and there's nothing we can do to stop it so long as we remain unclean. But when we go into the sweat we bring all these good, strong, hard, things inside to help us. The stones, the wood, the water, the fire. We pray and sing and call upon the Great Spirit, the Creator, to help us become clean again and wash all the badness from us. The ghosts and the bad spirits can't follow us into the sweat. The have to stay outside and when we come out we are cleansed and they don't recognise us any more. They stand around the sweat saying to each other 'That man I made bad, that man I made trouble for, where is he? Where did he go? He went into this place I can't go into, but he didn't come out again. Where is he? Where can he be?' They can't see us anymore because we've been cleansed in body and spirit.

"Once you are clean the good spirits can see you and will want to help you because they can see all the evil has gone and you are pure again. So, my friend, now you know why we Indians do this thing called a sweat, and why it is so important to us," he concluded.

While we had been talking the fire had burnt down, exposing some of the stones that were now so hot they glowed red even in the bright desert sun. I had thought the fire would collapse suddenly as the layers burnt through. But instead, it burnt down slowly, shuddering from time to time as the logs gave way internally under the weight of the rocks until the whole had settled in an orderly fashion at the bottom of the fire pit.

At last Blue Horse stood up and walked slowly to the pit. He looked carefully at the rocks for a few moments before declaring, "They're ready. Let's go sweat!"

I held him back for a moment. "Does the same apply to skin-walkers?" I wanted to know. "If you sweat, will they not be able see you anymore?"

He shook his head. "A skin-walker isn't a ghost or a spirit, it's a man changed into an animal. So it's not the same thing and it doesn't work the same," he replied gravely.

"Do you really believe a man can turn himself into an animal?" I asked.

He replied with a single emphatic "yes," and, saying no more, strode over to the sweat, removed his clothes, dropped on all fours, and crawled through the low, semi-circular, entrance. I fetched a large iron pitchfork and, two at a time, forked eight big rocks into the pit in the center of the sweat. When I'd finished, and was seated inside, Blue Horse closed the door by pulling a piece of old carpet across it, and pitched us into deep darkness.

The heat inside the sweat was hotter and dryer than any sauna I'd ever experienced. In the dark, the sweat lodge seemed smaller inside than it did on the outside, and at first I worried about accidentally putting my foot on the hot stones that glowed dully in the center. Through the dark came the sound of a bunch of sage twigs being dipped into a bucket of clear water and stirred by Blue Horse, who had gathered the fresh sage earlier that day. Sage is held to be sacred and is used in most Indian ceremonies because it helps to purify the body and soul. Blue Horse began to chant in Navajo, and a series of fierce hisses issued forth as the twigs were used to splash water onto the hot stones. Then came a blast of superheated steam that took my breath away and left me drenched in perspiration and feeling parboiled.

As the sweat went on Blue Horse continued to pray and sing his Medicine songs in Navajo, accompanying himself on a water drum that he beat in a tight rhythm. Occasionally Fox came and passed much needed water into the sweat lodge. She also made sure there were drinks ready for us when we emerged between rounds, but she did not enter the sweat.

"A lot of Navajo ladies still won't enter the sweat lodge when men are inside, because they don't think it's proper, even though it's considered OK for men and women to sweat together these days," Blue Horse explained as we took a break between rounds and stretched out in the afternoon sun, which now seemed re-markably cool despite the thermometer showing 110 degrees Fahrenheit.

Back inside the sweat, Blue Horse left the door open so there was enough light for him to point out the willow rods that formed the structure of the sweat, and have much deeper meaning than their simple nature would imply.

He explained, "The two strong rods making the doorway are your parents. We call them the mother and father, because they make the entrance and your mother and father gave you entry to the world. They run from east to west, which is the course of a man's life, which begins with his own dawn and ends with his own sunset. The two rods above them are the grandmother and grandfather, they run north to south because they have already gone on before us. But if you look carefully, you'll see they sup-port the mother and father, just as your mother and father once supported you. Then there is a rod in each corner that represent the four seasons. If you look up, you'll see the four seasons cross at the center of the roof, and where they cross they form a star. That is the morning star and it shines down from Father Sky, who is at the center of our lodge to bless us as we gather here to cleanse ourselves and pray."

Next he directed my attention to the three big hoops of willow that went round the walls and helped give the lodge its shape. "The lowest of them is only a few inches from the ground and that represents all the creatures that crawl and burrow in the earth and Mother Earth herself. The next one, which is a few inches higher, represents all the animals that live *on* the land. The deer, the elk, the cougars, the foxes, and the wolves. It also represents ourselves and reminds us that we are not only on the earth, but *of* it, as are all creatures put here by the Great Spirit to live on his earth. It reminds us who we are and that we should live in harmony with all living things. Finally, the third hoop represents the birds of the air and Father Sky and above that, all the way to the star in the middle, is the universe. So, you see, my friend, although this sweat lodge of mine is only a little place, and takes up only a tiny space on the earth, inside it contains the whole universe. You should think carefully about what I have just said, because there is much to learn from it," and with that, he fell silent.

Eventually, it was time to start the final round and I forked in the last of the rocks. Then I crawled inside once more and took up my cross-legged position opposite Blue Horse, who closed the door and in the darkness began to again sing Medicine songs. By now my eyes had adjusted enough to be able to see a little in the darkness of the lodge, and when he had finished his songs, I was able to see that he took from his Medicine Box some special herbs, which he scattered on the hot stones. These gave off a strange smell, the like of which I had never smelt before, and he encouraged me to breath in the smoke, saying it would clear my mind.

I did as he said and after a while a strange clarity of mind did indeed begin to dawn. Problems that had been plaguing me for weeks now seemed easy to solve, and my sketchy understanding of his Navajo medicine songs improved so dramatically that I was able to join in the words. When the smoke from the herb had cleared, I saw him take some new thing from his *jish* and throw that on the stones as well. This time a cloud of little blue stars appeared on the rocks, glittering and twinkling like pale sapphires. For a few moments they lit up the darkness with a soft pale blue light, before slowly going out one by one. But Blue Horse was still not finished. Once more he threw something onto the fire. Again the blue stars appeared, but now some of them shot out of the fire and rose into the air, where they moved about in the darkness, circling in the space above our heads in a breathtaking display.

"This Medicine is very special," Blue Horse said, holding up the little white doeskin bag from which he had taken the blue stars. "It's very expensive, but I wanted to share it with you. It's made out of a root and also the skin of a blue bird, that's why it sparkles blue. Because it comes from the earth and the sky, it's especially powerful. There's something else in it that comes from a tree. The tree lives midway between the earth and the sky and so when you grind them all up together, that gives the Medicine even more power. I don't have much of it, and it's hard to get and very expensive. Only the oldest, wisest, most powerful Medicine Men can make it. But today I want to share it with you, my white brother, because you have a good heart." And he reached out in the darkness and shook my hand.

I responded in Navajo, saying: "*Nizhóní,*" meaning 'It is beautiful.'"

I do not know if you can hear a smile, but, if you can, I'd swear I heard Blue Horse smiling at me through the darkness.

"*Nizhóní,*" he repeated with great satisfaction. "*Nizhóní.*"

Half an hour later the sweat was over and we lay around in the sunshine drinking water, until we had recovered enough to stagger back to the house for something to eat.

Baa' and Fox had prepared a meal of roast mutton with tortilla bread and strong coffee. I wolfed it down, being extremely hungry after all that hard work and sweating, but noticed during the course of the meal that Blue Horse did not appear to be comfortable.

"It's my back," he confessed, wriggling around in his chair when I asked him about it. "I worked in the uranium mines for twenty-seven years and it didn't do my back any good."

Some of the largest uranium mines in the world are to be found along I-40 going west from Albuquerque, but with the collapse of the old Soviet Union in the 1980s and the end of the Cold War, there was no longer much need for their products. The result was that the mines were all closed and the workers fired—including Blue Horse.

He rubbed the small of his back gently. "I hoped the sweat might do it some good, sometimes it helps a lot. But it's not given to a healer to heal himself," he added ruefully.

At least I now knew why he had been so keen to invite me to share the sweat lodge with him. He was incapable of chopping all that wood and heaving those rocks about by himself and so he had got muggins to do it for him!

"We have a saying in England that 'a man who would be his own doctor has a fool for a patient,'" I said, and everyone laughed.

Then I told them what had happened to me in the Louisiana swamps.

Before heading West, I had been driving around Louisiana when a chance rainstorm of almost supernatural ferocity forced me off the motorway and into the vastness of the Atchafalaya swamp, which lies a little to the west of New Orleans. The storm was so intense and the rain so heavy that the swamp, which is larger than some European countries, expanded. It began to overflow the roads as I drove and at times almost seemed to be in pursuit of me. At length, and to my great relief, I found myself in the little Cajun French town of Breaux Bridge.

There I found a wonderful bed and breakfast establishment in a grand old antebellum house built on stilts over the Bayou Teche river, owned by a larger-than-life genteel lady, Madame Cecile.

Madame Cecile made it her self-appointed mission to keep me entertained by introducing me to every aspect of Cajun life, and I ended up staying for weeks. I went canoeing and catfish-netting. I met real moonshiners whose illegal brew of alcohol rivalled the best Bourbon whisky. I went to cockfights, dust dances, pig roastings, and crawfish eating contests. I even visited an illegal gambling den.

All this would have been no more than an interesting diversion on my journey, had Madame not decided that I should meet some *traiteurs*. I was unfamiliar with the word, but *traiteur* in Cajun French means "healer" and is applied to those men—the few who remain, at least, are mostly men—who heal by laying on hands.

Madame drove me to a rundown trailer park near the back of a large and smelly chemical works in the Lafayette suburb of Maurice.

"There he is," Madame cried excitedly when we arrived at our destination, motioning towards an old man and a fierce-looking hound standing outside a battered trailer. At eighty-eight years of age, Monsieur C.J. Broussard was indisputably in better nick than his dog and considerably less battered than his trailer.

"This dog," he said to me excitedly, after we were introduced, pointing to the well-built cur with floppy ears that lollopped about at his feet. "This dog's great, great, great, I can't remember how many greats, but her great grandam was sold to Batista. Yes, Batista! The last dictator of Cuba before the communists took over. Batista, he liked fighting dogs and this one comes from a line of the best." The old man's disclosure that she was a fighting dog certainly accounted for her battle-scarred appearance.

C.J., as he told me he preferred to be called, invited us into his trailer and as I followed him up the rickety wooden steps, I spied a couple of shivering Chihuahuas huddled underneath.

"Also your pets?" I inquired.

"Her lunch," he replied, jerking his thumb towards the fighting bitch. I like to think he was joking.

Inside the trailer, an ancient television blared away at full blast and Madame Cecile indicated to me that C.J. was a little deaf. He may not have had his hearing, but he still had his manners and he turned the offending instrument down to a quiet burble the moment we entered. Then he waved Madame and myself onto an old sofa before settling himself into an ancient-looking armchair.

At Madame's urging, C.J. explained some of the duties of a *traiteur*.

"I'm often called to the dog pit to stop the bleeding when animals are injured," he said, pointing a finger towards his dog. "But I don't like the fights any more and I wouldn't go if they didn't keep calling for me to help. I can't let the animals suffer. They call me to cockfights, too, and I've saved birds worth tens of thousands of dollars. You see, if you have the ability to heal you must use it, no matter what. You cannot refuse to use your gift if you are asked for help."

He was a man small in stature who, despite his obviously limited means, retained about him a polish that spoke of better days. He was smartly dressed in good quality casual clothes and, despite his age, still had a full head of thick, dark, hair that was immaculately clean and well barbered. Before he could continue with his story, the sound of footsteps on the wooden stairs outside interrupted. The door handle rattled and an old man walked in. He was tall, thin, erect, stern of visage, and with a pronounced De Gaulle-like nose and steel gray hair. He entered the room wearing the sort of checkered siren suit I thought had gone out of use when Winston Churchill stopped wearing them at the end of World War II. Monsieur Learcy Aubey was a legendary *traiteur* and had come to visit C.J. who, it transpired, had once been his pupil. He was eighty-five and was, along with C.J., a D-Day veteran. As my father also landed on D-Day, we talked for a while about the *debarquement* and the role the two had played. C.J. had been stationed in Ipswich and remembered it fondly.

"I'd have loved to go back there sometime," he said. "But I've left it too long. There ain't going to be no one there who remembers me after all this time and that's for sure."

"Maybe that's not such a bad thing," said Aubey with a smile. "No jealous husbands waiting to shoot you!" We all laughed, although the remark earned Aubey a cuff from Madame.

After a while the conversation turned back to *traiteurs*. As the two men talked, in marked French accents, about their work, it was hard not to be impressed by their quiet confidence in their art. They did not boast about it, still less did they try to explain it. They simply told their tales and left me to make up my own mind.

"First of all, you have to understand that a healer can't heal everything," C.J. warned me. "Sometimes he can cure a patient and sometimes he can't, just like a doctor. You go to the doctor and he gives you medicine and sometimes you get better and sometimes you don't. If we could cure everything then no one would die and that's not God's purpose. We're meant to die and there's nothing anyone can do about that—not the best doctors, not the best *traiteurs*, not anyone. I've cured people with double pneumonia and I've cured people with cancer and you can believe me, or not, as you please." Then he told the following story.

"One day I had a call from a man saying his wife was in the hospital dying of cancer. The doctors told him to phone the family and get them there quick, but instead he decided to call me. To be honest it didn't sound too hopeful. A *traiteur* is pretty much like a doctor in that the earlier he's called in the better, because when things have gone too far there's a limit to what I can do. But the man was desperate, so I went to the hospital and did what I could. The next day I got a call from the husband to say his wife had improved so much the doctors were sending her home. The hospital couldn't explain it, but she was on the mend. That was ten years ago and do you know, the husband has since died, but the wife I cured is still alive."

As the old men reminisced it became apparent they believed unquestioningly in their ability to heal. They also believed that their day was done and that the modern world was sweeping their ancient art into oblivion.

"I don't treat people anymore," Aubey complained. "People abuse me." He explained that a *traiteur* was not only obliged to treat all who came for his help but was not allowed to charge for his services.

"Even your worst enemy deserves to be treated if he asks for help," Aubey said, sounding very serious. "God did not give us this gift so we could refuse to help people. But sometimes I have people ringing me up five or six times a week for treatment. I say to them 'if I can't cure you after three or four tries I can't cure you at all so go to your doctor,' but they don't. They won't go away and I can't refuse to treat them, so they only thing I can do is to give it up altogether."

Unlike C.J., Aubey was an educated man, a retired schoolteacher who had never wanted to be a *traiteur*. He said he had been aware of his power from early in his life, but chose to teach physics and chemistry until, one day, he set his pupils an exercise about medicine in the Middle Ages.

"My pupils came back with all this stuff about folk medicine and faith healing. When I read their homework I saw that fate was speaking to me and realised I could no longer avoid my destiny and I would have to start to heal again," he said. "Even in the 1940s and 1950s there were no doctors in the swamp. There was no way in or out except by water and it could take days to get a casualty out of the swamp and to the side of a road. After you got to the roadside, you had to flag down a vehicle and persuade the driver to take you the ten hours' drive to the hospital in New Orleans. By the time they arrived, most people were already dead. Today there's a fine new road and we can be in New Orleans in no time, but it was different then, and most folks in the swamp would call on the *traiteur* for help before they did anything else.

"I can cure you of anything from a cold to cancer. I can stop the pain in your broken leg and I can make your warts disappear. I can unblock your sinuses and stop the bleeding if you have a bad cut. But nowadays there are a lot more people in the town and few *traiteurs* and it's impossible to cope with the demand. We're not allowed to ask for money and so we rely on people making donations to us. But often they don't, or can't, and things have become so bad I've heard of *traiteurs* these days *asking* for payment. No one should charge for what God has given for free. It also means the young people refuse to become *traiteurs*. If they can't make money, they can't buy cars and houses and that's what everyone wants now. It doesn't help that the young people don't even speak French any more," he concluded in disgust.

With a heavy heart C.J. concurred. "In the old days there was a *traiteur* in every village and in between fishing and hunting and trapping there was time to go around healing. Maybe they would get a chicken, or a sack of crawfish, or a piece of pork belly for their trouble but never money. Now everyone has a *job*. They have to work, work, work, to make money to buy *things*, so why would they want to cure people when there's so little in it?"

Later, when we had finished our coffee, Aubey took C.J. into a corner where they stood talking earnestly in French, from time to time casting glances in my direction. After a while Madame Cecile, who had been sitting quietly beside me, leaned over and whispered, "They want to give you something. I'm not sure what because I can't quite hear. But whatever it is, accept it gracefully because it's something that's important to them."

The old men came back and Aubey did the talking.

"You may not realise this, but you're one of us," he began.

"One of what?" I asked.

"You're a *traiteur*," he explained. "We can see it in you."

I began to protest, but the old men brushed my protests aside.

"When people are first confronted with this power they often shy away. But there's no mistake, you're a healer," Aubey insisted. C.J. explained, "We're old men and we don't have much time left. We have no successors and when we die everything we know will die with us. We've often prayed that someone would come to us before it was too late, someone we could hand on our knowledge and prayers to. Our own people don't care about what we do any more, so we would like you to take this power to the people of England. Perhaps it'll be of some use to them."

I had come to the U.S. to get away from England, and to find some much-needed freedom. Becoming successor to a dying breed of Cajun folk healers was definitely not what I had in mind.

"What happens if I can't do it, if I can't heal?" I asked.

"Either you can heal or you can't," Aubey assured me. "If you can't, there's no harm done. If you can, you might be able to do some good in the world."

I didn't think I was able to heal, but I was curious so I decided there was little harm in humouring these two old gentlemen.

"There is a prayer for everything and some prayers are very general and cover a lot of healing," C.J. told me, while Madame Cecile excused herself to the kitchen for more coffee. "Normally a *traiteur* learns these prayers by heart, but because there is so little time you'll have to write them down. But you should learn them as soon as you can, because then they can never be lost. In an emergency you may find you can't remember exactly the right prayer, so a general healing prayer will often work just as well." We three men went to a back room where C.J. invited me to sit down at a battered old desk and pulled up a chair beside me. Then a strange thing happened. As I was preparing myself with pen and paper to write down what he instructed, I suddenly felt a great pressure on my head and shoulders. A pressure so strong my head was forced down to my knees in a gesture of supplication, while at the same time my hands seemed lifted upwards in a gesture of prayer. I thought at first that C.J. or Aubey had shoved me in the back, but then after a few seconds the pressure lifted. When I was able to straighten up, I found C.J. and Aubey smiling at me, looking not in the least fazed by my sudden downward dive.

"What happened?" I asked. I wasn't scared, just intrigued.

"Don't worry, I've seen it before," C.J. reassured me. "Although not usually as dramatically as that. It's the power coming alive in you and waking after a long sleep. We told you we could

Photos taken along famous Route 66, the highway that runs from Chicago, IL to Santa Monica, CA

▲ Winter snowfall on the reservation

▼ Monument Valley in Navajo Country

Tse' yaa' ak' ahi: The store's name translates as "The Grease Under the Rocks," a pun that relies on the hot stones that are used in traditional Navajo cooking, the Navajo belief that grease, particularly mutton grease, is good for you, and a rocky outcrop behind the store

A satellite dish painted with a traditional Navajo pattern

Navajo Express trucking company

An altar set for a Navajo wedding

The shaman ties his drum

A Medicine Man divines in the fire to see whether witchcraft or other spiritual pollution has caused a patient's ill health

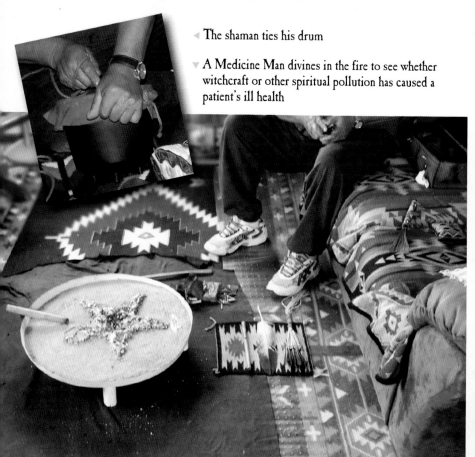

Navajo women sort peyote
medicine after a trip to Texas

◁ Navajo elders set
up camp in the lush
mountains of
Mexico to instruct
local Indians in the
ways of the sacred
peyote Medicine

The author's walk in Canyon de Chelly ends in an unexpected 500 foot sheer drop

The author stands outside in the early morning after an all-night ceremony on the reservation

The author in the beautiful Canyon de Chelly

see the power in you. Now you've felt it yourself. Aubey and me spoke true, so don't be afraid, the power has come to guide you."

"But how will it guide me?" I asked.

"You'll see. Things will start to happen," C.J said.

"What things?"

"It's impossible to say," he replied. "All I can say is that you'll know when it happens. But what will happen, or how, or where, or when, who can tell." He shrugged and then began to recite his healing prayers. I picked up a pen to write and, just as quickly, put it down again. He was reciting in Cajun French and I hardly understood a word!

"I don't know them in English," C.J. protested when I asked for a translation. "I thought you would understand." My French is Parisian, rusty and limited, but I asked him to recite the lines again, slowly this time, in the hope I might glean something.

Whether it was the power coming alive in me, or merely that I was concentrating harder the second time, I don't know. But to my astonishment, I found I could understand every word. Checking back each word with C.J. to make sure I had it right, I wrote down the prayers.

"That's very good," he said when we'd finished. "Most people take a long time to get those prayers. You got them right away and that shows you have power. Make sure you use it wisely."

This was all fine and dandy until the first time I tried to do it, which oddly enough happened in a restaurant in Lafayette, Louisiana's state capital. Madame Cecile had assembled a dinner party of some of the cleverest and wittiest people in the town and I'd been retelling the story of meeting the *traiteurs*, when one of the guests unexpectedly revealed himself as the Medicine Man of an Indian tribe. He didn't look like an Indian, but no one else at the table contradicted him, and I guess they would have known if he wasn't.

He either didn't like what I said, or didn't believe it, and asked me if I could get heat into my hands. The *traiteurs* had shown me how to do this by putting my hands together before laying them on to heal people, but I had not actually done it for real. Remembering Aubey's advice that I could "either do it or not," I put my hands together as I'd been taught and immediately felt a surge of heat between my palms. The heat increased the closer I brought them together and decreased as I moved my palms apart. Soon I found I could "play" the heat between my hands like a squeeze box, even twisting it about in the air.

My fellow guest seemed suitably impressed but when I tried to end the demonstration the heat would not go away, and soon my palms were burning like hot coals.

"My hands are burning," I told him.

"Didn't they tell you how to get rid of the heat?" he asked in astonishment.

"No," I gasped. My hands now felt as if they'd been placed under a hot grill. "Help me, I'm on fire!"

"It's like this," he said, and quickly showed me how to wipe one hand across the other in a special way. Sure enough, within a few seconds the heat faded and my palms returned to their normal temperature.

The next day, back at Madame Cecile's B&B, I opened a cupboard while looking for some coffee and an avalanche of stuff fell out on me. There were bolts of cloth, bowls, knives, forks, and goodness knows what else.

"It's stuff for the Indians," Madame Cecile, told me when we'd picked it all up. And she explained how some Navajo Indians had come to stay at her B&B during the local promotion of a film about the use of their difficult language as a code during the war.

"People gathered all these gifts for them, but they left before we could present them," she said.

The map showed that if I took Route 66 as planned, the road would take me straight past the Navajo reservation.

It is astonishing that the only Frenchwoman in the swamp with something to take to the Navajos met the only Englishman who was going that way, and so ensured he would wind up on the reservation. As C.J. said, "Things will start to happen."

When I'd finished my story, Blue Horse smashed his right fist into his left palm and bellowed, "I knew there was something about you! I knew there was. I couldn't figure out why I let some *bilagáana* from *Tóta'* come to a cedar ceremony with me. I couldn't figure out why I let you hang around camping under a tree. Now I know. You have power! You're a healer. I knew it, I knew it!" And he took off the Stetson he had mysteriously put on to eat his meal and threw it across the room.

"I knew it, but I couldn't believe I was seeing it in a *bilagáana* from England," he repeated, and he put his hands over his face and leaned back in his chair so far I thought he would topple over backwards.

"Why didn't you tell us this before?" asked *Baa'*, straightening the slightly battered Stetson she had retrieved from the other side of the room, and plunking it down on the table in front of her husband. "Why do you want to hide it if you can heal people?"

"I didn't think it would count for much with a real Medicine Man," I told them honestly. "In any case I haven't had much practice and I don't know how well I can do it."

Heaving himself upright again Blue Horse shook his head sadly. "Man, you have no idea how rare the power to heal is. It's rare among us Indians and we go looking for it, and it's so rare among you white people nobody bothers to look at all. Like those French guys told you, you can either do it or you can't. If you can't then no amount of trying will help. But if you can, then the more you practise the stronger you will get," Blue Horse assured me.

"I've only tried a couple of times," I said, remembering my fellow student at the university who I'd tried to help with the pain from his broken leg. At the time, he assured me I'd eased his pain, but I wasn't certain if I had done anything, really. I had put it down to the placebo effect and the amount of beer he habitually drank.

"Fix my back for me," Blue Horse suddenly demanded.

I gulped. Then, remembering that a physician must always appear confident if anyone is to have confidence in him, I told him as nonchalantly as I could, "Sure, lie down and take your shirt off."

A few minutes later, and with a curious *Baa'* and Fox in attendance, Blue Horse was lying face down on his bed with his shirt off, while I tried to get some heat into my hands. The heat came easily enough but I found that, as the *traiteurs* had warned me, I could not remember the right prayer. In fact, I couldn't remember any of their prayers at all. Then, very slowly, the words began to return. Laying my hands on Blue Horse's broad back, I began slowly to move my hands over him until I found a part I sensed was particularly sore. I concentrated on this and, as the prayers began to flow, felt the heat in my hands intensify.

I had little idea of what I was doing, but whatever it was, it appeared to work. Half an hour later Blue Horse was cantering around his kitchen regaling whichever relatives happened to be passing through with the Tale of How the *Bilagáana* Cured His Back. Not surprisingly, their reactions varied from disbelief to shock and awe.

The next morning, instead of driving straight past my tent, Blue Horse stopped his truck and called to me through the window. "I'm going over to Window Rock to see a man who needs help. Wanna come?"

I have never climbed into a truck so fast in all my life.

CHAPTER SIX

Spirit of a Snake

NOW BEGAN ONE OF THE MOST FASCINATING and interesting periods of my life. During which, to all intents and purposes, I slipped back into the Stone Age.

It is well to remember that less than two hundred years ago some Indian tribes of North America were Stone Age people. Their use of metal was minimal and stone was the first choice, for many the only choice, for tools that required a sharp edge. Arrowheads, knives, and spear blades being obvious examples. Such Stone Age technology is now a thing of the past, and few Indians make stone blades today except to sell to tourists. But the Stone Age beliefs and learning that underpinned their society and its stone technology have proved far harder to destroy, and among the Navajo they are still strong and vibrant.

When I accompanied Blue Horse on his visits to the sick and needy, I was doing no less than accompanying a Stone Age shaman. Everything he knew and taught, he had learnt and been taught, by men who had learnt from others in a direct succession back to the last Ice Age and, conceivably, beyond even that. This is not to say that techniques and ideas have not changed over the millennia, it would be extraordinary if no adjustments had been made. But the basic ideas, beliefs and practices, I believe to be largely unchanged. The fact that similar practices and beliefs can be found among tribes scattered widely across the Northern Hemisphere, both in the New World and the Old, tends to support this belief.

Walking and talking with a Stone Age shaman may sound romantic, but the first thing I discovered about life with a Medicine Man was what exceedingly hard work it could be. I had fondly imagined that a Medicine Man sat about most of the day waiting to be consulted and, on being so consulted, sought in turn the oracles before returning to impart the will of the divine to a breathless and appreciative audience. *Nothing* could be further from the truth.

We often had to drive long distances—hundreds of miles in some cases—to visit people who telephoned out of the blue asking for help. For reasons I could never understand, people often phoned at between two and five in the morning. Others came knocking on the door at similar hours, wanting help for sick relatives who waited swathed in blankets in their trucks.

I had finally given in to the family's concerns about skin-walkers and was sleeping regularly on the sofa, so it was usually me who answered to door to these callers. I did my best to be polite, but at four A.M. it could be testing. The pressure from people in need was unrelenting and went on day and night, seven days a week. Blue Horse complained to me privately about how much it tired him, but he never once turned anyone away.

"A Medicine Man cannot refuse to treat anyone," he told me, echoing the code of the *traiteurs*. "If people need my help, I have to help them."

Those who called at the most eccentric hours were usually asked to call back at some more convenient hour, although remarkably few of them did. It often seemed that if they could not be treated at three A.M., they did not want to be treated at all.

In many cases people were too sick or were too old or lived too far away, to come to Blue Horse, so he had to go to them.

Most Navajos, particularly those living in the more remote parts of the reservation, do not have anything an Englishman would even recognise as an address and finding their homes was frequently a saga in itself.

Try following directions like this: "Go up the highway about ten miles and you'll see some juniper bushes growing close to the road; turn north up the track there. After about eighteen miles you'll see a yellow truck outside a trailer and just after that there's a track going west. You can't miss it, there's a dead cow right beside it. Make sure you turn at the dead cow and not at the dead horse. If you turn at the dead horse you'll go wrong. After about ten miles you'll see some more juniper bushes near the road, turn south and we're up there about fifteen miles."

In a juniper forest there is never any shortage of bushes growing close to the road. But what was surprising was how many yellow trucks and dead cows and horses lay littered about the countryside when one started to look. Largely thanks to Blue Horse's uncanny ability to sense the proper direction, even at night, we always managed to find the right place in the end.

Or try to guess what might be the matter with someone who describes his symptoms thus: "I feel the flood waters of the San Juan River in spring flowing through my left thigh, and the cry of the raven echoing in my heart." Whatever it was, I'm glad to report he made a splendid recovery.

By far the most numerous calls came not from people who were sick in the way Westerners would understand it. Rather, they were victims of malicious witchcraft. Some people even attributed the extreme illnesses and deaths of their relatives to witchcraft and so, to the Navajos, it was a serious matter.

Sometimes Blue Horse would look into the fire to divine the cause of their problems, only to tell them they had not been witched and were merely having a run of bad luck. In such cases he would administer a traditional blessing by scattering cedar on the fire and wafting smoke and holy water over the people and their home with his eagle feather, in much the same way as a priest might give a general blessing to an enterprise or building in Britain. But more often the people had been witched and the hunt was on to find the "witch bundle."

Blue Horse would walk through the house accompanied by me and the senior males of the family, checking in various places where a curse could have been hidden. Sometimes it was hidden inside the home, but more usually we found them buried outside under a window. A window is seen as a weak point in a home's defenses through which the evil can penetrate more easily.

Blue Horse's ability to find these witch bundles was absolutely uncanny. Even a small house has several ground floor windows, and it was noticeable that he almost unerringly went to the right one. When he was sure he had found the spot, Blue Horse would call for a spade and then, with one dramatic swoop, lift out a shovel full of earth and tip it out on the ground. Then he would drop to his knees while everyone crowded round to look as he broke up the clods with his hands. Finally, with a whoop of triumph, he would break open a clod and produce the curse, which he would hold it up for all to see. When I asked how he did it, he said that when he blew his whistle and prayed, he heard a voice telling him where to look. Sometimes the curse was buried many miles away and we had to go in search of it. In such cases the hunt could go on for hours, but these were comparatively rare and most curses were found in or around the home.

In Britain it is not easy to bury things and make it look as if the surface has remained undisturbed. In that part of New Mexico and Arizona it is even more difficult, because the top layer of dust is bleached by the sun to a much lighter colour than the underlying sand. Yet, in not one of the many witchings I attended, did I see the slightest sign of the earth having been disturbed prior to our arrival.

In most cases Blue Horse did not know the people, or where they lived, until they contacted him and asked for his help. When we arrived at a house he was never out of my sight, and there no possibility of him slipping outside or sneaking into another room to hide a witch bundle of his own. As he rarely knew more than a few hours in advance where he was going, there was also no chance of him slipping round a few weeks earlier and planting curses himself. Eventually, I was forced to discount such ideas, although for a long time his own explanation — that it was prayer that guided him — was not one I found easy to accommodate.

While out on these witchings we often worked late into the night, sometimes well past midnight, in all weathers, in remote parts of the reservation. To cap it all the rewards were often meagre, for the clients pleaded poverty. As we worked for donations only, there was no mechanism by which we could ask for more. On one occasion we drove 150 miles, worked all night, and were rewarded with a small meal and five dollars between us, before driving 150 miles back again.

During this period Blue Horse performed some spectacular feats of divination and worked some extraordinary cures for which I could find no easy explanation.

My original idea had been that if I accompanied him and observed at close quarters, I would soon find out whether a Medicine Man's art was all hocus-pocus — as all good, educated white Western men and women are taught to believe — or if there might be something in it. I blush now to think of the sheer stupidity of regarding ten thousand years of Navajo learning and wisdom so lightly.

I am not sure I rationalised it all so neatly at the time. Rather, I tended to concentrate on the companionship of an extraordinary man and the rugged grandeur of the countryside amidst which I now lived.

Few outsiders get the chance to see so much of the wild, empty desert country that makes up the greater part of the Navajo reservation. It is a land of rocky canyons, gullies, and gulches. Rocks, cactus scrub, dried up riverbeds, towering cliffs, and deep valleys. Groups of semi-wild horses dot the landscape and here and there sheep and cattle are herded. Sometimes it is so empty that one can look across the sage scrub from horizon to horizon without seeing any evidence of human presence. A few Navajos in these remote parts still live in earth and wood hogans, at least for part of the year, while they raise corn, tend their herds, speak their own language, and live in a traditional manner without electricity, gas, or running water. They also make do without telephones or television or electric light and do not seem to miss them much. They cook over wood-fired stoves, light their homes with oil lamps, and either dig a well outside for water or drive miles to fill large plastic tanks at the wind pumps dotted across the desert that raise the precious liquid from deep underground into communal tanks.

This may sound idyllic to some, but for the seventy thousand Navajos who have no running water — that's roughly equivalent to the population of the state capital of Santa Fe — it's no joke. They have rights to water from the San Juan River but the Federal Government in Washington has failed to provide money for the necessary pipeline. Most Navajos reason there is no pipeline because more water for Indians equals less water for white folks, and less water for white folks equals fewer votes for white politicians. Whatever the reason, it's a scandal that in the twenty-first century so many people, many of them elderly and infirm, have no running water in the richest nation on earth. But scandal is nothing new in U.S. politics.

Blue Horse soon realised it was far more fun being chauffeured about in my speedy little Cougar than driving himself in his big Ford truck, so soon we travelled almost everywhere in my car. Although we went a lot faster, given the often appalling state of the roads, we were hardly safer and I frequently wished we had taken his truck. As I drove gingerly along the bone-jarring, potholed tracks, Blue Horse would often give a running commentary, partly in English and (when the subtleties of that language eluded him), partly in Navajo (the subtleties of which always eluded me).

I ought to explain that the way I have made Blue Horse speak in this book is not the way he really spoke. His English was limited and his accent so thick I often had to ask him to repeat things over and over before I could understand. When I learnt more Navajo things improved a little, but not much. The situation was not helped by the fact that, after years of working with noisy machinery in a uranium mine, he was partially deaf.

To give one example of many, we had several conversations over several days about something he called a "Cardboard Cadillac." I had not the slightest idea what he was talking about, knew only that the idea amused him, and to please him, nodded and smiled on cue. Belatedly, I realised he was actually saying "Cowboy Cadillac" (pronounced "*Carbor Cadlak*"), Cowboy Cadillac being a slang term for the kind of big Ford pickup truck he drove.

To make it easier for the reader I have translated his words into more or less standard English. Any attempt to imitate in print the way he really sounded, with his bizarre syntax, strangulated vowels, dangled participles, and highly idiosyncratic grammar and vocabulary, would have been a challenge too far for this author.

However, the following is a fairly good example of what I came to call his "Little Bighorn" approach to the English language: i.e., it was a massacre.

"Wild Indian live here, *Chizchillie*. Wild Indian," Blue Horse would say, using my Navajo name, "Curly Hair," and pointing with a sweep of his arm to the rocky and lonely countryside through which we were speeding. "Wild Indian got many wives. Fat one for winter, keep him warm. Thin one for summer, not eat much *dibé bitsi* (mutton), cheap to keep. Wild Indian no like *bilagáana*. You keep head down, *Chizchillie*. He might want scalp you."

One day he was talking exactly like this when we rounded a corner to find a lone Indian horseman eyeing us from the top of a distant bluff. The man was so perfectly placed he could have been put there by a Hollywood film director. To cap it all, after watching us for a few seconds, in true Hollywood style, he turned his horse and disappeared down the other side of the bluff.

Blue Horse was exultant. "Wild Indian!" he shouted, pointing after the rider. "He see *bilagáana* come, so he real wild now, man. He ride village fast, fast. He say, '*Bilagáana* come! Fetch warriors! Fetch war-paint! Fetch scalping knives! People come quick! Bring bows, bring arrows, bring guns. *Bilagáana* come! *Bilagáana!*'"

My only response to this was to reply rather weakly, "I'm on your side, *bilįį dootł'izh.*" But I didn't get the impression his fellow tribesmen would have been much impressed by my sudden affiliation to their cause.

The truth was that when he was talking like this, Blue Horse was only half joking. If the American Indians could catch a leprechaun tomorrow and be granted one wish, it would be that the white man would disappear immediately and NEVER COME BACK. True, all the benefits of our so-called civilisation that Indians enjoy like trucks, cars, TVs, aeroplanes, hamburgers, ice-cream, sugar, air-conditioning, movies, mobile phones, computers, and so on would disappear with him. But, on balance, most Indians would grin and bear it. Actually, most would just grin.

There is even a Navajo joke about a man who really does catch a leprechaun, or at least the Navajo equivalent. And while the joke is as much about the matriarchal nature of Navajo society as it is about the white man, like all good jokes it makes some telling points.

Holding tight to his captured leprechaun, the Navajo demands, "I want you to make all the white men disappear immediately!"

"Well now," says the little man. "I'm only a very small leprechaun and that's a very big wish. Perhaps you've got something a bit more reasonable I could do for you?"

"OK," says the Navajo. "I'm getting divorced and I want you to fix it so that I get everything and my wife gets nothing."

The leprechaun thinks for a moment, then sadly shakes his head, and asks, "Now, what was that first wish again?"

When Blue Horse was in a less jovial mood he would point out Navajo places of historic interest. I regret to say the reason they were historic was often because of their bloody association with the evil doings of white men.

"Here *Adilohii* come," Blue Horse told me somberly one day. *Adilohii* literally means "rope thrower" and is the Navajo name for American frontiersman Kit Carson. "*Adilohii* and U.S. Cavalry round up Diné people like animals. Kill Diné people. Kill sheep. Kill cattle. Cut down fruit trees. Drive people long, long ways away to *Hweeldi*. [*Hweeldi* refers to Fort Sumner in eastern New Mexico, approximately three hundred miles east of the traditional eastern boundaries of Navajo territory.] Many die. Women, children, old people, warriors, all die in concentration camp U.S. government set up. White man eats well at *Hweeldi*. Guards with guns eat well. Man from Bureau of Indian Affairs eat well. Visitors from Washington eat well, and all the time Navajo people starve to death. Everybody dying. Big people, little children, old people, young people, all get sick, starve, die. Some say, 'Make treaty now, or they wipe us all out.' But others say 'If we make treaty, will white man let us go home to Dinétah? If white man not let us go home to our land, better we fight till we all dead.' So Medicine Man catch coyote and gather all people around. Then he say, 'If coyote run east, north, south when I let him go, we fight because white man never let us go home. But if coyote run west, white man let us go home to Dinétah and we can make treaty.' When Medicine Man let coyote go first he turn north. Then he stop, turn, and run west straight as bullet. So Diné people know they go home. The next day General Sherman, big soldier chief from Washington, say to Navajo people 'You can go home.' Then we make treaty. Make big prayers and get big reservation. We stay here now forever. This our land, Navajo land."

When I checked in the university library I found the above was a pretty accurate oral account of what happened to the Navajos in the 1860s, right down to the story about the coyote. The tribe was rounded up and forced on a series of winter death marches by the United States, during which hundreds, possibly thousands, died on the march and in the concentration camp that awaited them at the other end. Pregnant women whose time was close were shot and killed by American soldiers so that they would not hold up progress. These winter death marches were a common terror tactic of the United States genocide policy against Indians. Their purpose being to ensure that as many Indian men, women, and children died as was possible, and in this they were extremely successful.

When the survivors reached *Hweeldi*, the records show that things were as bad as Blue Horse said. There was little food, the water was contaminated, the nearest source of firewood was nine miles from the concentration camp, and the Navajos had no horses. Given this sad history, and there is much more, it was a wonder that I was so well received among the Navajos. But, in almost all cases, I experienced only the greatest kindness and hospitality from them.

The difficulties of conversation with Blue Horse were not helped by his insistence on playing his favourite 1960s British rock bands at ear-splitting volume on the car stereo. He was no fan of easy listening music and so I played the Rolling Stones, The Who, The Beatles, The Troggs—a special favourite—and several others, more or less continually and loudly. On top of that he liked to drive fast and was constantly urging me to speed up, even when we were already travelling at a breakneck rate over tracks that were hardly safe for a horse and cart. In between singing bursts of his favourite songs, he would urge me to "get past that car!" and "put your foot down!" and "hurry up," until we were travelling at such speed that I would have been thrown into jail if a policeman had seen us. Fortunately, in that remote part of the world, policemen are as rare as pixies.

We must have been a strange vision, Englishman and Medicine Man, hurtling along at 120 miles per hour in a cloud of red dust, shouting at the tops of our voices as we joined in the chorus while The Troggs hammered out "Wild Thing" or "Feels Like a Woman" at full volume.

One day our luck ran out as we roared past Standing Rock, a small settlement deep inside the reservation, shouting and bellowing in a mixture of Navajo and English while The Troggs' lead singer Reg Presley howled "I Can't Control Myself." It was hardly surprising that we failed to notice a police car parked among the juniper bushes at the side of the road. It was only when I heard a distant siren, and looked at the speedometer to find we were travelling at 127 miles per hour, that I realised there was a problem.

I caught a glimpse in the mirror of a police car lumbering along more than a mile to our rear. I could see his emergency lights flashing, and while he was obviously going as fast as he could, he had no chance of catching my sleek, sporty little Cougar. Unfortunately, with its big front and rear spoilers, the silver Cougar was so distinctive and unusual for the area, that an all-cars alert was bound to result in us being stopped sooner or later.

I decided the only wise course was to pull over, but this was not at all to Blue Horse's taste and he urged me to outrun the *siláo* (policeman). My refusal sent Blue Horse into a sulk, but it also gained me an unusual insight into the power of a Navajo Medicine Man.

When the young tribal policeman finally rolled to a halt behind us, I was alarmed to see him clamber out of his car with his gun already in his hand. Looking in the mirror I could see he was extremely annoyed, as any policeman who has been covered in a thick blanket of dust by a high-speed sports car is apt to be. I knew he had been too far behind to accurately record my speed, so he could not charge me with a specific speeding offence. But if he decided to cut up rough, a few hours in a cell while my documents were "checked" was the least I could expect.

However, the moment the policeman saw Blue Horse everything changed. The two had a rapid conversation in Navajo, which I couldn't follow, during which the policeman visibly relaxed and holstered his gun. When he had finished speaking to Blue Horse he switched into English, checked my license, give me a mild verbal warning about the dangers of going so fast on such poor roads and, after I had duly apologised, retreated to his car smiling broadly. In fact, he almost bowed out, and drove away waving in a most friendly manner.

Watching him go, I turned to Blue Horse in some astonishment to ask, "What did you say?"

He shrugged matter-of-factly and replied, "I asked after his family."

"You know him?"

"Not really, but everyone knows me," he said proudly, even if it was a slight exaggeration.

"I was sure I would get a ticket!" I said, slightly flabbergasted.

"He wouldn't have given *me* a ticket," Blue Horse said huffily.

"You weren't driving. I was!"

"It's the same thing," he said, crossing his arms and staring straight ahead through the windscreen, making it clear there would have been no fuss at all if I had followed his far more exciting advice and made a run for it.

As the police car disappeared into the distance, it dawned on me that you would have to be an extremely bold young Navajo policeman, indeed, to give a speeding ticket to a senior Medicine Man like Blue Horse.

After this, and much to Blue Horse's disgust, I tried to keep the speed down to a maximum of eighty miles per hour. "Too slow," he would complain. "Too slow!" But in truth, at thirty-five miles per hour over the fifty-five miles per hour speed limit on Navajo roads, it was still much, much, too hair-raisingly fast.

Meanwhile, evidence of Blue Horse's extraordinary Medicine powers continued to accumulate. Try as I might, I could make no sense of what I was observing when they were set against the normal parameters of our Western world. Eventually, I decided the only thing to do was to keep my wits about me, record what I saw as accurately as I could, and hope that when I had seen enough I would gain some understanding.

One day we were called to see a man of about forty years old, who had been suffering serious neck pain for some years. The pain had recently become so bad he could no longer raise his arms above his shoulders and had been forced to stop working. His wife, a qualified nurse, was keeping the family going during this crisis, and had helped him obtain medical treatment at the hospital in Farmington where she worked. But nothing the doctors had recommended had done any good.

"All they do is take x-rays and give me pills," he complained over the phone. "They can't find anything on the x-rays and the pills are useless. They don't do anything to relieve the pain."

Mr. Yazzie lived in the Chuska Mountains that lie near the northeastern edge of the reservation. The Chuskas are beautiful alpine hills. Steep and heavily wooded, they were so difficult to negotiate in the days before roads that some Navajos avoided the U.S. Army's attacks on them by fleeing to these hills and successfully holding out for years. In fact, some of these holdout bands never surrendered to the United States, and retired undefeated at the signing of the 1868 treaty. The Chuska Mountains rise to almost ten thousand feet, but because the surrounding land on the western side is so high—about six or seven thousand feet above sea level—they look nowhere near so tall when approached from that direction.

It was high summer and stiflingly hot as we drove through Window Rock and took the road that ran beside Red Lake. When the road divided again, we took the left hand fork to go to Tsaile and Lukachukai, along the Western edge of the Chuskas.

For several days I had been failing to translate The Who's stuttering song "My Generation" into Navajo without losing the meaning. Even Blue Horse was fed up with the game and so, for once, we travelled in silence, with only the hissing of the car's air conditioning working at full blast to disturb us.

There was no visual clue as to how high we were climbing, as the road ahead betrayed no more than a gentle upward slope as we drove along. So it was only when the dashboard gauge showed the outside temperature, dropped from near a hundred degrees to closer to seventy-five, that I realised how high we had climbed and that we must be nearing our destination.

The Chuskas were well off our usual beat and this was one of the longest journeys I remember making within the reservation. It took hours to get there and when we finally arrived, we found that the family was a typical mixture of the traditional and the modern that is becoming an increasingly widespread feature of Navajo families.

Mr. and Mrs. Yazzie lived in a smart mobile home, but had a traditional hogan in the back. The children, a girl of ten and a boy of twelve, played computer games and watched movies on their DVD player, but also attended traditional ceremonies with their parents. He was a carpenter with traditional views who had finally put his foot down and demanded to be treated by a traditional healer after modern medicine had repeatedly failed. Mrs. Yazzie was Navajo enough to believe in the tribe's traditions and wanted to help him this way. But she probably had more faith in the hospital's battery of modern equipment than she had in Blue Horse and me, although she was polite enough not to say so.

When we turned in at the gate, the sacred fire was already burning, and the two children jumped down from the ponies they were riding bareback to welcome us.

It was decided to use the hogan for the ceremony because its thick earth roof and wooden walls insulated it from the heat of the day and it was cool and welcoming when we went inside. When all was ready I brought in a great heap of glowing charcoal and everyone, including the children, sat cross-legged in a circle on the floor around it, while I fashioned a five-pointed star from the coals. But the moment Blue Horse placed his crystal at the tip of the point aimed directly at him, I sensed something was wrong.

From my place at his right hand, I could see Blue Horse kept shifting his gaze alternately from his crystal to the fire. From time to time he looked intently at Mr. Yazzie, as if there was something he could not work out or understand about him. Ominously, he said not a word. This was most unusual because normally Blue Horse was relaxed during ceremonies and tended to sit back and chat amiably.

It was dark inside the windowless hogan, and from where I was sitting I was not able to see into the crystal. But when I looked into the fire I saw a small snake. It was coiled up near the beginning of the track through the charcoal that indicated the patient's passage through life. Snakes are a bad omen but this one was so small, and so far in the past, I did not think it could mean much. Which only goes to show how wrong you can be.

There are several Navajo words for a snake, of which *"tł'iish"* (try lisping and hissing at the same time) is probably the most common. When Blue Horse began to talk at last, he used this word a lot. He spoke in Navajo for a while and then, quite unusually, stood up and went over to Mr. Yazzie. Standing over him, he held out his right hand, palm down. Keeping it about six inches away from his patient's body, he began to move his hand slowly over the man's head, and then down over his neck and shoulders. It struck me at the time, and the image has remained with me ever since, that he looked like nothing so much as a soldier sweeping slowly back and forth with a mine detector.

The big turquoise and silver ring he wore on his right hand glinted in the firelight as he swept to halfway down Mr. Yazzie's back. There he stopped, and equally slowly worked his way up again, until he reached a point about one-third of the way up his patient's neck. There he stopped and touching with one finger a certain point on his neck, asked "Is that where it hurts most?"

"Yes," Mr. Yazzie said. "That's exactly the place."

"Did you ever kill a snake?" Blue Horse asked.

Looking surprised by the question, Mr. Yazzie replied to the contrary, "No, I've never killed a snake."

"Are you sure?" Blue Horse asked again.

"I'm sure," Mr. Yazzie insisted, sounding slightly affronted.

At this Blue Horse left him, and reseating himself at the fire, silently pointed to where the snake was coiled among the coals.

"What do you see?" he asked me in a whisper.

"I can see a little snake," I pointed.

Blue Horse nodded and was silent for a few more moments before turning back to his patient. Speaking softly he told him, "A long time ago, when you were about twelve years old, you were in the yard at your parents' home. Your father had sent you to clean the yard and you were angry. While you were in the yard you knocked over some boxes and there was a little snake underneath one of the boxes. . . ." He got no further before Mr. Yazzie suddenly cut in, "Yes, yes! That did happen. I'd forgotten. I wanted to play with the other boys and sweeping the yard took a long time because it was so big. I was angry, so I kicked over the boxes and there was a snake hiding under one of them. 'I'll get you,' I thought, and I took a hoe and chopped its head off. I don't know why I did it."

This outburst visibly shocked his wife and children, who clearly thought him the gentlest of men. Mrs. Yazzie sat silently shaking her head, while her daughter wailed at her father, "You said we should always be *kind* to animals!" The boy shouted, "Snakes are bad medicine. You always tell me not to go near them."

When they had quietened down a bit, Blue Horse continued, "The snake's spirit is still angry with you. It entered your body while you were sleeping and curled up round your neck. It says it waited a long time to get its revenge, but now it's making you hurt so bad at the exact same spot where you chopped off its head."

"It's true," Mr. Yazzie wailed, wiping away a tear and tapping with a finger at the point on his neck Blue Horse had indicated in his examination. "That's the same place where I chopped its head off. Please tell the snake spirit I'm sorry and to stop hurting me!"

Blue Horse said he would do his best and threw more cedar on the coals and began wafting fragrant smoke over everyone with his eagle feather. "Bless yourselves in the smoke," he said. Then he began to pray and continued praying for an extremely long time.

It was four days later when I answered the phone at Blue Horse's house to find Mr. Yazzie on the line. His neck was completely better, he said and he was going back to work.

"How did you do it?" I asked Blue Horse, when I had the chance to talk to him alone. I received the usual reply of "prayer," but this time I wanted to know more.

"That's not good enough. I want to know how you do it," I said, probably sounding more demanding than I intended. At this, Blue Horse, who was sitting at his table mixing tobacco with sweet herbs and licorice in a large steel bowl, looked up sharply.

"Prayer is not good enough for you?" he said in astonishment and his face clouded with anger for a moment. "If prayer's plenty good enough for the Great Spirit, it should be plenty good enough for you!"

A fraction of a second later a large neon sign appeared above my head and began flashing "Stupid White Man" in garish colours. I was obviously going about things the wrong way. "I didn't mean prayer isn't good enough for me," I assured him, realising my mistake. "What I meant was: how do you make a man's neck better using prayers?"

"The Great Spirit," he replied, speaking the name humbly and pointing a finger to the heavens. Clearly believing no further comment was necessary, he returned to mixing his tobacco.

I shut up for a few moments to give myself time to think. Then tried again. "How did you know about Mr. Yazzie sweeping out the yard? About the boxes? About the snake? It was so long ago even Mr. Yazzie had forgotten about it."

His face softened. "Oh, you want to know about that?" he smiled, as if I was asking something of such childlike simplicity it was hardly worth the explanation. "That's easy."

I waited, but he said no more, and instead went on silently mixing his tobacco round and round. Not sure what to do, I went to the stove and made some coffee while I waited for him to finish with his tobacco. When his mixing was done, I put the coffee in front of him, sat down, and tried again.

"Well," he began, slowly sipping at the coffee, as he considered my request. "As you know, the Navajo people are not the Navajo, we are the Diné. A long, long time ago, so they say, the Diné lived beneath the earth. One day a big flood came and they had to climb up a long reed to escape. When they emerged they found themselves here in Dinétah. The earth had given birth to us, so to speak, and so we Diné are from the earth and of the earth. We are Holy People of a Holy Land. We and the land are one. We and the land are the same thing, the same substance, the same being, and cannot be separated. This is true of all living things, whether it's a man or a grub or a tree or a bird or anything at all. All living things are part of the earth and the earth is part of the universe. So, you see, all things in the universe are linked together for all time, whether in the past, the present, or the future. Because this is so, it is possible to know all things that have been, that are, and that will be. That is, if you are wise enough. . . ."

He paused for a moment to sip more coffee before beginning to complain, not for the first time, that I was asking questions of the wrong man.

"You know there are Medicine Men among the Diné who know much more about these things than me, yet you keep asking *me* these questions," he said, sounding a little put out. "But if you are too lazy to find anyone else to ask, I'll do my best to explain," and he held out his right hand. "If you look here, on the finger of my right hand, you can see I wear a big silver ring with a turquoise stone set into it. If you look carefully, you'll see there is an eagle cut into the turquoise. This right hand is my Medicine hand and the eagle helps me to control it and keep it holy. If I lift my right hand like this," he demonstrated in the way he had held his hand over Mr. Yazzie, "I can use it like an x-ray to see what's wrong with you. It's not an x-ray exactly, but I'm trying to explain it so you can understand. For now it's enough for you to know that it helps me see things that other people cannot see.

"You say you have a sore ankle and knees because you got smashed up in a parachute jump. Maybe that's the reason they're sore, maybe it isn't. I don't know because I haven't examined you. But if I ran my hand over you, without even touching you, I would know. You saw me run my hand over Mr. Yazzie's sore neck, and when I did, I found the spirit of the snake we saw in the fire was lurking there. I've told you many times that the fire shows us what we need to know, always it does this, it never fails. This time I found the snake spirit in Mr. Yazzie's neck and I asked the spirit, 'Why are you here? Are you angry with this man?' And the snake spirit said 'He cut my head off for no reason' and told me the whole story. That was how I knew everything that had happened. Then the snake said 'Now I am getting my revenge by making the man's neck sore in the same place he cut off my head. I'm still angry with him. So I will destroy him by making him so sore he can't work.'

"Of course, this is no good to Mr. Yazzie and he wants me to make the snake stop hurting him. To do that I have to say a big prayer to the Great Spirit. People have different names for the Great Spirit. You can call him God, Jesus, Yahweh, Allah, or whatever you want, but really it's all the same thing. We Indians don't give him a name because we don't *know* his name, and that's why we just say the Great Spirit or The Creator.

"I burn cedar on the fire to purify the air and we bless ourselves with the smoke. Also the smoke rises to the Great Spirit and the perfume pleases him, so he will listen to my prayers. Then I say the prayers and ask the Great Spirit to speak with the spirit of the dead snake. I explain that the man is sorry and that he was only a child at the time and didn't know any better. Now that he is a man, he understands that he did wrong, and he wants the spirit of the snake to forgive him so it can be at peace and so his neck will stop hurting.

"I can't ask this of the snake spirit myself. I have to ask the Great Spirit to do this for me because he knows the snake and I don't. He knows me, he knows you, he knows Mr. Yazzie, and he knows the snake. He knows all living things because it is the Great Spirit who caused all things to be. If he accepts my prayers the Great Spirit will say to the snake spirit 'you can leave the man alone now and be at peace.' Then the snake spirit will obey the Great Spirit, and Mr. Yazzie's pain will go away forever."

I was silent for a while. Then I asked, "The snake's spirit spoke to you?"

"Sure," he said.

"And that happens a lot?" I asked.

"A lot," Blue Horse said.

"And four days later Mr. Yazzie is better," I said, leaning back in my chair and reaching for my coffee. It was a statement, not a question, but Blue Horse thought it was a question and replied, "It takes four days for prayers to reach the spirit world and get something done. You know that."

"Yes," I agreed. "I'm beginning to think I do."

CHAPTER SEVEN

The Grave

ONE EVENING WE DROVE EAST on Central Avenue in Albuquerque to rendezvous with a man who was due to meet Blue Horse and me in the car park of a twenty-four-hour Walgreen's chemist and general store.

"I don't know these people and they said their place was difficult to find, so they arranged to meet me here," Blue Horse explained as I pulled his truck into the busy car park.

There was no on to meet us, so I suggested he phone them.

"I don't have a cell phone," he reminded me.

"Use mine," I offered.

"I didn't bring the number because I don't have a phone," he repeated slowly, looking at me as if I was several prayers short of a full ceremony. The only thing to do was wait.

After about ten minutes, when no one had appeared, I went into Walgreen's and bought some milk and bread. I was walking back towards Blue Horse's truck when several vehicles, including a battered old tow truck, pulled into the car park. A few seconds later an Indian wearing a garage mechanic's overall stepped out of the tow truck and began walking towards the store's entrance.

"That's him," Blue Horse said, pointing to the driver of the tow truck.

As he had never before clapped eyes on him, I don't know how he knew, but he was right. The man was plainly surprised to be hailed by us, but not so surprised as I was when he admitted he had completely forgotten we were coming, and had come to Walgreen's only to buy some headache pills.

Trailer parks can be of all sorts, from the rough to the pleasant, and as we drove into this one my impression was that it looked unusually prosperous. Once through the entrance we followed the mechanic along a smooth tarmac drive flanked by grass verges until we stopped outside a large, comfortable-looking trailer, which atypically boasted a covered carport and topiary growing in neat little white barrels around the outside.

Inside the trailer was neat and tidy and for a while we sat drinking coffee and making small talk with the equally neat and tidy Navajo housewife, while her husband went outside to get the fire going. My Navajo was improving and I could make out that both husband and wife had been ill.

When the charcoal was brought in, Blue Horse threw cedar on the ashes and wafted the smoke through the room to purify the air. When that was done I looked into the fire to see what might be revealed. Almost before I had time to focus Blue Horse had already divined the cause of the trouble and was on his feet and heading towards the trailer door.

For a portly gentleman, who was a good fifteen years older and few stone heavier than me, he could move like greased lightning. Outside, night had fallen and low clouds obscured the moon and stars. I could just make out the dark outline of Blue Horse disappearing round the back of the trailer as I stumbled out of the door after him. The back yard was littered with junk. In fact, it was as cluttered as the front was neat, with old tyres, motor car parts, and heavy gym and weight-lifting equipment scattered about everywhere.

Blue Horse had obviously seen in the fire that the curse was somewhere back here, although I had not seen anything myself. Soon he was blowing his whistle and searching among the debris, while I pointed a powerful flashlight so that we could negotiate our way through the clutter without breaking our necks. After a while he detected something under some wooden pallets, but was unable to reach it because of the enormous amount of iron-mongery placed on top.

"How long has this been here?" I asked the mechanic as we strained to move some weight-lifting equipment and a set of car wheels.

"*T'óó ahayóí nááhai,*" —years—was the reply.

It took the combined strength of me, the mechanic, and Blue Horse to lift the heavier pieces from the pallets. When the way had been cleared, Blue Horse picked up a crowbar and, while I held a flashlight for him, levered out a strut from one of the pallets. Kneeling down he shoved his hand inside the gap and felt around before letting out a yell of triumph. "Got it!" he shouted in Navajo and raising his arm above his head held up a witch curse for all to see.

We examined it in the torch light and found it to consist of a piece of leather that had been bound round a split stick with a leather thong and what looked like some human hair. The leather was perished, showing that it had probably been there for a considerable time, and when Blue Horse peeled it back it tore.

"This leather comes from a corn pollen bag," Blue Horse said, holding it up to the light. "Pollen is sacred and by using part of a pollen bag they are profaning the sacred and trying to make their curse more powerful."

The stick turned out to be painted black. It was slightly pointed at one end and when unwrapped, it fell into two halves. I kept the torch beam steady while Blue Horse held it in his palm and pointed out the crude figures that had been scratched on the inside face of each half. One figure was of a human being and beside it was scratched a lightning symbol and an arrow point.

"When the lightning strikes, do you get a pain in the knee?" Blue Horse asked the mechanic.

"Yes, I do," he confirmed.

"Here's why," Blue Horse said, pointing to the symbols. "See the lightning symbol? That's to attract the lightning. See how the arrow points right at the figure's knee? That figure is you and the arrow is to guide the lightning so that it pains you when it strikes. You're lucky. If it had been pointing at your heart you would have been dead by now."

When he had done with his explanation, I held out the bag of ash and Blue Horse quickly dumped the curse inside. Later, we burnt it.

I always remember this particular de-witching, partly because of the strange way in which Blue Horse intuitively recognised a man he had never seen before. But mostly because after I'd loaded all our equipment back into the truck, Blue Horse gave me ten dollars out of the donation he had received. It may not sound much, but to me it was wealth indeed, for it made me feel like a real Medicine Man's apprentice at last. I was not, strictly speaking, any such thing, for we had made no kind of formal arrangement and Blue Horse had not yet adopted me into his family as he was later to do. But I was learning at the feet of one of the masters, and if I wasn't exactly what most Navajos would have in mind when thinking of a Medicine Man's apprentice, I was indisputably his friend, assistant, bag-carrier, general facto-tum, and driver: not bad for a *bilagáana* boy from North London.

A few days later we were asked to go to a small Navajo farm. When we arrived the story we heard was that several years previ-ously the mother of the family had died, and the family believed she could have been the victim of witchcraft. Now her mother, the grandmother and matriarch of the family, was also ailing and no one knew what was the matter with her. The family told us the doctors at the prestigious Presbyterian Hospital in Albuquerque had examined her twice, and sent her home each time saying they did not know what was wrong with her and there was noth-ing they could do. Naturally, the family suspected witchcraft and after bringing in a number of Medicine Men, none of whom had been much help, they had been advised to call in Blue Horse.

Haltingly, the old lady herself told us that she was constricted in the throat and could not eat and had difficulty drinking. As we talked she constantly brought up saliva, which she dribbled into a paper cup because she was unable to swallow it. Despite apparently not having eaten for some time, she was hugely fat with a belly that overhung her thighs, and she wore a vast dress. She was deathly pale, and so short of breath she frequently gasped for air as she spoke. After a short while she tired and had to be helped to another room, where she lay down to recover.

"She used to drink those little cans of condensed soups, but she can't even get those down now," said one of her grandson's wives.

The family's suspicion, bolstered by the white doctors' bafflement, was that whoever had cursed and killed their mother was now trying to do the same to their grandmother. I am not qualified to make any kind of medical judgment, but it was not necessary to be a doctor to see that the old lady was unwell. The question was: how ill was she, and what was wrong with her? This was one of those cases where I would dearly have loved to know exactly what the hospital thought of this woman's condition. It would have been helpful in assessing what happened next and what impact Blue Horse had on her recovery. Unfortunately, as so often in these cases, that information was not available.

I set up the travelling fireplace and, when all was ready, Blue Horse placed his crystal in front of him, looked into the fire, and asked a series of questions. When he was satisfied, he announced the source of the trouble was not at the house but further afield. Taking with us two of the older grandsons—actually men in their forties—and a large bag of ashes to neutralize evil, we set off in Blue Horse's truck to find the curse.

"Where are we going?" I whispered as we climbed in.

"I don't know," he whispered back.

"How are you going to find this curse if you don't know?" I asked. I always felt a bit on edge at this point in the proceedings, in case we found nothing.

"You must learn to have faith in the ways and traditions of my people, *Chizchillie*," Blue Horse replied quietly. Suitably chastised, I reverted to silence and with the two grandsons sitting in the back of the truck, we set off fast out of the farmyard, scattering geese, chickens, and sheep in every direction.

It was still early afternoon and there was plenty of daylight as we drove away from the farm. After a couple of miles along a dirt track we came to the top of a hill. There Blue Horse swung the truck off the track and pulled up under the shade of some cottonwood trees. As soon as the vehicle rolled to a halt he seized his drumstick and whistle and jumped out, calling to us to follow. Then he began to pace back and forth, blowing on his whistle and holding his right arm outstretched at about shoulder height, while his right hand jerked back and forth in a most unusual manner. This is a Navajo divining technique known as "hand trembling," which is used to discover—among other things—the direction in which evil may lie. It was the first time I had seen him do this and at first he appeared to have no success. Then, after several long minutes, he turned to the grandsons and asked, "Is there a cemetery near here?"

"Over there," said one of the grandsons pointing. "It's a couple of miles away, over the other side of that hill." At this Blue Horse appeared satisfied and we all climbed back into the truck and drove to the cemetery following the grandson's directions.

Indian graveyards are generally a lot more colourful than their English counterparts, and this one was a typical riot of colourful flags and ribbons flying in the wind. Traditional symbols were strewn over many of the graves, along with plastic flowers, beads, and other offerings. I should add that Navajo graves are often only mounds of earth without gravestones or any other marker to indicate the name of the occupant, a feature that was about to become significant.

Once in the graveyard, Blue Horse began walking up and down between the rows of graves, blowing his whistle and holding up his hand, which continued to jerk around alarmingly. I had little idea of what he was doing, but it did not seem the best moment to start asking questions, so I kept quiet and tagged along a couple of yards in the rear.

Suddenly, and without any warning, he gave a yell and threw himself on top of an unmarked grave mound. Lying prone he commenced to dig frantically with his bare hands in the soft, crumbly red soil. Then, with a whoop, he rolled over on to his back and held up a witch bundle for all to see.

"Here it is," he announced, still lying on his back with his big round belly in the air. "Here's the cause of the trouble!"

I glanced at the grandsons and saw them rigid with shock and looking as thunderstruck as any two human beings could be. Eventually, one of them managed to stammer, "But . . . but . . . but that's our mother's grave!"

I checked carefully and there was absolutely no clue as to whose grave it was. It was just a mound of earth identical in every way to many others in that graveyard. There was nothing that could have told Blue Horse who the occupant was, and he could not have known in advance, as he had never heard of the family until they telephoned him.

If Blue Horse was pleased with this feat he gave no hint of it and, still lying on his back on top of the grave, announced calmly, "They put it in your mother's grave to give more power to the curse. It's the connection between your family past and present that gives it that extra power to do evil to your grandmother."

A man of his shape could not easily right himself from the position he occupied and so I helped him to his feet. When he was upright again and had dusted himself down, he unwrapped the bundle to reveal a piece of old pottery. It looked exactly like some bits of pottery I had seen in the Maxwell Museum at the University of New Mexico that were hundreds of years old. The condition of this piece was poor, however, and it was so saturated with water that it broke easily like soggy chipboard. String had been wrapped round the pottery shard in such a way that it formed the shape of an arrowhead.

"Something broken, something sharp, that's what they curse with," Blue Horse uttered the now familiar refrain, pointing to the makeshift arrowhead. There were a few other bits and pieces in the bundle that I wasn't able to identify because the grandsons were so frightened they snatched the bag of ash from me and demanded the bundle be immediately placed inside to make it safe. Back at the farm they built a large fire at astonishing speed, and threw the bag and its contents into the flames in such haste, they accidentally burnt a stone arrowhead Blue Horse had given them to ward off evil.

Only when the burning was completed to the grandson's satisfaction did we go back into the house, where another surprise awaited us—granny was sitting up holding a plastic spoon and eating from a can of cold condensed soup.

"She suddenly felt better," one of her grandson's wives explained as we walked in. "It's the first thing she's eaten for nearly two weeks."

When everyone had settled down, I brought in more charcoal, and was asked to form it into a perfect circle in the fireplace, so Blue Horse could give the house and its occupants a blessing. Dried cedar was sprinkled on the embers and with its fragrant smoke, the house—and all within it—was blessed.

Finally, Blue Horse performed a healing rite of a type he did only occasionally. I watched in awe as he took a pair of metal tweezers and selected from among the embers a piece of charcoal about the size of fifty pence coin. Holding it firmly in the tweezers, so as not to burn his fingers, he blew on it until it was hot and red, and then put it in his mouth. Holding it between his teeth, he began to blow his hot breath over the grandmother. There was no trick involved and I could see the heat of the ember lighting up his cheeks from the inside as he blew on her a special kind of blessing and cure for evil. When he had blown hot breath all over her, he returned the charcoal, still red hot and smoking, to the fireplace. I had brought that charcoal in myself, direct from the fire, and knew full well that it was hot as hell. Later, as we drove away, I asked how he managed to find the mother's grave so unerringly among all the others. At this stage I was still willing to believe that coincidence, or plain luck, might account for some of his feats of divination. So his answer was instructive.

"When I stopped on the hill to pray and blow my whistle I could feel something," he told me. "That's why my hand was moving the way it was. It was telling me the source of the trouble was not far away and in which direction it lay. I guessed that wherever it was, it was probably in a cemetery, and that's why I asked the men if there was one nearby. When we got there I could feel something pulling at my hand again, so I knew we were in the right cemetery, but I still didn't know where to look. That's when I began blowing my whistle to call to the good spirits and listen for the voice that tells me where things are hidden. After a while the voice said, 'There. In that grave.' That's when I went to the grave and dug out the curse."

I asked, "And it's correct that you've never been to that cemetery before and that you've never met those people before today?"

"No, never," he confirmed. "You were there when they phoned up and you took the call, so you know I never heard of them before."

This was true and I sat silent for a while before asking: "Did the old lady start to eat again because you found the curse and broke its power?"

"Yes," he said, sounding very definite. "That's exactly why she felt better and she'll continue to improve from now on," he added with a smile.

A few days later I had confirmation of this when the family telephoned to say there had been a considerable improvement in their grandmother's condition and she had begun to eat solid food once more.

Perhaps if I had been a different kind of man I could have accepted all this more easily. In fact, the more I saw of the extraordinary things Blue Horse did, and the more he attributed it all to the power of prayer and the intercession of good spirits, the more puzzled I became.

Looking back on these incidents, and many others I recorded in my notes, it is interesting to observe how, during this period of first acquaintance with the powers of Navajo Medicine Men, I repeatedly ran for shelter in comfortable, white, middle-class notions whenever I was faced with something I could not understand: there had to be a trick, surely? The alternative was that well educated white Anglo-Saxon Protestants like myself did not, after all, know all there is to be knowed. Eventually, I found some comfort in reasoning that even if Blue Horse was not going around at dead of night planting curses in advance, I couldn't be absolutely sure he was not slipping things down his sleeves, or indulging in some other form of trickery as yet unknown.

However, it did not take long to detect a flaw in this line of reasoning, because one, he often wore sleeveless T-shirts, particularly as the weather warmed up, and two, I was so close to him during most of these happenings that if he had been slipping witch bundles down his sleeves, or from up his trouser legs, or from anywhere at all, I really should have noticed.

Needless to say, I didn't mention my doubts to him and instead I kept my eyes open, tried to keep my brain engaged at all times, and hoped that some piece of evidence would eventually turn up to clarify matters. To be brutally honest, I steeled myself in case Blue Horse—wonderful, engaging, and endlessly interesting individual though he was—was secretly practicing a bunch of tricks and fooling me along with everyone else.

Some weeks had passed since the events described above and Blue Horse had fallen ill with gallstones. He had returned from hospital having been operated on and was convalescing at home. He was an extremely bad patient who would make no concessions to his condition, and one evening I arrived to find him playing air-guitar around his kitchen, while The Who hammered out "Won't Get Fooled Again." *Baa'* comforted herself—and me—that this was marginally better than his preferred alternative, which was hauling wheelbarrow loads of dirt to fill the potholes in the track that ran from the road to his house.

I managed to persuade him to sit down while *Baa'* made coffee, and we were on our second cup when the telephone rang. Signalling to him to stay seated, I walked over to his desk and picked up the receiver, only to find someone on the other end speaking Navajo too quickly for me to understand. I was forced to passed the telephone to Blue Horse and a couple of hours later, and against the advice of both myself and *Baa'*, we were on our way to help a family who lived somewhere north of Wide Ruins in Arizona. The only concession I was able to wring from him was that I did the driving, which was not much of a concession because I almost always did the driving.

We soon found ourselves on a mean-looking NHA development deep inside the reservation. NHA stands for "Navajo Housing Authority," or "No Happiness Allowed," as the Navajos joke. This is rather unfair to the NHA, many of whose developments are modern and pleasant, or so they seem to me. Unfortunately, this was not one of them. The family we sought lived in one of the identical single-story homes that lined the unkempt and heavily littered streets. The houses may have had numbers at one time, but none were on display when we got there, and after driving around fruitlessly for a while, I stopped to ask the way from some young men lounging on a street corner.

By now it was dark and Blue Horse was alarmed, "Be careful, *Chizchillie*, people are mean," he cautioned. But it was OK and the boys willingly pointed out the correct house. As we parked outside, Blue Horse whispered, "Make sure you lock the car. There are a lot of witches around here, and some of them are good too. Be sure they can't leave anything in the car."

Inside we found a single mother with at least seven children, so far as I could count. Poverty is always relative, and while no one in the house was in danger of starving, the family was obviously hard up. None of them was well dressed and the only light came from a single bulb in the main room. That is, if you didn't count the super-size, wide-screen TV in the living room, which was on permanently and illuminated most of what the little bulb could not reach.

As we sat round the charcoal, the family complained that nothing ever worked for them. They had lived in the house, which had been newly built, for six or seven years. But they had no money and all their attempts to make any seemed doomed to failure: the money simply drained away. They were unhappy, too, that the eldest boy, who was about fourteen or fifteen years old, was being blamed for many things that happened locally, like vandalism and theft, all of which he insisted had nothing to do with him.

It had all the classic hallmarks of a witching and after a while Blue Horse saw something in the fire, called for a paper bag of ash, and with me and the eldest boy in tow, went in search of the curse.

First we searched the boy's bedroom, which contained four car wheels with the tyres attached stacked one on top of the other. The stack reached almost to the ceiling and left little room for anything else besides the bed. Blowing his whistle, Blue Horse checked the walls for hidden cavities but, finding nothing, he directed us outside.

It was dark and cold in the backyard, which, as we often found, was strewn with bits of junk that in the dark made it as dangerous as a minefield. After a fruitless search Blue Horse demanded that the side, east-facing door of the house be opened and insisted we enter and exit the house that way, and no other, from then on.

Shortly afterwards he found a spot where he wanted to dig and dispatched the young man to find a shovel and a flashlight.

"You're not doing any digging," I told him. "You'll only burst your stitches."

To my surprise, he acquiesced easily enough, and when the boy came back he directed him to give the shovel to me. Then, pointing to a spot on the ground in front of the boy's window he told me to dig.

"Careful," he cautioned. "Don't dig too deep. Don't damage anything. Just make a shallow hole."

There was a slight depression at the spot where he pointed and I thought it might indicate something had been buried there. But there was nothing. Then he pointed to a spot about three yards away, nearer the bedroom window, where there was no depression.

"Dig there," he said, excitedly. "Be careful not to go too deep."

I tipped out the first shovelful of earth in the full glare of the powerful flashlight the boy was holding and at once saw the witch curse. It was a bundle about eight inches long and the biggest curse I had ever seen up to that time. My first thought was that it at least answered one vital question: As I had dug it up myself there was no question of Blue Horse planting it this time.

Once again the curse had obviously been in the ground for a considerable time and it showed signs of decay when he unwrapped it. It consisted of a piece of black sweatshirt-like material about two feet long. This had been cut into the shape of a snake, with a snake's head shaped at one end and with two holes cut for the eyes. Inside was a piece of tree bark with drawings on it and an oblong piece of white paper that had been tightly folded to the size of a small square.

"Hold the flashlight steady," Blue Horse commanded. Taking the strange piece of paper, he unfolded it and began to examine it in the torch light. At first he could see nothing, but then he announced, *"béeso"* — money.

When I looked carefully under the light, the white paper still retained slight markings showing that it had once been a dollar bill. It could have been a photocopy of a dollar, as it is difficult to bleach the colour out of real dollar notes, but there was no doubt as to what is was supposed to be.

Dropping the paper into the ash, Blue Horse told me, "The point of the single dollar drained of all colour is to drain all the money out of the house. It will drain it right down to the last dollar, so the people here only ever have a dollar in the house." Which was exactly what the poor woman had complained about.

Blue Horse sent the boy for some petrol and newspapers and burnt the sweatshirt snake, along with the bark and the piece of rawhide that bound it all together. But he did not burn the dollar.

"The best thing to do with this dollar is to take it to the river and throw it in to wash away the evil," he told the family.

"But there's no river for miles," the boy objected.

Blue Horse had a bright idea. "My *bilagáana* friend will throw it in the Rio Grande for you," he said pointing to me. This perked the family up no end. The Rio Grande is a big river and so it must be big medicine and bound to wash away evil by the ton. The dollar bill was wrapped up in a piece of newspaper along with more sanctifying ash and presented to me.

"Don't forget, now," said the woman, obviously wondering if a *bilagáana*—especially one from England—could be trusted with such an important task.

"I won't forget," I promised, nor did I. But before I could fulfill my promise, Blue Horse performed another feat of divination so startling that it put into the shade all else I had seen so far.

The next day was Sunday and I awoke early after spending a restless night on Blue Horse's sofa, musing over the events of the night before. By now I had been working with Blue Horse for about ten months on and off, but had still been unable to rid myself of the security blanket that he might have been slipping things down his sleeve. The moment I dug that curse up myself, the security blanket was unceremoniously whipped away and I was not a happy boy. I knew *I* was not driving around planting curses or slipping them down *my* sleeve. So if I wasn't, and Blue Horse wasn't, what the heck was going on?

I was still pondering all this when there was a knock on the door and I opened it to find Mrs. Graymountain and her son Otto standing outside. Mrs. Graymountain was an elderly Navajo lady of slim, almost elfin appearance and beguiling charm, whose late husband had been half Navajo and half German, hence her three sons named Manfred, Luther, and Otto.

Mr. Adolf Herman Graymountain had been one of those fortunate individuals who know how to make money, and with good business sense and some shrewd investing, he had set up his family for life. Mr. Graymountain had died some ten years earlier and two of his sons had left the area to seek their fortunes elsewhere. But Otto, who was in his thirties, still lived with his elderly mother in the large house built by her husband.

Blue Horse had been called in to help the family some months earlier. I had accompanied him and remembered it vividly because it was one of the first witchings I attended. Blue Horse had been successful in lifting the immediate threat, but now there was more trouble.

Over coffee Otto explained the problem, "I've been putting off coming to see you, Blue Horse, but this morning as I drove into town a *mą'ii* [coyote] crossed in front of me going west towards the setting sun and the land of the dead so I knew we had to come straight away. It's a very bad sign!"

I already knew from our earlier encounter that the root of this family's trouble lay in an incident twenty years earlier, when one of Mrs. Graymountain's family members had killed a young boy in a traffic accident. To revenge themselves, the boy's family had employed a well-known witch man to curse the Graymountains and, as a result, Medicine Men had to be called in periodically to lift the curses. It was only comparatively recently that they had come to Blue Horse. Navajos with difficult problems often consult a number of Medicine Men until they find one powerful enough to lift the curse. In a similar way patients in London with difficult medical conditions sometimes trail from one consultant to another.

To calm them down Blue Horse offered to cedar there and then to see if he could divine what was going on and I was sent out to light the fire. When the charcoal had burned down to the right consistency, I brought in four shovelfuls and placed them in the center of the travelling fireplace, which I had set up in the living room.

Blue Horse peered long and hard into the fire and I saw he was also staring deeply into the crystal. It was a long time before he began to speak and when he did his words were somber.

Turning to Mrs. Graymountain Blue Horse said, "When you buried your husband ten years ago, you buried him with a bead bracelet you gave him for protection from witches."

Bead bracelets of a special kind are often used by Navajos to give protection from witchcraft. From the way Blue Horse was speaking I guessed he was not asking a question, and this turned out to be the case.

"Yes, I did," Mrs. Graymountain confirmed, adding, "My husband didn't follow our traditional ways. But because I was worried for him with all this witching going on, he agreed for my sake to wear a bead bracelet to protect himself. Because he had worn it in life, I wanted him to have it in his grave."

Blue Horse took a deep breath and still looking into his crystal, told her, "Shortly after your husband was buried the people who cursed you dug up his body and took the bead. All these years they've held on to it, waiting for the time to use it against you. When you came to me for help they saw and they knew. They know my power is great and so they've decided to use the bead now to make the strongest curse they can and finish you off.

"The bead your husband was buried with has been turned into a curse and buried somewhere near your home, along with some bearskin, and some other things I must not name. But have no fear, tomorrow I'll come and find the bracelet. When I've found it, I'll bring it to you so you can recognise the bead you gave to your husband and be sure I am telling you the truth. When that is done I will destroy the evil and lift the curse from you forever."

This last bit had all been in English, which was mostly for Otto's benefit as his Navajo was not a lot better than mine. Mrs. Graymountain spoke perfectly good English and Navajo and would understand. But the fact that Blue Horse spoke in English, so that no one in the room could misunderstand, underlined how seriously he viewed the matter.

Upon hearing this news, Mrs. Graymountain was understandably extremely upset. Letting out a long "Ooooooh" sound, she slumped against her son in a semi-faint. Otto held her to prevent her from falling and I fetched her a glass of cold water.

When she had recovered a little, Mrs. Graymountain sobbed to her son, "I can't bear to think of your poor father being treated in such a way. He was a good man."

Otto tried to comfort her by saying to Blue Horse, "But we visit my father's grave regularly and we've never noticed it was disturbed."

Blue Horse nodded sagely, "They did it very soon after he was buried, while the ground was still soft and easy to dig. They go at night and take things, then shovel all the earth back so you would never know."

By "things" I knew he meant urine from the corpse and body parts with which to make curses, but naturally he did not mention this in Mrs. Graymountain's presence.

"I thought it was over after the last time you came," Otto said sadly. "Things improved a lot."

"Yes," Mrs. Graymountain agreed between sips of water. "But then they started to go bad again."

Blue Horse explained, "When I came last time and removed the other stuff it scared them. That's why they're using the really bad stuff now."

By the time they left we had managed to cheer the Graymountains with the thought that on the morrow their ordeal would be over. But the whole business left me worried. We had all heard what Blue Horse said and if he failed to produce the bead it would be disastrous to his reputation and probably finish him as a Medicine Man. I went to bed that night wondering how on earth he was going to pull it off. It was true that on every other occasion he had delivered the goods. On the other hand I had never heard him prophecy anything so definitely, or define it so precisely.

The next morning people came and went as usual until, at about noon, Blue Horse and I drove about an hour west until we came to one of those "eat as much as you like" diners. Apprehensive, I was not in the mood to eat, unlike Blue Horse, who displayed not the slightest sign of concern and ate more than enough for both of us.

Watching him shovel down jelly and trifle on top of the banquet he'd already consumed, I was tempted to ask things like: "How on earth are you going to do this?"; "Don't you realise that if you fail you're finished!"; or "If it's all a trick tell me now and I'll try to think of a way out for us."

When I finally plucked up courage to cautiously approach the subject of how he was going to make good on his pledges, I received his usual explanation: "Prayer."

"Prayer?" I echoed.

"Prayer," he said firmly.

There was nothing else I could do except wait for events to unfold.

We left the restaurant and drove north to the Graymountains' home. We at once began the cedar and, after the tobacco had gone round and we had all blessed ourselves in the holy smoke, Blue Horse began to recount what he could see in the crystal. First, he told us he could see the witch bundle and that it was buried at the side of the house. Then he asked if there was some way to leave the house and get round to the side unseen.

"Sure," said Otto. "We can go out the back of the house. No one will see us if we go that way." This struck me as odd, as Blue Horse had never shown any reluctance to be seen at work during the all the months I had been accompanying him. I didn't have to wait long to find out why.

Still looking in his crystal he announced ominously, "That man, the one who's witching you, he knows I'm here and he's watching us. He doesn't like it that I'm here."

This made Mrs. Graymountain and Otto extremely nervous. Holding up his whistle and his drumstick, Blue Horse quickly reassured them, "Don't be afraid, there's nothing he can do about it. I have my whistle and my drumstick and he's seen them too. He knows he has no power over us."

He continued to look into the crystal for a while longer and then asked Otto to fetch a shovel. Then the three of us slipped outside, leaving Mrs. Graymountain sitting beside the fire nervously twining and untwining her fingers.

With his whistle and drumstick firmly in one hand, Blue Horse drew an imaginary line on the wall. "The curse is right under here," he said, beginning to draw another imaginary line down the wall. While he was doing this I checked carefully to make sure there was no sign of disturbance on the surface, and saw none.

Once again I did not want him to risk his stitches and when he called for the shovel I stepped forward to take it from Otto. As I did so, a red Ford pickup truck appeared and began heading across some waste ground straight for the house. Otto saw it first and froze. He turned deathly white and seemed to be trying to speak, but no sound came from his lips. He pointed to the rapidly approaching truck and I heard him gasp, "It's him. It's the witch man!"

Caught unawares, Blue Horse stared open mouthed for a moment. "I never thought he'd come himself," he said. Then he tried to calm Otto by repeating three or four times, "He can't harm us. I've got my whistle and drumstick." But even he looked a little panicky.

"He must know what we're doing!" Otto whispered hoarsely, looking as if he might faint.

"He knows, all right," Blue Horse said. "I told you he could see us. He knows who I am and he knows what we're doing. But there's nothing he can do about it." And he held his whistle and drumstick up high for all to see.

The witch man's truck came to a halt on top of a small knoll about eighty yards away, from which point he had an excellent and uninterrupted view of us. I could make out no more than a faint outline of a man behind the windscreen, but there was no doubt that whoever was in the truck could see our every move.

Speed was of the essence and Blue Horse had not the patience to allow me to dig for him. Quick as a flash he seized the shovel and thrust it into the earth at the spot he had indicated, which was about six inches from the wall of the house.

"Quick. Get round the corner," he cried, speedily lifting out a shovelful of earth, and we ran round the corner into the family's back yard where we were out of sight of the witch man.

I brought up the rear and did not take my eyes off that shovel of earth. As Blue Horse needed two hands to hold the shovel as he ran, there was no chance of him slipping anything into the little pile of earth balanced on the blade. If he had, I would have seen.

Once round the corner and out of sight, Blue Horse tipped the earth onto the bare ground and we began to examine it. The witch bundle was plain to see and on further inspection proved to contain pretty well everything he said it would. There was a piece of bearskin about two palm breadths long and one wide. Remember, bears are extremely bad omens to Navajos, and so only a Medicine Man is allowed to handle any part of the animal. When he opened it, it had strange drawings on the inside of the hide.

Examining these drawings Blue Horse explained, "It's a sand painting of a lightning-being. It's to bring bad luck, danger, and death to you."

A few seconds later he pulled out a bead bracelet. It had been wrapped inside the bearskin and proved to be a single turquoise bead attached to a distinctive kind of wristband.

I do not recall if he made any comment about it at that moment, although he would have been justified in allowing himself to do so. Instead, everything was put into a bag containing the sanitizing ash and taken inside for Mrs. Graymountain to see.

To avoid introducing evil into the house, the bag could be taken only as far as the outer hall of her impressive home. There, in my presence, Mrs. Graymountain examined the bead and its attached wristlet and identified it as the one she had given to her husband and with which he had been buried.

A little later, when Otto and Blue Horse went outside to burn the bearskin and the other stuff in the curse, I was left alone with Mrs. Graymountain and took the opportunity to gently question her myself.

I would not normally have done this, but the circumstances were so unusual and the claim so extraordinary, I wanted to be absolutely certain there was no mistake.

I asked Mrs. Graymountain, in English, if she was really sure the bead was the one she had given to her husband, the same one he had taken to his grave.

"Yes," she replied without hesitation. "That's the bracelet I gave him. He wore it for me and I would recognise it anywhere."

So there it was. Blue Horse had dug up the bead as he predicted he would, and Mrs. Graymountain had recognised it as he said she would. The bearskin was also present as he said it would be, and all this was predicted in my presence and found in my presence. And also in Otto's presence who had no reason to want to be cheated. Further, Blue Horse had looked in the fire and had seen the witch man watching us and the man himself had duly appeared.

What on earth was I to make of it? All I could say for certain was that these things happened. I had seen them and I wrote down what I saw. But I had the uncomfortable feeling that events were taking on a momentum of their own.

When I started to accompany Blue Horse I had never expected things to go so far. Now I had encountered events that seemed to emanate from beyond the grave. Events for which I had no explanation were plunging me deeper into a world over which I had no control. I wondered if I ought to be frightened, but no fear came. Instead, I felt a strong need to carry on and see where all this led.

CHAPTER EIGHT

Sacred Sacrement

ABOUT THIS TIME I HAD MY first experience of peyote, the sacred cactus. Most reference books will tell you that Indians eat peyote in order to experience "hallucinations." As with so much written by whites about Indians, it isn't true.

To the Indians peyote is a sacred sacrament, every bit as sacred as the bread and wine at Holy Communion, and is permitted to congregants only under the most rigorous and testing of circumstances, as I shall shortly relate. It undoubtedly produces some strange effects, but I cannot say they are hallucinations. Indeed, they seem only too real. The explanations I was given by Blue Horse and other Navajo Medicine Men for some of the episodes that befell me when taking part in prayer meetings where peyote was ingested were based on the assumption that what was experienced was indeed reality.

Peyote, which Indians invariably call Medicine, and botanists *Lophophora williamsii*, is certainly powerful stuff. A ground-hugging cactus, *Lophophora williamsii* grows wild in parts of southern Texas and Mexico and exactly what chemical effects it has on the brain no one really understands. What is incontestable is that it has had a beneficial effect on many tens of thousands of people, mostly Indians, who use it in their religious rites. It can return drunks to sobriety, addicts to normality, evildoers to good citizenship, and it buttresses the righteous in times of trial.

In order to understand the experience, it is necessary to undergo it many times, and the best description I can offer will inevitably fall well short of the real thing. As near as I can fathom it, peyote seems to retune the brain to several different realities that in normal times it either ignores or are lost to it. Like a radio that tunes easily to the strongest signal in the area, so the brain seems to tune to what, for the sake of argument, might be termed "everyday reality." However, if a radio is retuned, it is possible to pick up dozens or even hundreds of stations, the existence of which the listener may have previously been entirely unaware. It may be that when "retuned" by peyote, the brain becomes aware of many more realities than merely that of the everyday. The trouble is, at least to start with, it is difficult to control which reality you drop into.

To give a simple example, during one all-night peyote ceremony I turned into a fly. Or at least I thought I did, and flew out through a tiny hole in the hogan roof. Soon I found myself walking among the clouds. I could see the moon shining below me and on my face could feel the chill breeze of the night air. As suddenly as I had flown out, I found myself flying back into the hogan and in less time that it takes to tell, was back in my place sitting cross-legged on the floor.

Being a good white man the first thing I did was to analyse the experience. I immediately looked for the hole in the roof through which I had supposedly flown—and there wasn't one. "That proves it," I thought to myself. "It was just a hallucination. There is no hole and even if there was, I could not have flown through it because I didn't know it was there."

But as the dawn came up, I saw there *was* a tiny hole in the roof, and it was exactly at the point where I thought I'd flown through.

"How can this be?" I asked one of the Medicine Men and told him my story. When I'd finished he gave me a rather pitying look before replying, "A fly doesn't have time to think when it needs to move fast. Remember all the times you tried to swat one? How many times did you succeed? If a fly stopped to think about where it was going it would be dead. Instead it knows instinctively where there is a hole in the roof. It doesn't even know that it knows, but it does know. When it moves that fast it goes straight through without any effort or thought."

"But why would I turn into a fly?" I persisted.

"You are a part of the universe and a fly is a part of the universe, so why shouldn't you swap places from time to time? Why shouldn't you be a fly, and why shouldn't a fly be you? You may once have been a fly and you may be one again, and the fly may once have been you and could also be you again. Why are you so surprised by this?" Then, mellowing slightly, he added, "We've all walked on the clouds looking at the moon and felt the wind on our faces. It's a sign that you are growing closer to the Great Spirit and the Great Spirit wants you to know there is more to his creation than the world you see around you."

However, all that came later. My first experience of peyote was rather tame.

It may be remembered that Gray Fox Lady had recently presented Blue Horse with a new great granddaughter. As he already had twenty-four grandchildren and twelve great grandchildren, and the total was growing fast, I sometimes joked that he was founding his own tribe. However, there was a problem with Fox's daughter, Santi. She was nearly six months old, but was failing to thrive. Santi was Fox's first baby. Fox was a devoted mother and she had her own mother and her grandmother *Baa'* to help her bring up the child. Yet despite the best efforts of these experienced women, Santi frequently fell ill in a way that came to form a perplexing pattern. She would be ill for a while, then better for a while, then ill again with jaundice and fever, then better again. The periods of wellness were getting shorter and the periods of illness getting longer, so she was taken to the hospital in Farmington. The doctors could offer no explanation for her illness beyond suggesting that she might "grow out of it."

Even to a casual observer like me it was clear that at times little Santi was a very sick baby. Then, just as everyone was becoming alarmed about her, she would suddenly become well again as if nothing had happened. This went on for some time until the three women—mother, grandmother, and great-grandmother—decided the cause of the child's illness was that her afterbirth had not been treated in the proper traditional manner.

When a Navajo baby is born the afterbirth is routinely handed over to the mother. Usually the mother keeps the umbilical cord and buries it somewhere near her home to guarantee that no matter where the child roams in later life, it will always come back to home and mother. The rest of the afterbirth, including the placenta, is passed on by the mother to the maternal or paternal grandmother. The grandmother is then expected to treat it with certain herbs and prayer, and bury it safely somewhere on the reservation. Once again the intention is that this will bring the child home to Dinètah, the Navajo Heartland.

If the grandmother is careless, or does not use the correct protective herbs, or does not use them in the correct manner, the afterbirth may be discovered by an animal and eaten. If this happens the child is bound to fall ill, and if the animal is a bear then the child will surely die. The women had become convinced that a bear had found Santi's afterbirth and if something was not done quickly she would die. So they prevailed upon Blue Horse to hold an all-night Medicine ceremony with peyote, to force the bear to relinquish the afterbirth and allow Santi to become well again.

I should make it clear that these were three highly intelligent, forceful women, one of whom had recently accompanied the tribal hierarchy to Washington as a financial adviser. Any idea that they were ignorant peasants or, heaven forbid, dumb Indians, should be put out of mind. They had jobs, credit cards, cars, computers, mobile phones. Yet, when the modern world and its medicine failed, as it frequently did, they had the advantage of being able to fall back on an older culture, where they could seek redress through customs and ceremonies whose roots reached far into the distant past.

The Navajo were never nomadic, teepee dwelling Indians. Rather they were settled herders and farmers, yet religious ceremonies like this are often held in a teepee rather than a hogan. The reason being that when the peyote religion came to them it was brought by teepee-dwelling plains tribes like the Kiowa, Cheyenne, and Comanche. Despite the fact that most Navajos had never seen a teepee before the 1950s, almost overnight it became "traditional" for Medicine ceremonies to be held in a one.

On the appointed day I was cheerfully clearing weeds from the teepee site in advance of helping the Navajos to put it up, when Blue Horse took me to one side.

"I want you to understand that what will happen tonight will test you to the limit mentally and physically," he confided. "The peyote Medicine is the most bitter thing you will ever taste. It may cause you to throw up. You will have to stay awake all night praying and singing with us, you will sit cross-legged on the ground for twelve hours and there will be only one short break at three A.M. for about ten minutes. That's a modern thing, when I was young we had no break. Whatever people in London do with drugs, put it out of your mind. The Medicine is not a drug it, is a holy thing that demands your body and your soul. There will come a time during the night when you will think you cannot stand the pain of the way you are sitting another second. When you think you must sleep no matter what. When your thirst becomes so great and the heat of the fire so fierce that you would gladly die rather than go on. Don't look for any relief because there is none and that's the way things should be. The Medicine is not for the weak or the faint-hearted. It is not for the coward or the casual user, for such people break like reeds and the Medicine does not want them." He paused for a moment, before answering my unspoken question. "If I thought you would fail this trial, I would not allow you to attend our meeting. But you will not fail, because when you think you cannot take any more pain or sleeplessness or heat or thirst, you will remember these words: 'There is no harm that can ever come to you through the Medicine.'" With that he went on his way, leaving me wondering what on earth I had let myself in for.

Incidentally, I never did get to help put up the teepee. Putting one up is a ticklish business and if done incorrectly the whole thing can collapse in the night, sometimes with fatal consequences. So this *bilagáana* was only ever allowed to help take the teepee *down*, which, as Blue Horse cheerfully observed, "any idiot can do."

It was now that I finally discovered what a shade house was, all those months after Reuben had first taken me into one. After a Medicine ceremony, a feast is traditionally served, but *Baa'* and the ladies complained that the summer heat made it too hot to cook inside the house. So we men were instructed to build a *cha-ha'oh* (shade house), which turned out to be nothing more daunting than a lean-to arbour. With an axe and a few willing hands we threw one up in a couple of hours, cutting saplings to make the sides and taking green boughs of juniper and scrub oak to cover the roof. Inside we dug a fire pit and put in a barbeque so the women could cook the meat and fry-bread in comfort.

The ceremony began at about nine P.M., with Blue Horse presiding, or "running" the meeting, as the Indians say. When I entered the teepee the light outside was fading, while inside a fire was already burning bright in the center and the sweet smell of juniper smoke hung in the air. Between the fire and the Seat of Honour, which as in a hogan is on the west side, a low mound had been built as an altar using clean, damp sand taken from a nearby creek. This altar was a half-moon made of damp sand, about three feet long and a few inches high. It was perhaps six inches wide at its widest, with the ends tapering like the horns of the half-moon. Placed at the center of the half-moon, and resting on a bed of freshly gathered sage leaves, was an enormous peyote button at least two inches across. This kind of button represents the mythical peyote ancestor, who is viewed in rather the same way that Christians view the Holy Spirit. Sometimes called "Father" or "Mother" peyote, these special buttons are often carried in a small box of pure silver, lined with soft velvet, and may be passed down the generations.

A teepee appears much bigger inside than might be imagined from the outside. Even a medium-size teepee, which this one was, will easily hold thirty people spread out in a single line around the sides; while a large teepee will hold many more.

Blue Horse took his place in The Seat of Honour and signalled to the three other officials who are always present to assist the Medicine Man in the smooth running of a peyote ceremony. They are the Cedar Chief, who sits on the Medicine Man's left and is responsible for keeping up a steady supply of cedar to throw on the fire; the Drummer, on the Medicine Man's right, who takes care of the small water drum, which he beats to accompany the singing of prayers during the ceremony; and the Fire Chief, who importantly sits by the door to control who comes in and out of the teepee, and whose main responsibility is to keep the fire burning bright during the twelve hours of the ceremony.

Of these three the most interesting was John Begay, another Medicine Man and friend of Blue Horse who was serving as Drummer. He was young for a Medicine Man, being in his mid-thirties. A short, squat, strongly built man of great authority, he wore a grave expression and round, owlish glasses, which gave him the air of an intellectual. John once told me, "I'm one of the last of those who grew up speaking Navajo and learnt our traditions in the old manner. Behind me there's just a big black hole full of kids playing computer games, drinking, and speaking English. They don't know anything about our traditions and care even less." A powerful Medicine Man in his own right, John was related by clan to Blue Horse and had been invited to sit at his right hand to assist in this difficult and highly personal case.

Baa', Fox, and Fox's mother *Asdzáán łibá* (which means "the Gray Lady") sat on the women's side with baby Santi swaddled and placed on a traditional Navajo cradleboard that lay on the ground between Fox and the child's father, Jimmy Tso. Soon the other friends and relatives who had come to support the family with their prayers drifted in and took their places. When all was ready, the meeting began with the traditional smoke. The smoke is very important because it underlines the meeting's unity and determination to act together for the good of the patient. During the smoke, the patient's need for physical or spiritual healing — or often both — is explained.

Unlike the cedar ceremony, where the Medicine Man rolls the smoke and the same smoke goes round to everyone, in a Medicine ceremony everyone rolls their own, which is not as easy as it sounds. For a start, when I tried to put the dried cornhusk into my mouth to wet it, it stuck to my tongue. Although I'd watched Blue Horse roll a smoke many times, I'd never done it myself and was well on the way to making a botch of it, when the Indian sitting next to me leaned over and whispered, "If you can roll a joint, you can roll one of these."

"I hate to admit it," I confessed. "But I don't smoke and I haven't had much practice rolling anything."

"In that case, think good thoughts while you roll your smoke, and then you will find it much easier," he assured me. So I did, and it was.

When the smokes were ready the Fire Chief lit a special fire stick from the fire in the center. It was nearly two feet long and was passed from person to person until everyone had lit their smokes and begun to pray. Then the teepee was filled with the sound of personal prayer, while the smoke carried the prayers to the Great Spirit.

When the smokes were done each person rose in turn to place their stub beside the altar. The stubs, each representing the life of the person who left it, remain there until near the end of the ceremony when they are consigned to the fire. After the stubs had been put in place, the prayers and songs began and for a couple of hours the teepee was filled with the singing of shrill Navajo Medicine songs, sung to the accompaniment of the hypnotic beat of the water drum and the rhythmic shaking of a gourd rattle. Only after this concentration of prayerfulness and humility before the divine, did the sacred peyote begin to circulate.

Peyote comes in a number of forms, of which the most common is a kind of rough, dry powder made of ground up cactus that has been dried in the sun. This can be eaten raw or boiled to make a tea. Both were served at this meeting and the first to come round was the dried powder. Blue Horse was not kidding when he warned the Medicine was the bitterest thing I would ever taste. I scooped about half a teaspoonful into my mouth and found it so intensely bitter it took considerable effort not to vomit immediately. Next the tea came round in a metal bucket with a single cup from which everyone drank. On this first acquaintance I thought it smelt awful; it tasted awful too. But somehow I managed to keep it down.

"The Medicine needs to know you are strong enough to take it, that's why it makes itself bitter to you," Blue Horse told me. "All good medicines are bitter to the taste." He laughed at my obvious discomfort.

The only effect I noticed was that the fire seemed immediately to brighten and chase away the deep shadows inside the teepee. Prayers and singing continued nonstop for Santi, and the peyote went round twice more, but it seemed to have little effect on me, probably because I took only a small amount.

By about four A.M. I was feeling pretty well done in. My back was killing me and my buttocks were so tortured from sitting cross-legged on the ground for seven hours, I thought my pelvic bones were going to come out through the flesh. The fire inside the teepee was insufferably hot and, on top of that, I had managed little rest the night before and had now been about thirty hours without sleep. As Blue Horse had predicted, I was tired, hot, thirsty, feeling rather sick from the peyote, and seriously wondering whether it was all worth it and whether anything worthwhile was going to happen. Then, without warning, there was a loud crack and a large spark flew out of the fire and landed a few inches from Santi, who was lying fast asleep in her cradleboard in front of Fox.

Blue Horse was so fast off the mark that I saw his gaze tracking the spark even as it flew through the air. When the spark landed, Fox bent forward and knocked the glowing ember away from her baby, back towards the fire. As she did so, I saw her look anxiously at her grandfather, who nodded slightly to her and then leant over to speak to John Begay. It was obvious from their demeanour that something important had happened that the Navajos understood, even if I did not.

The two Medicine Men conferred for a long time and I saw them looking deep into the fire. Blue Horse pointed periodically with his drumstick but from my position I could not see what they were looking at. Whatever it was it must have been a difficult and complicated set of signs to interpret because the discussion went on for some time. Eventually they reached agreement and then the real drama began.

Blue Horse began to ask questions of the baby's father, Jimmy Tso, which were partly in Navajo and partly in English, because Jimmy's Navajo was not good. I heard *Baa'* chip in, and then Fox's mother *Asdzáán łibá*, the Grey Lady—although the name can also mean "light skinned"—started talking, mostly in Navajo, about "*shash.*" *Shash* in Navajo means "bear," so I knew at once that something bad was being indicated. Also, the three women became tense and strained as the questioning went on.

I heard Jimmy protest, "My grandmother knows what she's doing. She mixes it with all the right herbs and everything. She knows what to do." But the women were not satisfied and more accusations began to fly about his grandmother's fitness to carry out the correct treatment of the afterbirth. Finally, Jimmy shouted at them, "You can go and look, but you won't find it.

My grandmother knows all the secret places. She knows what she's doing!"

It was clear the three women believed his grandmother had botched the job and that a bear had found the afterbirth and eaten it. But Jimmy continued to resist these accusations and defended his grandmother stoutly, which, given his formidable trio of accusers, was a very brave thing to do.

Now Blue Horse began to ask more questions, but the answers didn't seem to take matters much further and after a while he stopped to confer with John Begay some more. At the end of this consultation he picked up his whistle and blew several high-pitched notes. Getting up, he walked over to Santi, Jimmy, and Fox and blessed them by wafting cedar smoke over them. He also seemed to be speaking words of reassurance and evidently something had been sorted out. After this Jimmy and the three ladies seemed to relax and from then on the meeting rolled forward good humouredly with prayers and songs, and everyone in a much better mood.

When at last the first rays of the morning sun came up they struck the main pole directly above Blue Horse's head. And when the teepee door was thrown open the rays fell directly on Blue Horse. Then, as the sun rose higher, a dagger of sunlight cut across the center of the teepee floor and straight through the remains of the fire. The teepee appeared to have been pitched quite casually, but when I saw this, I realised it had been placed with startling precision to catch those first rays.

The meeting ended at nine A.M., after which there was a break while people rested. Food was served at noon. Shortly after, people began to drift home and when everyone had gone I helped Blue Horse take down the teepee and pack it away. Only then did I stagger inside and collapse on the sofa into a deep sleep.

When I awoke, feeling stiff and sore all over, it was evening and Jimmy had departed for his job in the oil field at Farmington, taking Asdzáán łibá with him. None of the women wanted to cook and so I offered to take Blue Horse, *Baa'*, Fox, and the baby out to eat.

"I'm feeling good," Blue Horse told me as we drove along the highway looking for somewhere that was open. "I don't get tired or sore at meetings because I've been doing it for so long. This is what I do, and it makes me feel good."

The only place open locally was a truck stop diner, which, regrettably, was not one of the better ones. As there was no other choice, we took our places at a not particularly clean Formica-topped table, and were soon drinking not very good coffee and eating not very good hamburgers. I was still mystified by exactly what had happened during the ceremony, so while we ate I took the opportunity to ask questions and at last heard the full story.

Fox explained, "Jimmy disagreed, but me, my mother, and my grandmother all thought something found the placenta, most likely a *shash*, and that's why Santi keeps getting sick."

I was about to ask for further explanation, when Blue Horse said something in Navajo to *Baa'* that I did not understand. I had the impression he'd spoken in Navajo deliberately so that I would not understand. When *Baa'* then immediately tried to end the conversation and change the subject, I was convinced of it.

"It's not necessary to worry any more because it's all been fixed," *Baa'* said hurriedly. Then, looking at Blue Horse rather uncertainly, she began to ask what we all had planned for the next day.

It was a dilemma. I had been treated as great friend of the family and had been shown much kindness and more of their traditional ways than any white man had any right to be shown. Nonetheless, I *was* white, a foreigner in their land, and this was intimate family business. They were torn, and I was making them uncomfortable, so the only thing I could do was back off.

"I'm very glad to hear it," I said. "I hope my prayers were of some help in all this and when I get the chance I shall pray for Santi some more."

Then was silence for a few moments during which Blue Horse appeared to be studying his burger with far greater attention than it deserved. *Baa'* seemed embarrassed and Fox looked for a moment as if she might cry. Then Fox said, "Tell him, Grandfather."

"I don't know," said Blue Horse, still looking at his burger.

Then *Baa'* chimed in. "Charles is practically a member of our family now. You should tell him."

"How is he going to understand unless we explain," Fox continued, cradling her baby and feeding her one of the French fries off my plate. "He knows things, he sees in the fire, he can understand."

Eventually Blue Horse bowed to the ladies' opinion and began to explain what had really happened in the teepee.

"It's always difficult sometimes to explain things because there is so much you don't know, but I'll do my best," he began hesitantly. "You remember the spark? The big one that flew out of the fire and nearly hit Santi? Well, that was what gave me the clue. When I looked into the fire I could see that something bad, something real evil, was trying to get the baby. That's when I called John over and when we looked into the fire we could both see that something had got at the afterbirth."

"Was it the *shash?*" I asked.

"No, it wasn't the *shash*, not necessarily, but something had damaged it," he said, but he would not tell me what it was.

"I could see it all in the fire," he continued "So I decided to put it right and that's when I used the whistle to call on the spirits to make things better. The spirits came to our aid and everything will be all right from now on," he concluded.

As an explanation it was a bit short on detail, but it was obviously all I was going to get. If I had been a Navajo it would have been clear enough, I suppose, but all I could do was take it at face value and thank Blue Horse for telling me. Looking over at baby Santi, who was gurgling happily to herself and chewing a French fry, I hoped he was right.

Then Fox told me how she had collected baby Santi's belly-button when it fell off. "I'll either bury it or keep it somewhere, so she'll have two things calling her back if she should ever go away," Fox said. "It makes it more likely she'll want to come back and see us, or come back and stay here."

"I have a friend," Fox went on, "who kept her baby's bellybutton in her purse. She kind of forgot about it and she couldn't understand why, as soon as the baby could walk, it kept going to the purse and playing with it. It was only when she remembered the bellybutton was inside that she understood why the baby kept being drawn to her purse. So you can see that these things are real and they work," she said.

It should be noted that after the ceremony, baby Santi recovered and became well again. True, she still suffered from the usual childhood ailments, but there was no return of the mysterious periodic bouts of sickness and fever. She was one of many patients among the Navajo who I saw recovered or much improved by traditional methods.

However, I still found it difficult to decide whether the improvement I witnessed in Santi, or improvements that appeared to be wrought by Medicine Men generally, were real or not. I was not in a position to measure scientifically whether real improvements in long standing conditions had really taken place.

But I did have sixty thousand words of notes, soon to double, written down contemporaneously as Blue Horse and other Medicine Men divined the future, looked into the past, healed the sick, lifted curses, and undertook activities designed to help their fellow Indians. This was evidence of a kind.

And more evidence was walking around on two legs—the patients the Medicine Men had treated. They were usually only too happy to tell anyone who would listen, either in Navajo or English, that they felt better after being treated by traditional methods. The Medicine Man's work was at least observable and any researcher who can find a Medicine Man prepared to cooperate can see for himself. He may not agree with me, but he can observe the evidence as I have done and reach his own conclusions. The wonder is that more have not done so.

Admittedly my evidence had flaws. It was usually impossible to know how sick someone was before the Medicine Man got to work on them, or how much they recovered afterwards. I had to rely on the word of the patient and the patient's family as to how ill they had been and how great was the recovery. The family is usually in a good position to know when one of their number is ill, and when they are better, but their evaluations are, of course, not scientific in any sense.

The great American physicist Carl Sagan once likened science to "a candle in the dark." Science is about finding the truth, however unlikely or uncomfortable that truth may be. Sagan warned that the guttering candle flame of science, which sometimes seems to burn dangerously low, was all that stood between us and a tidal wave of pseudo-science, non-science, or simply nonsense peddled by armies of psychics, channellers, mystics, crystal ball gazers, self-styled witches, mad Christian creationists, mad mullahs, and associated loonies of all kinds.

I entirely agree with Dr. Sagan. However, my Navajo Medicine friends were anything but loonies. Without exception they were sincere and dignified people who had dedicated their lives to helping their fellow beings through use of their traditional ways. I felt I owed it to them to try to discover what effect for good they really had. If it was a placebo effect, the beneficial effect often observed when people *believe* they are being helped even if they aren't, then so be it. The worst that could then be said of Navajo traditional ways was that they complied with some very basic rules about good medical practice.

More than 2,400 years ago, Hippocrates, the father of European medicine, wrote in his treatise, *Epidemics*, that physicians should, "Declare the past, diagnose the present, foretell the future, and practice these acts. As to diseases, make a habit of two things—to help, or at least do no harm." Which is pretty well what I saw in Navajo medicine. Help was always intended but, even if it failed, it was certain that no one ever came to any harm from being blessed with cedar smoke and an eagle feather. The morale boosting effect on the patient more than justified it. On the other hand, if these traditional methods were producing genuine improvements in medical conditions, and these benefits could be scientifically measured, I felt the world needed to know about them.

It irked me that I was not in a position to organise a scientific study to evaluate the results the Medicine Men achieved. Still, I comforted myself that I had made a start by amassing enough evidence to suggest that *something* was going on. Even if I could not say what it was, I could still hope that one day I would be able to answer some vital questions.

A few nights after the Medicine ceremony for Santi, it was too hot to sleep in my tent so I lay out among the junipers looking at the stars and pondering all this. It was a cloudless, moonless night and the whole panoply of the firmament was spread out above me. There were millions, billions, trillions, zillions of stars stretching away to infinity and never had Shakespeare's line, "There are more things in heaven and earth, Horatio, than are dreamed of in thy philosophy," seemed more relevant.

This prompted me to remember that the Earth and everything on it, and everything in the universe, is made up of atoms. If I was small enough I would fall through the space between the atoms and exit our planet for good. There are particles that can do just that. These sub-atomic particles are so small that an atom is as gigantic to them, as to us it is small. Some sub-atomic particles behave in extremely odd ways—photons and electrons, for instance, can be in two places at once—and they exist in what is called the quantum world, where it turns out that reality, rather as in the peyote world, is not necessarily what you think it is.

In the quantum world, time can move backwards particles can suddenly materialise from nowhere. This is not science fiction but well established scientific fact and has been observed many times from the early 1970s onwards. Yet, despite being made up of atoms, we humans can do none of these things because, somewhere between the sub-atomic world and our own consciousness, something happens—and no one knows what it is.

Parts of quantum physics defy common sense. On the other hand common sense tells us the earth is flat and the sun goes round it. Common sense also tells us that a Navajo Medicine Man cannot speak to the spirit of a long dead snake or make a baby well by looking in a fire. At least, that's what it tells most white men, but it tells most Navajos completely the opposite. Common sense apart, reason suggests the quantum world appears so strange because we do not have the full picture. It is the large chunks of the picture that are missing, the parts completely unknown to us, that make the sub-atomic world look so crazy. If we knew the full story it would probably be nowhere so baffling—at least to a quantum physicist.

It occurred to me, lying beneath that bush under the stars, that if sub-atomic particles can appear out of nowhere and be in two places at once while time whizzes merrily backwards, was it really so ridiculous that a Navajo Medicine Man could look into the fire and see the past, present, and future? Or that he could find evil witch curses and beads stolen from a grave ten years earlier? Or intercede with the spirit of a dead snake to make a man's neck better?

Was it not reasonable to suppose that Blue Horse's world might look crazy to me because *I* did not know enough about it?

Perhaps the ability to cure was once innate in us all, but in our over-crowded, over-confident, fast moving society, we have lost the ability. Leaving few outside the medical profession who would dare to attempt to heal, while among the Navajo, there are many.

CHAPTER NINE

The Chanter

I HAD NOT SEEN REUBEN FOR A LONG TIME when, unexpectedly, I bumped into him at a funeral in Shiprock, a small
town on the northeastern edge of the reservation, where I had
gone to pay my last respects to Mrs. Yellowhair, an elderly Navajo
lady who had befriended me.

She had followed the traditional ways of her people but her
family, particularly her sons and grandsons, had become Mor-
mons and insisted upon a Christian funeral service. What I did
not know was, that out of respect for her, the sons had arranged for
the Christian funeral service to be followed by a traditional burial
carried out by a Medicine Man.

Sitting among the huge crowd packed into the church, I noticed a man standing at the back, wearing the traditional red and
blue prayer scarf of a priest of the native peyote religion. That
seemed slightly odd in a Mormon temple. He was, as the Navajo
would say, a *Hastiin Nééz*, a tall, fit-looking man of stern visage.
He appeared to be in his mid-fifties and stood a head taller than
most of those around him. His skin was unusually dark for a
Navajo and his hair was cut short in style of the Pueblo Indians.
In fact, I took him for a Pueblo Indian until I later heard him
speak good, clear Navajo.

The Christian service lasted a good two hours, with hymns, prayers, and long eulogies spoken by the sons, grandsons, granddaughters, nephews, and nieces. Mrs. Yellowhair had the most wonderful and loving send-off any family could have given her.

When the service was finished no one seemed inclined to leave the church and so, while they stood around talking, I slipped out to get my mobile phone from the car and make a few calls. As I approached my car I saw the car next to it had its bonnet up and that someone was doubled over working frantically on the engine. A second later the figure stood upright, wiped his oily hands on a rag—and at the same moment I recognised him, Reuben recognised me.

"Reuben!" I cried in astonishment.

"Charles! Man, am I glad to see you!" His face broke into a big smile.

"What are you doing here?" I asked.

"What does it look like, man? *Shichidí yícho'*!" he said, shaking his head in despair. "My car's busted!"

"Can you fix it?"

"No, man, I can't!" He declared grumpily and threw the oily rag to the ground.

"It's no good asking me," I told him. "I know more about the dark side of the moon than I do about engines."

"Well, ain't you just Mr. Wonderful," he replied. "I'm supposed to drive my boss to the burial service. If I can't get him there, I don't know what he's going to say."

This was the first I'd heard of there being another service. Reuben went on to explain that it was to take place at the family's home, which was on a small farm about thirty miles away.

"A lot of Navajos are buried at the back of their homes," Reuben told me, adding darkly, "That way we can make sure no one's creeping around at night who shouldn't be."

"Like skin-walkers?" I queried.

"Shush!" he hissed in alarm. "Don't talk about them around a dead body. It's like inviting them in."

I apologised and turned the conversation back to his problem. "I'd give you a lift myself, but I've not been invited," I said, explaining that I hadn't heard about the second service.

Indians can sometimes be very touchy about whites intruding where they are not wanted. As the family had not mentioned the burial to me, my instinct was to err on the side of caution and stay away rather than risk upsetting anyone.

"You're bound to be invited," Reuben assured me.

"I don't see why." I said.

"Because everybody knows you."

"They do?"

"Sure, when folks heard Blue Horse had got himself some *bilagáana* from England for a bag carrier, man, that one went round the rez so fast no skin-walker's ass could have kept up with it," Reuben said, magnificently ignoring his own advice of only a few seconds earlier. Then, realising his mistake, he slapped his face to atone for the mention of the unmentionable name and put his hands over his mouth like the monkey who spoke no evil. I couldn't help laughing.

"Man, you *still* laugh at the strangest things," he said, smiling. "You know, it's happened before with white guys coming around here swearin' blind they want to dedicate their lives to learning our Navajo ways. Usually they last a couple of weeks and the next thing you know they're in California running a Web site claiming to be Medicine Men. Navajo people don't like *that*. But you've stayed the course and stuck it out with us, and Navajo people kinda like *that*. So that's why everybody knows you and you're bound to be invited," he finished.

Even if it was true that everybody knew who I was—which it most certainly was not—I didn't quite follow his logic that an invitation to a burial automatically followed. But at that moment vast numbers of people began pouring out of the church. Soon the air was full of the sound of car doors slamming, people shouting, and engines revving, making conversation difficult.

Reuben looked at the size of the crowd and gave a low whistle. "Man, if there's one thing the Navajos like it's a good funeral," he said.

He continued to insist I would be welcome at the burial, and eventually I agreed to drive him and his boss.

"That's cool, man. Now, all I've gotta do is find the boss," he said, eyeing the throng. A few seconds later a tall, lean figure came striding towards us. It was the dark *Hastiin Nééz*, his red and blue prayer shawl blowing out behind him as he walked.

"Here he is," said Reuben.

"That's your boss?" I was surprised.

"Sure."

"What's his name?"

"We call him *Hataali*, The Chanter."

The Navajo word *hataałi* is usually translated into English as Medicine Man, and sometimes as "singer," neither of which is really correct. *Hataałi* means "chanter," the Navajo carrying within it the implication that what is being chanted is powerful magic capable of healing both body and soul. The same air of magic still hangs about the English words "enchanter" and "enchanted," both deriving from the verb "to chant." A phrase such as "One Who Heals in Body and Soul" is probably as close to the Navajo meaning as English can get. Certainly, it is best to think of a powerful Medicine Man such as The Chanter as someone who is in close contact with the world of the spirits.

"So you really are an apprentice Medicine Man at last," I said, congratulating him. "I hadn't seen you, so I wasn't sure if things had gone ahead."

"I'm sort of an apprentice," he allowed. "Most of the time I'm just a bag carrier and driver like you!"

"I'm an apprentice sometimes," I protested. "Blue Horse teaches me a thing or two."

"I wish my boss would give me more opportunities, but he can be real tough to work for. If I don't get it right, I get my knuckles rapped," Reuben confided.

"Will you introduce me?" I asked.

"Introduce yourself," Reuben advised, so I did. The tall man nodded slightly in recognition, but ignored my proffered hand. Thinking he might not have understood my Navajo, I tried again in English, but obtained the same result.

By now I'd sold the Cougar to save myself from bankruptcy, but for this special occasion I'd scraped together enough money to hire a beaten up little run-about from a Mexican outfit just off Central Avenue in Albuquerque. I'd nicknamed them "El Dodgy," and not without good reason—their cars were cheap but not smart, and brakes were an an optional extra that had been more or less left out on my model. Reuben looked disappointed when he realised he was not going in a fast, shiny sports car. But The Chanter turned not a hair as he climbed into the far from clean rear seat.

Reuben transferred a couple of Medicine bundles from his car to mine, as well as a water drum, and climbed in next to me. Then we went nowhere for thirty minutes while the tribal police formed all the mourners into one long convoy with an escort front and back.

"It's a narrow road and pretty dangerous," Reuben warned. "They don't want to risk another funeral by having this number people driving down all at once without an escort."

When we eventually started moving, Reuben and I chatted away amiably in the front, but during the entire journey The Chanter spoke not one word. I snatched occasional glimpses of him in the mirror and thought his bearing and demeanor resembled nothing so much as that of a Head of State being chauffeured between intergovernmental meetings. He took no notice of his surroundings, or of me, or Reuben, or our humble mode of transport, and appeared to be entirely preoccupied with his own thoughts. Even when the convoy came to a sudden and unexpected halt—and due to the lack of brakes I nearly buried us in the boot of the car ahead—he remained entirely unperturbed.

The Chanter was a famous and respected man who wore his authority easily. One of the most senior Medicine Men of the whole tribe, he often journeyed abroad as an ambassador for the Navajo people. I could not help feeling that Reuben had been extremely fortunate to apprentice himself to such a man, even if he was tough on him.

When Reuben said Navajos were sometimes buried at the "back of their homes," I'd imagined he meant a spot on some lonely hillside overlooking the old homestead. Nothing of the kind. This grave was only a few yards from the back door and as we drew up, the mechanical digger that had dug it was chugging away across a field.

At those high altitudes, well over seven thousand feet in this case, even in summer the weather can turn in an instant. While it had been sunny in Shiprock, now black clouds came over and hid the top of the mountain. Soon a cold wind started to blow and it began to rain as the sons prepared to lower their mother into her grave. At this moment, The Chanter stepped forward, holding his ceremonial gourd rattle and his eagle bone whistle in his hands. At the edge of the grave, in the rain and the mud, he knelt down on a rug and made ready to sing his Medicine songs.

"I will sing three songs. Anyone who wishes is welcome to join in," he announced sternly in Navajo, and then repeated himself in English.

"Come on, Charles," Reuben called, taking up the water drum. "You know some of these songs. Come and join in with us."

As the sons began slowly to lower the casket, I stood with several Indians singing the high-pitched, shrill Medicine songs while Reuben expertly beat time on the water drum. There was a perfect fit between the songs and the scene. The high notes and keening words formed a lament that had grown out of the land, people, and culture, and gave voice to their feelings far better than any Christian hymn could ever have done. In between songs there was only the sound of cold rain pattering on the coffin and the snorting of the horses in the paddock, while all around us people stood bare headed and grieving in the cold. When his final song was ended, The Chanter paused for a few moments before slowly bringing his eagle bone whistle to his lips and blowing several short, shrill blasts. He paused a moment more, then sounded one last, long, quavering note and it was over.

Swiftly spades were handed out and the sons set to work to fill in their mother's grave. They were all big men and the task did not take long, which was as well because by now there was snow mixed with the rain and despite wearing a good quality sailing anorak, I was feeling close to hypothermia.

"What's the weather like in England?" a man I'd never met before asked me, making conversation.

"Very like this. Cold and wet," I told him.

"You have snow in England?"

"Yeah, lots of it," I said, and he looked surprised. "But it doesn't last for long," I added.

"It lasts a long time on the mountain in the winter," the man replied, nodding towards the cloud-shrouded peak. "We believe each snowflake is one of our dead relatives come to visit us, so we're pleased if they stay around to see how we're doing. In the spring they turn to water and fill up the streams for us to drink and to water our crops and cattle. We're pleased to see the snow."

When all was done we retired with stiff limbs, frozen feet, and numb fingers to the local Chapter House, which is a kind of village hall. Here was mutton stew, fry bread, coffee, and more eulogies for Mrs. Yellowhair. Outside the rain turned to a downpour, flooding the car park and cascading in torrents down the gullies. Interestingly, all the Navajos, both Mormon and non-Mormon, were quite sure the rain—always so desperately needed in those high desert areas—had been sent by Mrs. Yellowhair.

"She knew we needed it," one of the brothers said.

"She wouldn't let us down," said another, and they all nodded in silent agreement.

During the meal I sat with Reuben, who naturally sat with The Chanter. The Chanter remained silent throughout the meal, merely nodding or shaking his head when Reuben spoke to him. The only exception came when he was called upon to speak of his memories of Mrs. Yellowhair. Whereupon he rose and delivered an oration of great warmth and feeling that lasted a good ten minutes and was admired by everyone. After which he resumed his seat and his silence. I was beginning to think I would never exchange a word with him when, without warning, he said something quietly to Reuben, at which Reuben turned to me.

"He wants to know if you're interested in our traditional ways," he said.

I was sure he knew perfectly well that I was, so I replied simply, "Aoó," pronounced "Oh!", which in Navajo means "yes."

Reuben turned to the Chanter to relay my answer, at which The Singer spoke again to Reuben, who turned back to me. "He wants to know if you would like to go to a Beauty Way ceremony?"

"Aoó," I replied, trying to fight down a rising sense of excitement. To be invited to a ceremony like this, by someone so elevated, was a rare honor.

Reuben turned to The Chanter and The Chanter said something to Reuben, who turned back to me. "He says it's near Red Mesa."

"I know Red Mesa," I told Reuben, whose back and forth head movements were beginning to rival those of a Wimbledon tennis judge.

Reuben turned to The Chanter, relayed my message, and then turned back to me.

"The ceremony is in a hogan," he added.

How long all this head waggling would have gone on I don't know but, fortunately, at that moment we were interrupted by a lady who wanted to talk to The Chanter, and Reuben and I were able to slip away to discuss the details.

A Navajo Beauty Way is a ceremony of personal and spiritual renewal that goes on for two nights and is performed when someone feels run down, tired, and drained. As its name suggests, the ceremony contains many beautiful and refreshing ideas and concepts, and includes many of the Navajos' most magnificent prayers.

"He likes you," Reuben confided, after giving me the time, date, and directions to the hogan.

"Then why won't he speak to me?" I asked, puzzled.

"Give it time, man. Give it time," he counselled me.

It seems odd to English people, but Navajos and associated tribes like the Apache often do not speak to people they have only recently met. I have heard of Indians who meet as strangers and do not speak to each other for four or five days, even though they may be working, eating, sleeping, and living cheek by jowl. Nobody bothers them, or encourages them to engage in conversation, as people reckon they will eventually speak to each other in their own good time. Invariably they do, and the odd thing is that once conversation begins, they carry on as if they have known each other for years. Reuben was gently reminding me that The Chanter was treating me perfectly properly by the norms of Navajo culture and I had no cause for complaint. A week later—and after another trip to El Dodgy's—I was driving through Shiprock on my way to Red Mesa in a vehicle held together largely by rust and apparently also devoid of brakes.

Shiprock takes its name from a huge volcanic plug created twenty million years ago that towers a thousand feet or more above the surrounding countryside. If viewed from some angles the rock does indeed resemble a ship under sail and amply justifies the name given to it by white people. But to the Navajos the place has another significance and a completely different name. To them Shiprock is *Tse'Bit'Ai*—Rock With Wings—and they say it is the bones of a giant bird that carried their ancestors from the north many years ago.

On each side of the rock are towering walls of solidified lava, so massive one could easily believe they had been built by giants. When viewed from the height of the nearby Chuska hills, they do indeed look like wings extending on each side of the head of a dead and decayed bird. The sun was going down as I drove by and Tse'Bit'Ai turned to gold and glowed in its rays. The sky changed successively to red, orange, and purple, and then all of them together, before the sun finally dipped beneath the edge of the earth.

At the town of Shiprock I took the fork out into the desert, following a lonely road that eventually leads to one of the great wonders of the world at Monument Valley, more than a hundred miles away. I was not going that far, which I was glad about, as the rust bucket I was driving would probably not have made it.

I was running late and it was pitch black by the time I reached Red Mesa, so I parked and went in search of the hogan on foot. In the dark I missed my way and to make things worse the moon had not yet risen and I had to make my way by starlight, with only the cicadas chirping in the underbrush for company.

I eventually located the hogan set back among trees behind a wooden house, but in the dark I could find no path that led to it. The house was surrounded by an eight foot wire fence and, in desperation, I eventually climbed over the fence and dropped down on the other side, only to find myself in a paddock where mustangs snickered nervously in the dark. A large dog came to look at me and, thankfully, slunk away again.

From inside the hogan came the compelling beat of the water drum and the singing of Medicine songs. It is rude to enter while a song is being sung so I waited at the door until the song had finished. Then, when all was quiet inside, I turned the handle, opened the door, and stepped inside.

The hogan was lit by two oil lamps whose flames guttered in the draught, casting dark and flickering shadows on the walls. In their deep yellow light I could just make out the shapes of many Navajos, both men and women, seated around the sides, some dressed in traditional clothes and some in normal working attire. In the Seat of Honour sat a Medicine Man I had never seen before. A big, powerfully built, impressive-looking man, he had two equally capable-looking assistants on each side of him.

At first I could not see The Chanter among the strange faces and rapidly shifting shadows. But as my eyes adjusted I saw he was on the Medicine Man's left, sitting cross-legged on a kind of makeshift bed, surrounded by all manner of strange objects. Next to him sat a woman and next to her was Reuben. Everyone looked up as I came in and I saw an expression of surprise cross the Medicine Man's face. He was clearly not expecting a curly-haired white man to come through the door and he darted a look at The Chanter, who nodded almost imperceptibly to indicate all was well and I could enter. I was as much surprised as the Medicine Man was, because up to that moment I had thought The Chanter was conducting the ceremony. Only now did I realise that he was the patient and the ceremony was being conducted for his benefit.

Reuben silently signalled for me to sit next to him and when I had taken my place, one of the Medicine Man's assistants rose and lay a brightly coloured, intricately patterned, traditional Navajo blanket on the ground in front of The Chanter. Several small bags made of deer hide, with rawhide drawstrings through the tops, were then placed on the blanket. The Chanter opened each bag in turn, took a pinch of the contents between his fingers, and placed each pinch on a piece of deer hide about a foot square that had been put in front of him.

Exactly what each bag contained I could not see, but it was possible to identify yellow and white corn pollen, cedar, and some other herbs including sage. When a pinch of each had been laid on the deer hide, the Medicine Man wrapped up the bundle with all the contents safely inside and placed it carefully beside him. A few moments later he asked for four male volunteers and, wishing to make myself useful, I started to stand up, only to have Reuben grab the sleeve of my shirt and pull me down again.

"Sit still and keep quiet!" he hissed—where had I heard that before? "He means *Navajo* men."

The Medicine Man, one of his assistants, and the four volunteers left the hogan taking The Chanter with them. I heard the roar of an engine outside and then the sound of a truck bouncing away along the rough track that led towards the mountain. Everyone stood up and began making for the door.

"Is it over?" I whispered to Reuben, wondering for a moment if I'd muddled the time and come at the end of the ceremony.

"No, man, it ain't over," he said yawning, and stretching his arms. "We're taking a break while they do the Stone Ceremony."

"What's that?" I asked.

"Can't tell you. The Stone Ceremony's secret and we aren't allowed to talk about it to outsiders," he replied, and yawned again.

I knew better than to pursue the matter and so, turning my attention to the display around the Chanter's bed, I asked about the stone objects. Some of which looked much like spear- and arrowheads, and there was also a piece of stone shaped like an axe head.

"They're sacred things," Reuben explained when I asked. But he confessed he did not know why they were sacred, or what they represented. "I'd have to be a Medicine Man to know for sure," he confided. "I don't want to tell you the wrong thing."

"Shall I ask the Medicine Man?" I suggested.

"Noooooooo!" he gasped, looking horrified. "This Medicine Man is very conservative. He doesn't want you here at all, but as you're The Chanter's guest there's not much he can do about it." And he laughed.

Most of the others had gone outside to stretch their legs, but we stayed inside talking. After a while the remaining assistant brought in a large plastic barrel from which he began scooping out handfuls of damp sand. With these he began to construct a pathway about three or four inches high and about six inches wide. By the time he had finished it ran in a semicircle from near the hogan door, around the battered old iron stove in the center, and finished under the edge of The Chanter's bed. The top of the path was flattened with a wooden batten traditionally used in weaving and, about a yard from where the path disappeared under the bed, the assistant made a circle of sand, which Reuben said represented a garden.

While this was going on one of the women removed the husks from two ears of Indian corn and, after placing the golden corn in a small tin dish, put the dry husks carefully to one side. She shelled the corn and then took it outside in the dish and began to winnow it, tossing it up and down in the fresh night air to allow the chaff to blow away. When she was satisfied, she brought the winnowed corn back into the hogan and, kneeling on a cushion, begin to grind it by hand between two traditional grinding stones.

The corn shone like drops of gold in the lamplight, and taking a few kernels at a time, she sprinkled them on a large flat stone about two feet long, which tapered and rose slightly at the far end. Then, taking a much smaller, flatter stone in both hands, she ground the golden corn to white flour with a simple, unhurried back and forth movement. As soon as she had a few tablespoons of flour she pushed it to the raised end of the stone for safe keeping, using a bundle of little white sticks that Navajo women traditionally keep for this purpose. Then she took a few more kernels and began the process anew.

As I watched her rocking gently back and forth on her knees, grinding the corn to make the flour, I felt a strange and unusual calmness creeping over me. It took time to remember that for the best part of eight thousand years, all my ancestors had watched their mothers, wives, sisters, and daughters performing precisely the same actions, in huts not dissimilar to the one in which I was now seated. Somewhere in my modern brain an ancient pathway was still open that associated watching a woman grind corn with home, hearth, and tranquillity. Although I had never before in my life seen a woman grind corn by hand, the deeper part of my mind must have recognised it as a signal that all was well, and I felt at peace.

When she finished, the woman had about half a small pudding basin full of white flour, some of which the deputy Medicine Man took and used to draw a thin white line along the middle of the raised sand path.

"That's The Chanter's path through life," Reuben told me. "He has to relive his life by walking through it again to regain his strength."

A little later The Chanter and the rest returned and resumed their places, while the Medicine Man began a long oration in Navajo. From this, I gathered that the path represented not only a man's life, but also the life of the Navajo people going all the way back to Dinétah, the sacred place, where the Navajo people first emerged into the world.

When he had finished, the Medicine Man switched into accented English and for my benefit kindly explained, "I'm reminding everyone of the strengths and values of our Navajo history. Of our understanding of the need for harmony and of the need to use the harmony principles of the Navajo in everyday life. We seek to be in harmony with all things. If a snake crosses my path and I am in a bad mood, I may throw something at the snake and that will make the snake angry. In that way we are both angry. Angry at each other and angry at ourselves and the world around us, and we need to hold a little ceremony so that we can seek to calm our anger. In that way harmony is restored not only in us, but in the world around us and in the universe.

"I am also reminding everyone of the need to teach our ancient ways through the telling of the old stories, and of the need to teach these things to our young people, so they can learn and not forget them. There are 120 secret and sacred words in the Navajo language that should never be used. Nowadays I hear some of them being spoken all over the place, all the time, and that's wrong. But it's also wrong that we don't teach our young people better. Too many young people believe tradition is something that will bind and constrain them, but this is not so. Tradition aids and strengthens us, as it aided and strengthened our ancestors. It told them who they were, why they walked the earth, and for what purpose their lives were intended. I know that to white people such things are a mystery, and many clever white men write long books in which they fail to find the answers to these simple things. But to we Navajos there is no mystery, for we are from the earth and *of* the earth, and our purpose is to be in harmony with all who dwell here, and with the Great Spirit, and with the universe."

After he had spoken, the Medicine Man ordered The Chanter to be wrapped in a colourful Navajo blanket. Then, accompanied by much lively chanting from the onlookers, The Chanter was led along the pathway of sand back to Dinétah. As he walked he was told to tread "right, left, right, left." I noticed that although the path looked quite broad to my eye, the Medicine Man had to hold The Chanter's left arm as he walked to, quite literally, keep him on the straight and narrow.

"It looks easy," Reuben whispered. "But it's not easy to walk through your life again. The moment you step on that path you find how narrow and hard it is and how easy it is to slip off and fall into sin. The Medicine Man helps him on his way and reminds us that we all need the help of others, and the help of the spirits, in our journey through life."

When The Chanter reached the end of the path the assistants helped him strip to his underwear, after which they liberally scattered white flour over him. Yellow corn pollen was also sprinkled on him and by the time the assistants had finished The Chanter looked as if he had been in an end of term school flour fight.

Now he was led to the "garden," where a jug of water was produced and his hair was wetted and washed using yucca roots, which produce fine, soapy suds and are the traditional Navajo "shampoo." With his hair rinsed, he was redressed and seated on the bed once more and a pipe was produced. It was now that I learned why the woman had earlier put the dried cornhusks so carefully to one side. Going to the stove in the center of the hogan, one of the Medicine Man's assistants lit one of the dry husks and used it to light the pipe, which he had filled with aromatic tobacco. The pipe was unlike any I'd seen before among Indians, being short and stubby and made of stone. By the time it reached me, the pipe was so hot it could be held only by wrapping it in a large bandana.

The Medicine Man looked at me keenly as I raised it to my lips but, thanks to Blue Horse's teaching, I knew what to do and blew one plume of blue smoke to Mother Earth, one to Father Sky, one straight ahead for myself, and then I blew smoke into my cupped hands and patted it all over my legs, body, head, and hair as a blessing, before passing the pipe to my left to the next man in line. When I looked at the Medicine Man he held my eye for a moment before giving a slight nod of approval, so I knew I'd passed a crucial test. By the time the pipe had gone round, and everyone had smoked and blessed themselves, it was nearly dawn. After a few more rounds of chanting, the sun came up and the first part of the ceremony was concluded.

I spent most of the day lolling around in the hogan, alternately napping on the earth floor and talking inconsequentially with the few Navajos who had stayed. Reuben disappeared and so did the Medicine Man and his assistants, while The Chanter went to sleep in the house where a decent bed had been prepared for him. It was not until late in the evening that the full compliment of friends, family, and supporters regrouped, and the second part of the ceremony got underway.

Now there was a lot more chanting and drumming, which went on for some time. Once more a beautifully coloured and patterned Navajo blanket was spread out in front of The Chanter, and all the things he valued, including his Medicine bundles, his prayer staffs, his wallet, and car keys were thrown onto it. Then everyone else was invited to add articles, and there followed a veritable shower of car keys, wallets, wads of cash, prayer staffs, and religious paraphernalia. There was even a U.S. government tax form and a couple of homemade CDs by local rez bands!

I had been content merely to observe, but Reuben suddenly jabbed me in the ribs.

"Quick. Put something in," he hissed in an urgent whisper.

"What's it for?" I asked.

"It's the blessing. Whatever you put in there will turn out good. Put money in and you'll get more back. Put your car keys in and the Great Spirit will make sure you drive safe. Put the Medicine bundles in and they'll be made more holy," he explained.

"And the CDs?" I asked.

"More people will buy them. They'll top the charts," he assured me.

From my inside pocket I fished out the little silver case my three children had given me before I left England and which contained two pictures of them: one taken when they were little and the other of them as adults. Of all the things I have ever owned it was by far the most precious, and whenever I looked out upon a sea of troubles, which was often, I touched it and prayed for the storm to modify. After placing it carefully in the blanket, on an impulse I threw in the keys to El Dodgy's finest. Reasoning that if I got home in one piece, no further proof of the ceremony's efficacy would ever be required.

The Medicine Man blessed The Chanter once more, this time by taking yellow corn pollen from a deer hide bag and placing a little on the soles of his feet. More was rubbed on his legs, his arms, and the top of his head, and then two lines of pollen were drawn under his eyes and a little rubbed on his lips. With this done the pollen then went round for everyone to bless themselves by scattering a little in front of them. As I did not know this ritual, I copied everyone else by throwing a little into the air and letting it fall in front of me.

Once more the Medicine Man switched into English, and addressing himself to me, he explained, "Yesterday you heard me say how important it is that our young people learn our traditions. Our traditions are the sinews and muscles of our way of life and like the sinews and muscles of the body they must be exercised if they are to stay healthy and strong. Our traditions are not rigid as some imagine, but extremely supple and adept. They change readily as the world changes around us and that is their strength and ours.

"Just now you saw how we use the corn pollen to bless ourselves, but during the last hundred years the way corn pollen has been used in this ritual has changed several times. Early in the 1900s people scattered it about in front of them like a blessing. When the influenza epidemic came at the end of the First World War, people scattered it in lines before them like a barrier. In the 1920s when the economy was booming they scattered it with their hands going upwards as if encouraging a tree to grow. But in the 1930s when the economy collapsed, they scattered it like a barrier again to keep bad things away from them, and they did the same in World War II. When people began to prosper once more in the 1960s they tended to scatter it more towards themselves like a blessing, and now it is once again being scattered as if encouraging a tree to grow. It changes with time because our people need the corn pollen to give them different things. Our young people need to know this so they can grow up in a Navajo way and benefit from the wisdom of our ancestors."

After an hour or more of songs, The Chanter was asked to rise and walk around the inside of the hogan praying. Dressed in a freshly laundered, pale-coloured shirt, gray trousers, and moccasins, he rose and wrapped a bright Indian blanket around himself. Then, beginning once again on his right foot, he went on his prayerful journey while the Medicine Man intoned, "We are all of the earth, we emerged from the earth and are made of what the earth is made of. The earth is made of what the stars are made of. We are the earth and the stars, we are one, we are men, indivisible, indestructible."

Whether he knew it or not, this was perfectly orthodox science. The basic component of human beings is carbon, and carbon is produced only in the heart of stars: human beings are literally stardust. A few moments later he slightly ruined the effect by adding, "That's why when we bang our heads, we see stars." I was never sure whether this was a joke or not.

When The Chanter returned to his place after his long, prayerful journey round the hogan, it was almost dawn. There was more chanting and singing and then, as the sun came up, the Medicine Man ended the ceremony with the great Navajo prayer for harmony and beauty:

Beauty before you,
Beauty behind you.
Beauty above you,
Beauty below you,
Beauty all around you
May you walk in beauty.

Hózhó náhásdlíí'
Hózhó náhásdlíí'
Hózhó náhásdlíí'
Hózhó náhásdlíí'

There is blessing
There is blessing
There is blessing
There is blessing.

The final refrain was repeated four times, once for each of the sacred directions.

When he had finished we tumbled out of the hogan to stretch our cramped limbs in the morning chill, contemplate the beauty of the colours of dawn, and bless ourselves in the first rays of the sun. As usual in the desert, the sky was streaked with amazing colours and the earth glowed in the early light. The mountain behind us, with its green slopes, shady glens, and tumbling streams, looked like the gateway to the Promised Land.

Refreshed we returned to the hogan and queued up to congratulate The Chanter on a successful ceremony. After which the Medicine Man warned him to take four days' rest, in order to give the prayers time to reach the spirit world and become effective.

"During those four days you must do no work," the Medicine Man told him. "You are not allowed to wash, particularly you are forbidden to wash away the pollen and flour we have scattered on your body and hair. You must not consort with any woman, nor cut meat, nor tend the fire, but we will allow you to clean the palms of your hands, so long as you do no more than that," he insisted. To all of this The Chanter readily agreed.

The Medicine Man, who was a very busy man, left shortly afterwards. Driving away in a swanky, top of the range land cruiser. The rest of us tucked into a breakfast of mutton stew and fry bread.

While we were eating I took the opportunity to ask Reuben why The Chanter needed to undergo a ceremony of renewal at all.

"It's like executive burn-out," Reuben explained. "You know how hard Blue Horse works with people callin' and comin' by every minute of the day and night. It's the same for my boss, 'cept my man gets international calls too, and since I got him on email it's only got worse. He travels so much these days he's got more air miles than a freakin' bird. After a while it gets to him. He has to take a break, get some renewal, and get some energy back. The Beauty Way is a great way to do it."

I'd never thought of a Medicine Man suffering from anything so garishly modern as executive burn-out. But whatever he was suffering from the Beauty Way certainly cured him. When I met The Chanter again a month or so later, he looked at least twenty years younger. People pay a fortune in London and Los Angeles to have surgery aimed at restoring their youthful looks. All I can say is, the results aren't a patch on what the Navajos can achieve for the price of a few ears of corn and a couple of nights praying.

Later I helped Reuben load The Chanter into the back seat of his truck, where he sat swathed in his brightly coloured blanket to hide the fact that he was still covered from head to toe in flour and pollen, and Reuben drove him home.

I must have passed a kind of test during that ceremony, because some time later Reuben called me on the phone to say The Chanter would like me to attend an all-night prayer meeting he was conducting. All-night prayer ceremonies are usually held in a teepee, although in this case it was held in a hogan. I remember it partly because it was the first of that kind of ceremony I'd attended in a hogan, but a far better reason was because it was at this meeting that I had my first peyote vision. It wasn't a great vision, but it was a start.

In a teepee there is a central fire that is kept burning all night, but in a hogan it is more usual to have a stove in the center, otherwise the smoke can be a nuisance. After the ceremony had been going on for a few hours the Medicine came round in the form of tea. Served up in a bucket which had pictures and Medicine symbols painted on it in blue and gold, it circulated left to right from the door in the Holy Way, accompanied by a little silver cup into which the tea was poured before being drunk. Everyone drank from the cup and there was no attempt to wash or clean it as it passed from person to person. This is normal because Indians believe nothing harmful can enter during a ceremony and that all gathered in fellowship are cleansed by their prayers. White people who worry about such things are best advised to stay away.

Soon the chanting and singing increased in its intensity and the sound level rose as everyone joined in. The result of this continuous, rhythmic, sonorous chanting, coupled with the pulsating beat of the water drum and the jingling of the gourd rattle, undoubtedly contributes to a lowering of consciousness, which must in turn increase the effect of the peyote.

Strangely, the peyote did not taste so bitter as before, nor did it smell so bad. So I took two hefty swigs and passed it on. It must have been powerful stuff, because during the next few hours I watched with interest as the rusty metal side of the stove turned slowly into a magnificent painting reminiscent of William Blake at his best.

A hugely powerful long-haired god appeared holding aloft a great silver trident, and driving forward a herd of plunging red and gold horses. Their manes and tails flying in the wind, the horses galloped across a pale blue-green sky, watched by nymphs and dyads floating among the clouds. It was a fabulous representation and I was sorry when, with the coming of the dawn, it faded away, leaving only a rusty panel on an old stove.

After the ceremony was over one of those odd complications that can bedevil any human activity arose. Reuben, who didn't have any more luck with cars than I did, had leant his *chidi* to a local resident who needed to drive to Shiprock, about forty miles away, to visit his sick mother. The man had assured him he would be back before the prayers ended but he had run out of petrol in Shiprock and, lacking the money to buy more, had hitchhiked home, leaving the car in the car park of a Kentucky Fried Chicken and Reuben and the The Chanter stranded.

"And I was doing him a favour! I try to live a good life and be kind to people and look what happens," Reuben fumed. "They'll be takin' the hub caps an' stealin' the wheels in Shiprock. And the engine, and my radio, and the seats. You couldn't leave a brigade of tanks in Shiprock overnight!"

The Chanter lived more than a hundred miles in the opposite direction to my way home. But as I had to go back via Shiprock, I offered to take them to get Reuben's car.

"Ain't no point, man," Reuben opined gloomily. "We might as well go straight home 'cause the only part of *shichidi* we're gonna find in Shiprock will be the scorch marks on the ground."

Despite my being mounted once more on one of El Dodgy's finest—it was only eighteen dollars a day including insurance, although I doubted they actually had any insurance—it was eventually agreed that I should drive Reuben and The Chanter to Shiprock on the off chance the car had survived the night.

We set off east, driving into the sun. I screwed up my eyes against the dazzling brightness, but apart from that the drive was no different to thousands of others I have made. I like to keep a watchful eye on the mirror when I'm driving, so I can see what's going on behind me. Out of habit I probably check my mirror a little more often than the average motorist. So I was surprised to glance up casually and find a car I swear was not there thirty seconds earlier, now so close it was almost touching the rear bumper. The road was dead straight and flat for miles and I should have seen it. That I had not, I attributed at the time to the sun's dazzle.

It was an odd sort of car, of a type and model with which I was not familiar. Painted a strange off-green, it had a blacked-out windscreen and blacked-out side windows, so no one could see who was travelling inside. Having appeared out of nowhere, it continued to sit irritatingly on my tail at seventy miles per hour. The road was straight as a die and there was nothing coming in the opposite direction to prevent it overtaking me. Yet the unseen driver persisted in driving a couple of feet from my rear bumper.

"Who the hell is this guy?" I said out loud to Reuben. He made no reply and when I looked he was fast asleep.

Every so often the car dropped back a few yards, then slowly closed up again, until it was only inches from my rear bumper. I was in no mood for games after a sleepless night and so the next time he closed up, I dabbed the brakes, hoping to frighten him into staying back. This had no effect, the most likely explanation being that, along with no brakes to speak of, my car had no brake lights either.

We were now tearing along a stretch of road that ran straight for the best part of five miles. It was empty in both directions and if the car behind was going to pass, this was the place to do it. So I slowed slightly to encourage him to come by. The strange car moved slowly onto the other side of the road and into an overtaking position, and I thought he had taken the hint. But, instead, he inched forward until his driver's window was exactly aligned with my front passenger window. As our cars raced side by side, I turned to get a look at whoever was at the wheel, but I could see nothing through the blacked out windows.

The car continued to inch forward, slowly overtaking me until eventually I could see the rear of the vehicle. The thing I noticed was an enormous aerial, much larger than necessary, attached to the boot and bent at an awkward angle that gave an extra air of oddness to what was already a decidedly rum looking *chidi*. At last the car pulled ahead in the opposite lane and I thought it would keep going and that would be the last I saw of it. Instead, it began to drop slowly back again, and after a few minutes resumed its position inches from my tail.

By now I had the impression that whoever was inside was sizing me up. If I hadn't been driving an El Dodgy special I might have put my foot down and tried to outrun him. Although the other car was far more powerful than mine, driving at full speed over desert roads is never easy. The roads may look straight, but they have steep crests and blind summits where they cross the many deep gullies carved into the desert floor. At the end of their long straights, desert roads often enter startlingly sharp twists and turns, where they descend with breathtaking suddenness into deep defiles or curve round low hills.

It takes more than ordinary nerve to keep your foot down while going over those blind crests and the steep twists and turns. Anything from a flock of sheep to an eighteen-wheeler truck could be approaching from the other way, and you would never know it until you met at full speed. Not many drivers have the stomach for this kind of thing, and I would like to have seen what the other driver, who by now was irritating me grossly, was really made of. However, the thought of trying to race in an El Dodgy rust bucket was not very appealing and so I held off.

By now we were travelling at eighty miles per hour and my steering wheel was vibrating violently as we raced up the steep side of one of the many blind summits. Near the top, the other car pulled out and once more came alongside with its speed matched exactly to mine.

Jabbing Reuben in the ribs I yelled, "Look at this! The guy must be crazy!" But Reuben hardly stirred.

The strange car lazily completed its overtaking and, having got in front of me, put its brakes on. There was no choice but for me to brake hard too. However, pressing the pedal had little effect and to avoid hitting him, I was forced to swing on to the opposite side of the road. If I'd been driving the Cougar I'd have put my foot down and overtaken him, blind crest or no blind crest, as by now all I cared about was getting away from the idiot.

But in an El Dodgy special this was impossible, so instead I slowed and began to move back to my own side of the road. As I did so I had a fleeting impression of the car ahead suddenly accelerating very fast. At the same moment the bright, blazing ball of the morning sun appeared over the crest and struck me full in the eyes. Momentarily blinded, I instinctively lifted one hand off the wheel to shield my eyes, and at that moment something huge, something monstrously enormous, shot out of the sun. The air was filled with a deafening wall of sound, a rattling, roaring, banging, and crashing that filled the world. Half a second later came the banshee scream of an air horn, as a fully leaden eighteen-wheeler juggernaut tore over the top of the rise and headed straight towards me, taking up the whole of his side of the road and half of mine.

I flung the rust bucket to the right and found myself careering along on the unmade verge. The worn tyres struggled for grip and the car skidded wildly from side to side in the loose dirt. Somehow I managed to wrestle it back on to the tarmac, but I oversteered and the car began to swing round. I tried to get it back, overdid it again, and we crested the rise going sideways in a pall of smoke and burning rubber. Don't ask me how, but somehow I managed to straighten up, and by taking my foot off the accelerator and dropping down the gear box, managed to bring the car to a halt at the side of the road. When I had time to think about it, I had good cause then to thank the Great Spirit for ensuring El Dodgy had supplied me with a car so lacking of brakes. If they had been working, the violence with which I tried to apply them in these circumstances would probably have caused the car to turn over, sending us spinning down the long, steep slope on the other side of the crest and into eternity.

For a few moments I sat white-faced and shaking, gripping the steering wheel with both hands. Later I discovered I'd unconsciously been gripping it so hard I'd bent it. If I'd delayed moving back to my side of the road by half a second the juggernaut would have hit us and we would all have been dead. If we'd been in the Cougar and I'd accelerated to overtake, we would all have been dead. If the car had any brakes, we'd all have been dead. It had been a damn close thing.

Roused by the violent movements of the car and a volley of unprintable language from my good self, Reuben was now awake, but groggy and disorientated.

"What the hell was that?" he asked rubbing his eyes. "I thought we'd crashed."

"Damn, right," I said. "We nearly did."

"What happened?"

"That car in front nearly did us in." I told him.

"What car?" asked Reuben, staring bleary eyed into the distance.

Looking along the road I could see no sign of the other car. The road was straight for miles and there was nowhere to turn off. Even if there had been, I would have seen the dust trail as it headed into the desert. But there was nothing. In my shaken state I could think of no explanation, other than it must have been travelling extremely fast to get clear out of sight so quickly.

Frustrated by his incomprehension and with my nerves frayed by the nearness of death, I exploded, "That car that followed us! That car that cut in front! That guy nearly killed us! You must have seen him!"

"I didn't see anything," Reuben insisted. "I must have been asleep."

I was about to let rip again when a strong, well-modulated voice interrupted from behind. In the heat of the moment I'd forgotten about The Chanter, who now leaned forward from the back seat and spoke.

"That was Death," he announced calmly. "Death drives a strange car with blacked out windows and a blacked out windshield. He has a big antenna on the back so he can hear all that goes on and everything people are saying. Sometimes he stalks the roads looking for victims to go riding with him and today he found you."

Still in shock, I blurted out, "What?! Takes them *riding*? Where does he take them riding?"

"There is a spiral road that leads to the Land of the Dead, and Death drives along it every day in his car," The Chanter replied. "When his car accelerated away so fast that is where he was going and that's why you can't see him anymore."

Before I came to the land of the Navajo I would have laughed off The Chanter's strange words—but not any more.

Reuben asked, "Where is this road." And he looked scared and his voice sounded squeaky.

"Everywhere," replied The Chanter. "That is why everyone finds themselves travelling it one day. No matter who you are, what you are, or where you are, the spiral road is there for you. One day it will open for you and you will walk to the center of the spiral where all must go. Or, sometimes, Death will take you in his car."

"But why would Death come for us on this road?" I asked, finding it difficult to get my head round the idea.

"He might as well find you on this road as anywhere else," The Chanter replied calmly, and in the mirror I saw him hitch his blanket higher around his shoulders. He was silent for a few seconds before adding, "He came to visit you today because you had a vision last night."

It was true, but I had not told him or anyone else about what I saw in the panel of the stove.

The Chanter continued, "Death knows this and came to see who it is that Mother Peyote has recognised as one of her own. Tell me, was the Medicine bitter last night?"

"No," I said. "It didn't taste bitter at all."

In the mirror The Chanter smiled, "That's because Mother Peyote is getting to know you and this alarms Death. He knows the Medicine will protect you, guide you, and help you. He is suspicious of another power entering your life. He fears the Medicine will weaken his hold over you, and so he came to look you over for himself."

Reuben asked, "I've heard it said that in the old days the great Medicine Men could raise the dead. Is this true?"

The Chanter shook his head. "Death cannot be held at bay forever and those souls that reach the center of the spiral cannot be brought back. For in the center lies the Land of the Dead where the dead dwell forever," he replied. "But sometimes Death can be thwarted for a while. If the Medicine Man is strong enough and brave enough, he can cut across the spiral road and intercept the soul of the departed before it reaches the Land of the Dead. Then it is sometimes possible to bring back the soul so that it can re-enter the body and return to life. It is a hard and dangerous task, and usually it is not possible. Even when it *is* possible, those who attempt it must be good men and strong, and they need the help, strength, and prayers of many good men around them."

I asked, "Is it possible that you can do this?"

But the Chanter made no reply. In the mirror I saw him hitch his blanket up to his ears, indicating he had said enough, and he put his head back against the headrest and went to sleep.

In Shiprock we found Reuben's car sitting undamaged in the car park of Kentucky Fried Chicken.

"I guess I was lucky," he said grudgingly, as we loaded the bags from my car into his. "It wouldn't happen twice."

When we had finished loading the car, The Chanter, who had been standing a few yards away, called us both over and pointed to a spiral he had drawn in the dust with a piece of stick.

"This is where the soul of the newly dead begins its journey," he said, pointing to the beginning of the spiral that wound from left to right in the Holy Way. Pointing to the center he said, "This is where the soul's journey ends and from where none can return." Then, with a dramatic gesture, he slashed through the top of the spiral with his stick, making a long, deep gouge.

"This is the route the Medicine Man must take if he is to intercept the soul on its journey," he said. "He cannot take the road itself, but must cut across it if he is to hope to rescue the soul on its journey. But the way is hard, the obstacles great and numerous, and there are many terrible dangers to be overcome. Even if the soul is found before it reaches the Land of the Dead, it still has to be returned to the Land of the Living. And the terrors encountered coming out may be every bit as terrifying as those found going in."

With that the lesson was over. No questions were allowed and a few minutes later Reuben drove The Chanter home, while I set off towards Blue Horse's.

Needless to say, I drove a lot more carefully going back than I did when I came.

CHAPTER TEN

Visions

FOR SOME TIME AFTERWARDS I wondered about the strange spiral and the strange things The Chanter had said about it. At the back of my mind was the certainty that I had seen that spiral somewhere before. But, try as I might, I could not remember when or where. Only that it had not been in the U.S., but in England.

One morning, while walking by the little chapel that stands near the anthropology block at the University of New Mexico, a man appeared who I had never seen before. His skin was weather beaten to the shade of old brown leather and his clothes were baggy and ill fitting. Long, unkempt hair protruded from beneath a battered sombrero set at a jaunty angle, and on his back he carried a pack so large his slight frame bent forward under the weight. What little could be seen of his face beneath his bushy whiskers wore a strange look of intense detachment, while his eyes appeared fixed on some distant, and as yet unrealised, horizon. Naturally, I took him for an anthropologist, but then something made me think again.

"He looks more like a pilgrim," I thought to myself and immediately the words *"The Pilgrim's Progress,"* flashed into my mind. The penny dropped, and I remembered where I'd seen the spiral road before.

As a young man I lived for a while in Elstow, Bedfordshire, where John Bunyan, the author of *The Pilgrim's Progress*, was born and lived in the mid-1600s. At least, he lived there in between his spells in jail for his religious views. What was believed to be his house was still standing, although much dilapidated at that time.

In the village lived an old lady who was friends with a vicar. This vicar, not the vicar of Elstow I hasten to add, found church life boring, and craving excitement, joined a gang of cattle thieves. With the vicar at the wheel wearing his dog collar to allay suspicion, they went by night to rustle cattle all over Bedfordshire, Buckinghamshire, and Cambridgeshire. The gang made many successful forays, but their luck ran out one night and they were all arrested and subsequently jailed.

As the younger son of minor aristocracy, the vicar was the only member of the gang with any assets, and some of his farmer victims got together to sue him for damages. To thwart them, his family dispersed as much of his property as possible among his few remaining friends, and that was how the old lady came into possession of a very fine, and very old copy of *The Pilgrim's Progress*. She delighted to tell me the story of the cattle-rustling vicar again and again and sometimes, when she had finished, she would bring out the book and let me leaf through its thick pages with their old fashioned print.

"Be careful with it, dear," she would caution as she handed it over. "I have to give it back when he comes out of prison."

The book had a map showing Christian's route from the start of his journey at the wicket gate to his destination at the Celestial City. This map, with the Slough of Despond, Vanity Fair, Doubting Castle, and other points en route clearly marked, was drawn in the shape of a spiral. With the Celestial City — the Land of the Dead by another name — at its center.

It seemed extraordinary that an artist in England, with no tradition to call upon, and a Navajo Medicine Man, with a tradition going back to the Ice Age, should both represent the soul's journey to the other world as a spiral path. I later learned that this journey is represented as a spiral in many ancient cultures. Perhaps it is one of those human universals that are hardwired into our brains. Things we all know instinctively, without knowing that we know them.

The Pilgrim's Progress is quintessentially English and Protestant—and seventeenth-century English and Protestant at that—and to some people it is a mystery that it has come to be admired by people so diverse as Moslem clerics, South Sea Islanders, Tokyo bankers, and just about anyone else you can think of. To me this is no mystery at all. *The Pilgrim's Progress* is a great visionary story simply told, and as such strikes a cord in us all.

Bunyan says in the opening lines that the story came to him in a dream as he lay in Bedford jail. "As I walked through the wilderness of this world, I lighted on a certain place, where was a den; and laid me down in that place to sleep; and as I slept I dreamed a dream."

Three hundred years earlier William Langland, the author of *Piers Plowman*, the greatest of all English visionary poems, told how he fell asleep in the Malvern Hills, lay down beside a brook, and dreamed such monumental dreams that he spent the rest of his life rendering them into that vast poem. Visionary dreaming is a long-standing part of our human heritage

I mention all this only because, unknown to me, my time of dreaming was fast approaching. At least, I have tried many times to tell myself it was a dream, but it is hard to say if the events I am about to relate were real or not. All I can say is they seemed real enough to me at the time.

It was September, temperatures had cooled, and rainstorms lashed the desert, soaking the cacti, drenching the junipers, and turning the parched sand to glutinous mud. At night the temperature plummeted, so when I slept out I needed two blankets inside my sleeping bag if I was not to shiver awake at four A.M.

I had not seen Reuben again for some time when word came that he was camped in a wickiup somewhere along the the northern border between Navajo territory and the state of Utah, at the bottom of the deep San Juan River gorge. ("Wickiup" is a word used by both whites and Indians to designate an Indian bivouac. Tribes of different regions have different ways of making them, and even within tribes the method of making a wickiup can vary according to the materials available.). It would be poetic to say Reuben had gone there to seek spiritual renewal in the awesome quiet and loneliness of the place. The truth was that his girlfriend had thrown him out and he had nowhere else to go. I wasn't doing much better myself, but I wanted to see Reuben before leaving for what threatened to be a long stay in England. So I gathered together the last vestiges of my former wealth and, taking my life in my hands, hired yet another car from El Dodgy and set out to find him.

It took half a day to get up to the San Juan, and I spent another couple of hours driving along the rim of the gorge, trying to spot his camp a couple of hundred feet below. It was impossible. I couldn't see a thing from the rim, so I abandoned the car and found a steep and perilous sheep track that took me to the bottom of the towering cliffs. Once at the bottom I walked up and down the riverbank shouting myself hoarse until it began to go dark.

I was about to throw in the towel and head for home, when I paused on the stony riverbank beside a large willow thicket. After a few moments I heard a strange wailing noise coming from the far side of the thicket, and in the fading light spotted a thin wisp of smoke rising into the air. Plunging into the undergrowth, I crashed my way through the willows and emerged onto a sandy promontory, where the dark brown waters of the San Juan lapped by on three sides. Lying stark naked on his back, looking up at Father Sky and bemoaning his fate, was Reuben.

"Bitch! Bitch!" he cried out loud to Father Sky. "And I loved her too!"

So obsessed was he with his woman troubles that, despite me making as much noise coming through the willows as a herd of buffalo, he had failed to notice my arrival. I announced myself by throwing a clod of earth at him.

"Charles!" he gasped, sitting up and looking round. "You're here!" He jumped up and embraced me. Then, clearly a man in the grip of obsession, he gushed, "I was going to marry her. I really, really loved her. Everything was fine until a couple of weeks ago and then she started in on me. I don't know why. Suddenly she seemed to hate me like I was some turd floating by. What have I done to deserve that? She asked me to come and live with her. I didn't suggest it, it was her idea. She'd been on me for months to go and live with her and I'm there six weeks and she throws me out! Why? I don't understand. I didn't do anything bad. I'm a nice guy. I love her! Why, why, why?" And so on, and so forth, ad infinitum. Doubtless he would have carried on for several centuries had I allowed him to do so. To stop his whingeing, I asked if he was hungry and it turned out he was, having run out of supplies the day before and having had no luck fishing.

Once his attention switched, he shut up long enough to put his clothes on, and for me to advise him that there was a little food in my car. In the fading light I could no longer find the sheep track that brought me down, and we had no choice but to free climb straight up the sheer cliff wall. It was not as bad as it looked and we found a surprising number of bucket holds and lesser holds and reached the top quite easily. It took a little more time to locate the car, but we found it in the end and retrieved some meager supplies of bacon, a few potatoes, and a handful of PG Tips tea for me.

It was dark by the time we started the climb down and neither of us was dressed for it. We were doing fine until my cheap trainers lost their grip while trying to negotiate a small overhang and I fell several feet onto a ledge. There was no harm done, apart from some bruises, but it proved how steep and dangerous the cliff was, particularly in the dark. Reuben traversed across and, leaning over, lifted me to safety with one arm. I hadn't realised until then how strong he was. We eventually slithered down to the bottom and after gathering some willow twigs for a fire, I began cooking our frugal meal outside the wickiup.

Reuben's wickiup was a traditional Navajo lash-up, about eight feet in diameter with the walls made of tumbleweed and sage piled about five feet high. There was no roof, but the walls curved in and narrowed at the top, so that any rain or snow would blow straight over, leaving the occupants dry inside. An ideal, I might say, that is by no means always achieved. To make an entrance Reuben had simply carved through the east-facing wall with a knife to create what looked like a large mouse hole. To get in or out we went down on our hands and knees and crawled through.

The night was overcast, the moon had not yet risen and the only light in the encircling darkness came from our tiny campfire. After eating, we talked inconsequentially for a while, during which time I tried to steer him away from the subject of his broken heart, and eventually we began to speak of peyote Medicine.

"It changes your view of everything when you take the Peyote Road," Reuben said.

I had not heard the term before and so I asked he what he meant by "the Peyote Road."

"It's the road you take that leads you to a better and more meaningful life. It doesn't matter who you are or how far you've fallen or how well you're doing or how good or bad you are. If you keep taking the Medicine and praying and living in a Holy Way, then after a while the world stops looking the way you thought it looked, and starts to look like something much better. You begin to see things that others can't, you hear songs others can't, you see the thoughts of others, and hear the voices of spirits whispering in the wind. You begin to realise that the world we're living in is only a tiny part of the real world, and there are many other worlds within this one, as well as outside it. That knowledge alone allows you to become a better person. But there's more, much more."

I asked him what he meant by "much more," but he admitted he did not know and excused his ignorance by saying that he had not yet himself progressed far enough to have accumulated such knowledge.

Later, as I advanced in my own understanding, I had dramatic evidence for some of this myself when, sometimes for weeks after Medicine ceremonies the earth itself seemed to come alive. Where previously I had seen only an oddly shaped hill, I now saw the face and body of a brooding warrior. Trees took on distinct, and not always kindly, personalities. An outcrop of rocks would change into a leaping deer, or a standing buffalo bull, and return to rock only when I drew close to examine them. When I walked away again they changed back into living things.

"The earth is alive," Blue Horse once told me. "All creatures come from the earth and return into it. You know that to be true, *Chizchillie*. But only when you take the Medicine and live in a Holy Way are you permitted to see these things for yourself."

As we talked, Reuben batted away a mosquito that had somehow managed to survive a couple of cold nights in the gorge.

"Take a look at that mosquito and think how different his world is to ours," he said. "All the other mosquitoes look huge to it and if you look at one closely, you'll see that it looks more like a *chįǧ'hyee'a dilohii*." (*Chįǧ'hyee'a dilohii* means "elephant," or more literally, "He Ropes With His Nose." This is a particularly charming example of how Navajo astutely avoids loan words from English or any other language.) Reuben went on, "That's how a mosquito looks to other mosquitoes. But to a mosquito we look as big as that cliff we just climbed and we move about as fast. While you or I are thinking a single thought, days of his life are going by. All his life takes place in the short time he has to hatch, fly about, drink blood, breed, and die. If you think about it, you'll see that the mosquito's world has nothing to do with our world, or ours with his. If we all disappeared tomorrow he wouldn't notice and would carry on as if we had never existed at all. The same is true of fish, or the night bird singing over there in the bush. We all exist in the same place at the same time, but the world of the bird, the world of the fish, the world of the mosquito, and the world of the man are all different worlds. They don't even look the same. The Medicine helps you understand all this, and once you understand, you see that what you thought was so, is not so. Once you know that, you can start to learn something."

"This is what The Chanter teaches you?" I asked.

"Yes," he replied gravely. "This and much more."

A few moments later Reuben crawled away from the firelight and went inside the wickiup. He emerged with a little wooden pipe and a pouch of white doe hide.

"It's some smoke from Mexico," he explained, drawing close to the fire and opening the leather pouch. "The old people like The Chanter don't approve. They believe the only medicine is the Medicine. But I'm more modern, I've been south into Mexico and north to Canada and Alaska and the tribes there use other things besides the Medicine. Here, try some of this," and he offered me the pipe and pouch.

"What is it?" I asked.

"I don't know the white man's name for it," he confessed. "In Mexico the Indians call it a smoke."

"What does it do?"

Reuben wrinkled his brow. "It's kind of hard to describe exactly," he said. "You know how the Medicine makes you see things differently? Well, this does too, but everything happens much faster."

"How much faster?"

"You go down fast to a different place where you see and hear things. Then it brings you up again," Reuben said. "There's a tribe of Indians in Mexico who become invisible once a year. They use it and I thought you'd like to try."

"They become invisible?" I was not sure I'd heard right. "Are you sure?"

"I talked to them and they told me," he insisted. "They become invisible and go into invisible houses and sit there all day and no one can see them."

"And if I smoke this stuff I become invisible?" I asked.

"No, I don't think you become invisible, but the ground opens and swallows you. Then it vomits you up and you come alive again. It's like you die and come back to life. Those Indians say that's a very holy thing to do."

"And you've done this?" I asked.

"Yes."

"And the earth swallowed you?"

"I went somewhere, that's for sure," Reuben said, still holding out the white doe skin pouch and the little wooden pipe to me. I could see in his face that he feared I would refuse.

While we were talking, the clouds had cleared and the night had become cooler. Above us the stars glittered like ice, while the moon rose over the rim of the cliff and bathed us in its cold light. By some geological oddity, on the rim of the gorge almost directly above us, there was a mound that rose sixty feet above the otherwise straight cut of the cliff. As the moon rose, it appeared to roll gently up the slope of this mound, rather like a large, bright yellow bicycle wheel. When it reached the top it paused for a few moments, before beginning its ascent into the heavens. It was a beautiful sight, and probably I would have been happy contemplating the vastness of the universe for several hours more, had Reuben not drawn my attention once more to the smoke.

"I'll watch over you," he assured me, offering the pipe and bag to me again.

"How will you watch if I become invisible?" I was only half serious.

"I really don't think you'll become invisible."

"Do I need watching?" I asked.

"I don't know," he confessed. "I'll watch anyway."

He pressed the pouch into my hand and, after a moment's hesitation, I opened it and found inside a few pinches of what looked like dried tea leaves. Except among them flecks of deep green flickered like phosphorescence from the sea.

"Is this all?" I asked, peering into the pouch. "It looks like tea leaves."

"Yeah," he confirmed. "That's all."

"And the green shiny stuff?"

"It's real," Reuben confirmed. "I can see it too."

"OK," I said. "I'll try it."

After carefully filling the little wooden pipe, I took a burning twig from the fire and touched it to the bowl, watched as the contents glowed fiery, and inhaled deeply. The "tea leaves" burnt remarkably quickly and after a couple of puffs were all done.

I waited for a few moments but nothing happened, so I took another pinch, filled the bowl again, and smoked that too. Now I became aware I was concentrating rather too hard on the pipe and, wrestling my concentration away, looked up to speak to Reuben, only to find he had gone. I had not seen him go and thinking he had gone inside the wickiup I stood up to follow. As I did so there was a deafening roar and something vast reared up over my left shoulder. A fraction of a second later a huge black tidal wave surged out of the darkness of the gorge and swept me away. I remember the silver disc of the moon performing a strange, watery parabola, and then I was spinning over and over, round and round, into total blackness and oblivion.

The next thing I knew I was inside something that at first appeared to be a room. Except the concept of "inside" was incomprehensible, as there was no "outside." There was neither inside nor outside—both existed at once, together, in the same place, and were all encompassing. From this outside-inside, inside-outside, I heard the voice of my grandfather, who had died forty-three years earlier, calling to me. I answered and was surprised to hear myself talking in the broad Lancashire dialect of my childhood. Try as I might, I could no longer speak standard English, perhaps because when my grandfather and I last spoke, that was the speech we used. I cannot recount what was said, but while we were speaking, a strange, bitter taste began to enter my mouth. It was an unusual flavor, but one I knew I had tasted before.

I searched my memory for that taste and suddenly, I was an infant again, chewing at the bottom of my great aunt's back door. When I was a little child I liked to gnaw at the wood at the bottom of her door, for what reason I cannot say. Now that taste, woody, bitter, redolent of old paint and varnish, flooded back into my mouth and mind. As quickly as it had come, the image and taste faded to be replaced by a strange noise: a hollow, echoing, ringing sound that seemed to fill the world.

"Oud Jimmy!" I thought.

Old Jimmy, or "Oud" Jimmy, as we would have said, must have been one of the last to wear wooden clogs in Lancashire, and it was the sound of those clogs ringing on the cobbles that now assailed my ears. I have only one remembered sight of him from my childhood, which I had forgotten until it returned to me in these visions. A small, wizened, bent old man, shabbily dressed in working clothes from half a century earlier. Walking gamely up the hill to his employment at the mill, as he had on almost all the days of his life, for I believe he began work when he was ten years old.

Every morning I heard him as I lay awake in the back room of my grandmother's house, or at the home of my great aunt two doors away. Especially on dark, frosty winter mornings, when the air was crisp and clear, the sound of those clogs would come pulsing between the cracks around the widow frames, oscillating down the chimney and up through the holes in the floor. There were factory hooters then that sounded for the morning shift at seven A.M. At first only those close by blew, then further and further off, all the hooters of Lancashire and Cheshire joined in until, around the corner Oud Jimmy's footsteps faded, the hooters ceased, and the morning once more fell still.

Again the scene shifted, and now a strange village floated in the air. Slowly, I realised that it was not the village that was floating but I, who was swimming in the cold English sea. Bobbing up and down, looking up at a village on the shore while the water lapped, lapped, lapped me by little waves, closer and closer to the land.

I awoke to find it was dank early morning. I was covered in mud, wet through and shivering violently on the cold sandy floor of the wickiup. At first I thought I must have fallen into the river, but further investigation showed I'd pissed myself. What concerned me more, however, was what I had seen. For all of those things had long been expunged from my consciousness, and if I had been put to the torture, I could not have told that once I chewed the bottom of the door, or saw a man who went to work in wooden clogs.

As the light improved I could make out the dark hump of Reuben's body slumped sound asleep on the opposite side of the wickiup. Feeling thirsty I crawled outside and made my way to the river's edge. Still on all fours I lowered my face into the mud brown waters and drank like an animal. The gorge was filled with mist, there was not a breath of breeze, and no sound was to be heard but the drip of moisture falling from the willows. Nothing moved until, out of the murk, the vague gray outline of an enormous bird appeared, flying silently only a few feet above the water. Then came another and another. No wing beat was heard, and they uttered no cry, as silently they passed like ghosts along the gorge.

Taking off my clothes I rinsed myself in the river using handfuls of mud mixed with grit to scrub my skin clean. I rinsed my clothes through and hung them to dry on some willows. Cold and naked, I gathered twigs for a fire while the mist condensed on my skin, turned to water, and ran in rivulets down my back and chest, on down my thighs, and off my knees to the ground. A coyote barked, the light began to brighten, the mist thinned, and from a bush a little bird began to sing.

What followed was a very strange day.

Reentering the wickiup, I soon had a good blaze going in the middle and set about cooking breakfast. The smell of sizzling bacon roused Reuben, who was never good in the mornings. "*Gohwééh*," he croaked, holding out his hand for a mugful like a junky for a fix. But there was no coffee, only PG Tips tea. Not that it mattered much, because like many Navajos, he put so much sugar in his drinks he could have been drinking petrol for all he could tell. In this case, there was no sugar. After we had eaten what little there was, and drunk black, sugarless tea, I took him to task for disappearing the evening before.

"You promised to watch over me. I could have fallen in the river and drowned," I complained.

"I didn't go anywhere," he protested indignantly. "You fell down and passed out. I watched you writhe around for a while, then dragged you inside for your own safety. You were shaking and mumbling and I looked after you 'till you lay quiet and fell asleep. You're ungrateful."

"Reuben," I said, quite sure of my facts, "after the second pipe I looked up and you weren't there."

"I was there!" he yelled, pointing through the entrance to the spot where he had sat. "I never left you."

"If you were there why couldn't I see you? I was only a few feet away."

"I dunno." He was silent for a few seconds before adding grumpily, "Remember those Indians who become invisible? Maybe, when they smoke, it's not them who becomes invisible, but everyone else."

"Maybe," I said, but I didn't believe it.

Later I went hunting with Reuben's little .22 rifle. We had eaten all my meagre supplies and had no money, so there was little choice but to go looking for birds and rabbits. Before I went, Reuben took me to the water's edge where he scooped up a big handful of mud and rubbed it into my hair.

"That's to get rid of the human smells like bacon and smoke, so the animals won't sniff the wind and know you're coming," he said. He took more mud and smeared it all over my still naked body, until I was covered in a thick layer of dark red mud.

"That's the traditional way to do it," he said, stepping back to admire his handiwork. "The mud will keep you warm even without clothes."

He was right. As it dried the mud protected my skin from the worst of the damp and cold, and later from the heat when the sun finally broke through.

Clothed only in mud, I hunted along the lonely banks of the San Juan River for hours. The camouflage worked and I had sight of many rabbits and birds. But there was something wrong with the gun and I couldn't hit anything. It took some time for me to notice that it was shooting about six feet to the left. I don't know why. When I adjusted my aim I quickly shot two big rabbits. I paunched them using a stone blade I made by smashing two stones together, threw the entrails into the river for the fishes, and proudly took the carcasses back to camp. When I arrived The Chanter was sitting outside the wickiup in deep conversation with Reuben.

"Hello," I said to The Chanter. "Have you come to see me?"

The Chanter looked up disdainfully and replied, "It is for the pupil to come to the master and not the other way round."

"I have come to you," I said, pointing back along the path over which I'd walked to the wickiup. But he took no notice and with a wave of his hand dismissed me. Somehow I could not go and remained embarrassed and motionless standing before him. Sympathetic to my plight, Reuben handed me a few fresh peyote buttons, and when I ate them they were not bitter at all.

The Chanter continued to refuse to acknowledge me and so, dejected, I wandered back to the river and made another stone blade to skin the rabbits. After throwing the bloody skins into the river to join the intestines, I slowly made my way back to camp again, carrying a freshly skinned corpse in each hand. With their long back legs and short fore legs, the rabbits closely resembled the bodies of still-born premature babies fresh from the womb. Their huge dead eyes stared from their little baby skulls, and their deathly white flesh was flecked with blood and muck as if from birthing.

The Chanter had gone, and in his place was a bag of fresh peyote buttons the size of a small sack. From a distance I thought the sack was The Chanter, as it occupied exactly the same place next to Reuben as he had done, and as I approached the two appeared to be in deep in conversation.

I gave Reuben the rabbits and he smiled and quietly thanked me, before opening the sack to give me more buttons to eat. Once more they did not taste bitter, instead they were chewy, like fresh, raw mushrooms. He told me to help myself, but I declined and instead lit a new fire outside the wickiup and began to cook one of the rabbits. While I was cooking I heard children singing a long way off, a song I did not know or understand. I asked Reuben if there was a school in the area, but he shook his head. Later I realised the singing was the sound of steam emerging from the broken ends of the wet willow twigs I was trying to burn.

The rabbit was half raw when we ate it, and afterwards I made tea in an old tin can; perhaps we put buttons in the tea, I don't remember. I know that I put my clothes on again. They were still wet but it didn't matter, because I needed to be decently dressed so that we could pray.

We ate more peyote buttons and drank more tea and Reuben fetched his water drum while I threw more wet wood on the fire. Then we sang and drummed and prayed and ate the sacred Medicine, until the moon rose over the cliff and ran up the side of the mound as before. It was now *hanlibąąz*, the time of the full moon and as its huge, yellow, disc hung poised in the act of lifting itself into space, I saw silhouetted against it the stark, black figures of three men standing on top of the mound.

They appeared so suddenly it was almost as if they had stepped out of the moon. For a few seconds they remained still as statues looking down on our little camp. Then, as the moon began its graceful rise, the three figures started to descend the steep slope. As they stepped over the edge of the lowering cliff they were lost to sight, but after a short while I heard them coming through the willows. Soon they entered our camp and stood at the edge of the little circle of light cast by our fire. It was impossible to see them clearly but I greeted them kindly.

"*Ya'at'eeh*," I said warmly. "*Shi Charles yinishye. Dóó bilagáana bá shíshchíín.* "Hello, my name is Charles. My clan is the White Man clan."

It was a standard Navajo greeting, but they took no notice and stood silently looking at us while deep shadows danced all around them. As they would not come any closer, I took a handful of dry leaves and grass I had been keeping as tinder and threw it on the fire, so that it flared up and cast a wider light. As the flames leapt I saw these men were not Navajos, but Indians of another tribe. They wore eagle feathers in their hair, which was braided and hung down to their waists, and instead of working clothes they wore deerskin and were wrapped in buffalo robes.

"They want you to go with them," I heard Reuben say, but when I looked at him, I saw that he had not spoken, but was seated resolutely on the ground playing his drum. One of the men held out his hand to me and the other two nodded and indicated that I should join them.

Standing up, I asked, "Where are we going?"

"West," someone said. It didn't sound like the English or Navajo word for "west" but somehow I knew what he meant.

"North," said someone else, and again it didn't sound like "north," but I understood.

Silently we walked out of camp, walked up the cliff face that previously I had found so hard to climb, and then turned west following the gorge of the San Juan. We entered Monument Valley in the moonlight and passed beneath the huge buttes and rock formations that have justly caused this placed to be dubbed the Eighth Wonder of The World. The moon shadows stretched for miles and were so deep and dark it was as if we walked through the Valley of the Shadow of Death. At length we came to the sea and turned north along the coast until we reached a river so wide, running through a gorge so deep, at first I could see nothing but the waters sliding by like an endless black velvet band.

In a patch of moonlight a canoe appeared. As it drew closer it revealed itself to be a traditional Indian birch bark canoe, paddled by a man holding an outsized paddle who stood, rather than sat, in the stern. Gently, the canoe grounded on the little stones of the shore and the boatman invited us by gesture to step aboard. I turned to see what my companions would do, and found myself staring at Reuben.

"I didn't know you were here," I said.

"I've been right behind you all the way, man," he told me.

"All the time?" I was puzzled.

"All the time, all the way," he repeated.

"Why didn't I notice?" I asked.

"I dunno."

"Where are we going?"

"Stop asking questions, white man, and you might learn something," someone else said sharply. "If you white people listened more and talked less we'd all do a lot better."

Except he didn't quite say that. Instead I heard the sound of a words fluttering around the canoe like strange birds, each one carrying a message that I did not understand, but somehow recognised.

When we were all aboard, the boatman pushed off and paddled the canoe out into the black waters. By now I'd seen a lot of Indians, but never one like this boatman. He was short, about five-foot-six, and his trousers were so long and wide they completely covered his feet, giving the impression he was growing directly out of the bottom of his canoe. His clothes were generally ill-fitting and dirty and his hair was long, black, and unkempt. But it was his face that riveted me. If you can imagine Ghengis Khan after six months on the booze—on a really bad day—then this fellow looked a lot worse than that. Eyes bloodshot, face raddled, body short and twisted as if by some deformity, he appeared not quite human. Yet he knew his job and landed us safely on the other side where, after we had disembarked, we set off once more walking into the night.

We travelled so far north it began to snow and soon the drifts were so deep I had difficulty walking. Someone gave me a parka made of fur to keep out the cold and a pair of snowshoes to help me walk. These were not the traditional native "tennis racket" snowshoes made of wood and sinew, but modern aluminum ones with built in crampons to aid my grip. Even with these firmly on my feet, I still sank up to my knees in the snow until I found the knack. After that I whizzed along through the arctic night for many miles, until we passed through the great northern forest and out onto the treeless tundra, where the Northern Lights came out in all their glory and splendour.

It was coming dawn when we rounded a bend between two snow-covered hills to see a thin plume of smoke rising from behind a dense thicket of dwarf willows.

"Over there," someone shouted, and we made our way through the thicket. On the other side was a little rectangular house made of bent willows, with walls two feet thick made of dense, spongy moss.

Behind the house we found three men, dressed in skins like Eskimos, who were pulling hard on a long, thick rope made of some kind of twisted hide. They were hauling with all their strength and panting and sweating, but so far as I could see the rope was attached to nothing and was merely lying on top of the snow. As we approached the three called to us and begged us to help them pull.

"This rope is tied to our brother's soul and we're trying to pull him free from Death," one of the men shouted frantically. "Please help us, or surely our brother will be lost forever."

I unstrapped my snowshoes and, taking my place on the rope, pulled with a will. All my companions joined in, but no matter how hard we pulled, we could not shift it one inch. Worse, something was pulling back, and pulling back hard, and we began to lose ground.

"Death is pulling him down!" one of the brothers cried in despair. "Pull harder!" We did, but to no avail.

After a while I abandoned my position and walked to where the end of the rope lay on top the snow. It was tied to nothing so, with the intention of showing the others they were victims of a trick, I bent down to pick it up. But when I tried to lift it, the loose end seemed to weigh a million tons. No matter how hard I pulled, it wouldn't budge! There was a stone axe with a wooden handle propped up against the side of the hut and, figuring the rope was frozen to the snow, I fetched the axe and hammered away at the rope to knock it free. Again, no matter how hard I hammered, the rope refused to budge.

"Don't pull from that end, white brother," the others cried when they saw what I was doing. "Don't cut the rope with that axe or our brother's soul will be lost. Take your place with us again for we need your strength."

I did as they asked and pulled until the sweat ran from me in rivers. But the contest proved unequal and, inch by inch, we lost ground.

Eventually, one of the three brothers fetched a stake of wood as thick as my thigh and six feet long and hammered it into the snow. When it had frozen firm he took the end of the rope and secured it to the top of the stake.

"At least our brother can't be pulled down any further," he announced, as exhausted, we flopped down in the snow to rest. Even as he spoke the huge stake quivered and bent like a fisherman's rod, but mercifully it held firm.

By now we were too tired to do more and so, when one of the brothers led the way into the hut, we all followed. Inside, lying on a pile of sumptuous furs, beside a small fire of willow twigs, was a fourth man. He lay pale and still and when his brothers pulled back the furs to examine him he was devoid of any sign of life.

The oldest brother pointed to a container made of thick, leathery birch bark that stood near the fire.

"We believe that by witchcraft our brother came to mix fish and meat in the same dish," he explained. "This is taboo among our people as it offends the Mistress who gave us the birds of the air, the animals of the land, and the fish of the sea. When we kill a creature and eat it, it passes through our bodies and the Mistress collects the pieces and makes it whole again, so that it can be hunted and killed again and we can eat. She gives us a never-ending supply of fish, birds, and game to feed and clothe us, on the condition that we never mix their flesh together in our cooking vessels. For if we do, she can never separate all the pieces and make the animals live again, and in that case all life will disappear from the earth, the sky, and the seas, and we will surely starve. By witchcraft our brother was made to break this taboo, and even though he was trapped into it by those who sent evil against him, it is for this reason he has lost his soul. The Mistress was angry and made him so sick that his soul was driven from his body and began its journey to the Land of the Dead.

"When he heard what had happened our Medicine Man made a big Medicine and his own soul left his body to go in search of the soul of our brother. But our Medicine Man is old and has grown weak, and when he found our brother's soul he lacked the strength to bring it home. So he tied a rope of walrus hide around him, because walrus hide is the strongest rope there is, and brought the end back to us. We hoped that we could pull our brother's soul up from the underworld, but we too lack the strength," he finished sadly.

One of the three men who had brought us from the San Juan now spoke, saying, "In a dream your Medicine Man came to us and begged our help, but we too are grown old. So we have brought you these two men who are full of strength and vigour. The young Navajo man is strong in the arm and leg and moves swiftly, while the white man is strong in his mind and believes in our Medicine. It is these two who will save your brother if he can be saved."

I looked over a Reuben and was about to ask something, but he cut me short.

"No more questions," he said and darted out of the hut.

Without stopping even to collect his snowshoes, he ran up the snow-covered hill behind the hut and disappeared down the steep slope on the other side. Not knowing what else to do, I followed and at the bottom of the slope found him standing by the bank of a frozen river. The snow cover had been blown off the ice by a stiff wind and the river formed a long, smooth, glittering highway that bent away to the right and disappeared between two far hills. Pausing for scarcely a second, Reuben stepped onto the ice and began to jog downstream towards the two hills.

"Come on," he called over his shoulder. "There's not a moment to lose." Pulling my fur parka around me for warmth, I followed as fast as I could.

It is remarkable how quickly, and with how little effort, it is possible to move down the almost imperceptible incline of a frozen river, and we reached the bend and passed between the two far hills in double quick time. As we came out of their valley I saw in the distance a great smoke rising into the sky and called out a warning, "The ice is on fire!"

Reuben laughed. "It's a waterfall," he called over his shoulder. "That "smoke" is mist and spray from the falls." He quickened the pace.

The river may have been frozen on top but it was obviously flowing fast and strong underneath. Before long a rumble could be heard that quickly grew to a roar as, moving at a cracking pace, we entered the thundering mist. It grew thicker around us with every step, and soon it was impossible to see one's hand in front of one's face. The thunder increased until it was all but deafening, and I realised we must be drawing close to the edge of a mighty waterfall.

Vainly, I cried out to Reuben, begging him to stop, or at least to slow down, but he plunged on ahead and was lost to my sight. Frightened and alone, deafened and blind, I came to a standstill fearing that one false step would take me over the edge and into oblivion.

Turning this way and that in the mist I shouted for Reuben, but soon gave up as I could not even hear my own voice over the roar of the water. Realising it was hopeless, I was about to press gingerly on, when I was struck by a new fear: that by racing ahead Reuben had plunged over the falls. If he had, the only way I could help him was to climb out onto the riverbank and climb down the rocks to the bottom of the falls. It was certain there would be a large pool at the bottom and in that pool I would find Reuben. But whether alive or dead, I could only guess.

With this in mind I turned to walk towards the bank, only to realise that after turning around while shouting and yelling, I was completely disorientated and had no idea in which direction the bank might lie. This was truly terrifying. One false step in any direction might take me over the edge to my death. Lost in a world of blinding white mist and deafening noise, I screamed once more at the top of my voice for Reuben, crying like a child for a parent. But my ears could detect no sound from my mouth and even if they had, it would have been to no avail as Reuben could not have heard above that din.

The best way to defeat panic is to sit down on the ground, because solid ground restores confidence to the mind, and gives it time to regain its composure. Shaking and sweating I settled myself down on all fours, and if the ice was not as comforting as the good earth, at least for the moment I was out of immediate danger. As the trembling in my arms and legs subsided and my breathing grew easier, I regained enough of myself to remember that by moving my head from side to side, and carefully turning round a few times, it would be possible to work out from which direction the thunder of the falling water sounded loudest. That would tell me where the edge lay and with my sense of direction restored, I could find the riverbank. Raising myself onto all fours, I was just about to do this when the mist darkened overhead and an enormous shadow spread across it.

Looking up, I saw the shadow form itself into an enormous head, stretched and distorted in the fog, in the same way the human face is stretched and distorted by wide-screen cinema and television. Fifty feet long and fifty feet wide, it was the head of a woman with strands of hair writhing in all directions like a head full of serpents. I tried to tell myself it must be an illusion, a trick of the mist or light. Then the vast, blackened face bent towards me and out of the mist a hand came from behind and gripped my shoulder.

So great was the shock that, even though I was still on all fours, I rose some considerable distance vertically, before crashing down onto the ice again, where I lay for several seconds winded and in pain. When I began to take notice once more, the first thing I saw was a familiar pair of boots a few inches from my nose Then the rest of Reuben appeared out of the murk as he bent down towards me.

"Man, am I happy to see you!" I shouted with relief. "I thought you'd gone over the edge."

Reuben was not listening, or more likely could not hear. Instead he pressed his lips to my ear.

"Did you see her?" he demanded. "Did you see the Mistress of the Animals?"

"That shadow?" I asked and, looking up, saw that it was gone.

"That was the she-god," he yelled. "The Mistress. The one the brother angered. Now she's mad with us for coming here."

"Let's go back!" I cried, scared out of my wits.

"We can't," Reuben shouted emphatically. "There's no way back until we've rescued the soul of the lost brother."

"How?" I yelled. "How are we going to do that? We don't even know where he is! We don't even know where we are!"

Reuben looked at me as if I was a simpleton and stamped his foot on the ice. "This is the road The Chanter spoke about," he roared. "The road to the Land of the Dead and beyond those falls lies Hell. Only the dead can pass beyond this point. The she-god guards the way to destroy all living things that go beyond the falls."

Scarcely were the words out of his mouth when the world began to grow dark again and the shadow once more loomed over us.

"We must ask her permission to go further," Reuben shouted, his mouth almost touching my ear.

Above us the great head wove its way back and forth in the mist, seeking us out amid the gloom, while we lay motionless on the ice hoping it would pass by. Unfortunately, after a short while, the she-god seemed to locate us and the great head bent closer, her wild hair lashing in all directions, and her she-god's breath coming hissing and steaming hot through the fog. From some-where I heard a woman's voice, deep and low, like no woman's voice I have ever heard, boom, "I AM HERE!" A pulse of white light shot through the mist and I thought our last moments had come. But even as I despaired, Reuben stood up, turned towards the vast head, and began to sing.

With his arms held out in a gesture of supplication he sang the most beautiful Indian song I ever heard. He sang of light and life, the good earth and greenery. He sang of the great waters, the mighty sky, the sun, the moon, and the stars. He sang of greatness and wonder and of all the eternal and alluring mysteries of being. And as his voice soared it sliced through the foggy gloom like a sword of light. The thunderous noise of the falls grew less, the mist thinned, and the great shadow slowed. Its terrible hair stopped lashing, and slowly it grew smaller and smaller until it dis-appeared altogether. It was only later that I realised Reuben's song had not been in Navajo, but in some other language I had never heard before. But of which, strangely, I understood every word.

By the time Reuben stopped singing the sun had come out. In only a few minutes it soaked up the mist to reveal that, what we had thought were mighty falls, was nothing more than a small cas-cade tumbling over a jumble of little rocks.

Quickly we headed for the riverbank and climbed out before making an easy descent of the little falls. About a hundred yards further on, the river was frozen again, and we clambered back on to the ice for ease of movement. As we did so, I looked back and saw an Indian woman dressed in traditional winter furs, standing near the base of the falls, looking at us.

"I get it!" I said to Reuben, pointing at the woman and laughing. "It's an ordinary woman. It must have been a trick of the light that made her shadow look like a she-god."

"If you believe that, white man, you'll believe anything," Reuben replied disdainfully. "That's the Mistress and I calmed her. It's only because I pleased her with my song that she's taken on the shape of a woman and allow us to pass."

We moved swiftly on once more until, around another bend, we found a group of fur-clad men who were beating on the ice with long willow sticks as they walked downstream. When we came alongside I saw they were chuckling to themselves.

"We're fishing," they replied, when I asked what they were doing.

"Why so happy?" I wanted to know.

"Our fish are happy little people and we laugh and chuckle to them so they're happy to be caught," one of the men explained.

Ahead big holes had been cut in the ice through which a net had been strung that reached deep down into the river. Beside each hole lay piles of frozen little fish. The ice was clear as glass beneath my feet and small pale-coloured fish, hardly more than six inches long, could be seen swimming towards the net. Behind them the men continued to beat on the surface as they drove them on, laughing. I wanted to stop and ask the fishermen more, but Reuben grabbed my arm and urged me forward.

"There's not much time," he warned. "We must hurry."

Leaving the men behind we entered part of the landscape where the river broadened out onto a plain. The light was beginning to fade, and that dark haze that gathers on gloomy winter nights was already creeping over the snow covered plain. The wind picked up as the sun dropped and soon it was blowing sharp and cold as a steel blade, and for the first time I was aware that my face and fingers were beginning to freeze.

We pressed on in the gathering twilight until we saw ahead of us a strange, dark hump lying on the ice in the middle of the river. At first I thought it was a dead animal, until Reuben gripped my arm and gasped, "That's him! That's the man we've come to save."

As we drew close the hump revealed itself to be a man dressed in furs. He was unconscious and lying on the ice with a walrus hide rope bound around his waist. His limp form was jammed across a circular hole that had been cut through the ice, and when we pulled the fur hood from his face, we could see that this was the same brother we had seen lying dead by the fire. What was more, he was alive.

"This is the soul," Reuben said. "You see, the man has died, but his soul is still living."

"It looks just like a man to me," I said.

"Of course it does," Reuben said. "It's his soul. But later it changes."

We tried to move the soul to make it more comfortable, but the rope around its waist was taut. We found the rope led through the hole and disappeared into the depths of the river, but when we pulled in an attempt to free it, something, or someone, pulled back and jammed the unconscious soul across the hole more firmly than ever.

After surveying the scene for a little longer Reuben explained to me, "You can see what's happened. The Medicine Man tried to bring him out by cutting a hole through the road, but he hasn't made it big enough. When he fixed the rope it only made things worse because it jammed it across the hole. No wonder we couldn't pull it out!"

"I don't understand," I said. "The Chanter said we had to cut across the spiral road. But we've been following it for miles and not cut across it at all."

"We cut across all right," he assured me. "Don't you see? We only got on to the road after the falls. Before that it was just a path the Medicine Men follow that leads *towards* the road."

The river at this point was about two hundred yards wide and on either side was a featureless plain with no trees, no bushes, no relief of any kind. I had the impression that somewhere, far off in the gloom and beyond my sight, there might be a line of low hills, but I could not be sure.

"What do we do now?" I asked.

For an answer, Reuben pried the unconscious soul of the brother away from the hole for a few seconds and pointed into the depths of the river.

"That's the way the Medicine Man went. He cut across the road like The Chanter said and made his escape that way. And that's the way we must go if we're to get out of here."

"What!" I gasped. "Down there? We'll drown."

"And if we stay here we'll freeze," Reuben said, not unreasonably.

"Let's go back," I begged, pointing towards the falls.

"We can't. To go back is death."

"Then let's stay here. I've had survival training, I can build a shelter," and even to myself I sounded panicky.

"With what?" Reuben demanded, pointing to the featureless plain.

"I can cut blocks of snow and make an igloo."

"The snow is powder. You might as well try to build an igloo out of sand," he said. "Even if you could, how would you heat it? We've no lamps, no candles, and no animal hides to lay on the floor to protect us from the cold."

"We can hunt!" I shouted in desperation, but I was talking nonsense, as one blast of the icy spears of the rising wind, or one glance at the endless vista of snow and the pale and cheerless dying sun, would have told anyone.

While we had been talking the soul had been jerked back across the hole.

"I wish those guys would stop pulling," Reuben said, sounding irritated. Taking a large steel knife from his boot, he bent down and cut the walrus rope, taking good care to leave untouched the circle of rope knotted around the soul's middle.

"I didn't know you kept a knife in your boot," I said, looking at him in some astonishment.

"I always do," he told me. "But it's a secret."

With the tension released, the rope hissed away over the edge of the hole and disappeared in an instant into the river. For a second I saw it wriggling like a snake towards the depths, and then it was gone.

Rolling the soul out of the way, Reuben went down on his hands and knees and began to enlarge the hole by hacking at its edges with his blade. After a few minutes he asked, "Are you brave?"

It was no time for false modesty. "Yes," I said. "But I'm not daft enough to jump through there."

Reuben made no reply but continued his work until things were completed to his satisfaction.

Standing up again he declared, "That's better. The hole's big enough for all three of us to jump through at once." But it did not look big enough to me and I said so.

"It's bigger than you think," he assured me. "Help me lift the brother's soul and we'll all jump together."

"I'm not going," I told him. "I'll go back up the river and I'll meet you at the hut."

Reuben pointed to the horizon, where the last tiny segment of the sun's glowing disc was about to disappear.

"When the sun goes down and the darkness comes, there is no return from this place. It's now or never," he said, and there was an earnestness in his voice that was unmistakable.

He picked up the unconscious soul by the hide rope still bound around its waist. Unfortunately, the poor thing sagged badly in the middle and its arms and legs hung down and bumped along the ice, forcing Reuben to half drag, half carry it, like an over-heavy suitcase.

"Help me!" he implored and, reluctantly, I took hold of the strip of thick hide. It was slippery with ice and I could not get a grip. So I slipped my arms under the rope and with the rope firmly resting in the crook of my arms, helped Reuben carry the soul to the edge of the hole. It still looked too small to me, not that it mattered much. Reuben could jump if he wanted but I had no intention of doing the same. I was about to say so once more, when the last flaming tip of the sun dipped below the horizon and the great shadow of night flashed across the land towards us.

At the same moment I felt a terrific bang in the ribs and the next second I was under water. Kicking and struggling, with my arms trapped tight by the hide rope, I found myself fighting for my life while bound to a corpse, or at least the next best thing to one. Unable to swim and further weighted down by my heavy fur parka, I began to sink rapidly into the icy water.

The water became dark and muddy as we plummeted towards the depths. I was vaguely aware that Reuben was somewhere nearby, but I could see nothing as I kicked blindly in an attempt to slow my descent.

I cannot tell the story of what happened next, because I don't exactly know what happened. It was more like a kaleidoscope of imagines than any cogent series of events. Dark shapes were swimming around me that I feared greatly, but what they were I could not say. At the moment of greatest terror, as fear piled upon fear, I began to scream and let out what little air was left in me. Then, just as I thought I must surely drown, I heard a voice say, "Look to the light."

At first I could see no light but, looking up, I saw a hole in the ice through which great shafts of sun were streaming, illuminating the water above me like powerful, downward probing searchlights. As I looked, I began to rise again. Slowly at first. Then increasingly rapidly, until I shot out of the hole like a leaping porpoise and found myself lying breathless next to Reuben on the ice. It was daylight and we were no longer below the falls, but back where we had started on the river at the bottom of the hill. On the other side of the hill was the hut and the brothers and their rope.

"Sorry I had to push you," Reuben said. "It was the only way."

"It's OK," told him, and sat up. As I did so I realised the brother's soul was no longer with us. Thinking it must still be in the water, I crawled to the side of the hole and peered in. The river was shallower and swifter here and I could see to the bottom only a few feet below, but there was no sign of him.

"We've lost him!" I cried to Reuben in despair. "After all that, we lost him!" And I beat my fists on the ice.

"No, we haven't," he called back. "He's over there."

Pointing over the brow of the hill he sprang up and began to run. Following his lead, I regained my feet, threw off my water-logged parka, and followed as fast as I could. Running down the other side we saw the brothers and their helpers lying on their backs in the snow still holding the rope.

Seeing us, they sat up and shouted, "It came free! We went to pull again while you were away, and all of a sudden it came free and we fell on our backs!"

Standing up, they began laughing and joyfully slapping each other on the back. As we ran by, the fourth brother came out of the hut and smiled and waved at us, and then all the brothers and the men we came with joined in a circle hugging each other and began to dance in the snow. But by now Reuben and I were al-ready entering the forest. The sun disappeared, the world became dark again, and the moon came out.

At the great river, the boatman was waiting and once more words flew around his canoe like colourful birds. This time they rested on my shoulders to impart their secrets to me alone; and for the first time I understood the true meaning of words.

Over the river in a trice, and still running, we hit the coast of Oregon. Here we turned inland and, picking up the pace, entered

Navajo territory to arrive on the San Juan as the moon began to set. Reuben found a good path and we ran down the sheer cliff and cantered through the willows into our camp, just in time to see the last of the moon's rays turn the San Juan into a fair stream of silver.

Standing on the edge of the river, watching the silver waters slip effortlessly between the high cliffs, exhaustion finally caught up with me. Heart pounding like a great drum, my head spun, my legs buckled and once more I was pitched to the earth unconscious.

It was daylight and a little bird was singing in the willows when I awoke. There was a smell of wood smoke and roasting meat and when I raised my head I saw Reuben was cooking the remaining rabbit over a small fire. Seeing me stir, he came over and washed my face with muddy brown water from the river. Looking down, I realised I'd been sick and went to clean up while he put the finishing touches to our breakfast.

"Could all that really have happened?" I asked when I joined him at the fireside.

"All what?"

"All those things we saw last night," I said.

"Sure."

"You saw it too!" I was a relief to know I hadn't imagined it all. "You saw the men in the moon, the boatman, the brothers, the Mistress. . . ." But Reuben quickly silenced me.

"You mustn't tell me about these things, I'm not a Medicine Man," he warned.

"But you were there," I said, not understanding why he did not want me to talk about it.

"I didn't say that," he replied. "What's important is that *you* saw it. If it was real then you don't need to know anything else."

"Oh, yes, I do," I told him. "I need to know a lot more."

"Like what?"

"Like, well, was it really real?"

Shaking his head Reuben looked at me pityingly and didn't even try to suppress the snort of derision that rose from him. "You white guys kill me sometimes. You don't want to learn a damn thing, any of you. I don't know why we bother with you!"

"I do want to learn."

I thought he would he would tell me that I had better believe what I had seen, but instead he said, "Then you must find a Medicine Man to guide you."

"Will The Chanter guide me?" I asked.

"No. Not The Chanter," he said.

"Blue Horse then."

"If you want it badly enough you'll find someone," and by his tone I could tell he meant it was up to me.

"I want it more than anything," I told him.

"Then you will," he said.

Turning aside, he removed the rabbit from the fire and taking a knife from his boot, with one deft blow chopped it in two and handed a portion to me.

"I didn't know you kept a knife in your boot," I said.

"Yes, you do," he replied curtly.

"No. I've never seen you take a knife from your boot, only from your pocket," I insisted.

Then I remembered.

"Except once." I said.

"Eat, *Chizchillie*, my friend," Reuben replied. "We can talk another time."

Taking a clump of grass he wiped the grease off his blade and slipped the cold steel back into his boot.

So I ate. And as I ate the fire begin to sing again, only this time its song sounded old and familiar. Although for the life of me, I could not quite put a name to it.

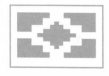